SHELTON STATE COMMUNITY
COLLEGE
JUNIOR COLLEGE DIVISION
LIBRARY

W9-BZM-362

DISCARDED

HB
87
.T93

Twelve contemporary
economists

DATE DUE

| | | | |
|---|---|---|---|
| | | | |
| JAN 10 1995 | | | |
| | | | |
| | | | |
| | | | |
| | | | |
| | | | |
| | | | |
| | | | |
| | | | |

# TWELVE CONTEMPORARY ECONOMISTS

# TWELVE CONTEMPORARY ECONOMISTS

Edited by

J. R. Shackleton and Gareth Locksley

A HALSTED PRESS BOOK

John Wiley & Sons
New York

Selection and editorial matter © J. R. Shackleton and Gareth Locksley 1981
Chapter 2 © J. R. Shackleton 1981
Chapter 3 © Gareth Locksley 1981
Chapter 4 © John Burton 1981
Chapter 5 © David Reisman 1981
Chapter 6 © Norman P. Barry 1981
Chapter 7 © Brian Morgan 1981
Chapter 8 © Josef Poschl and Gareth Locksley 1981
Chapter 9 © Martin Cave 1981
Chapter 10 © Maurice Peston 1981
Chapter 11 © Thanos Skouras 1981
Chapter 12 © Adrian Kendry 1981
Chapter 13 © Alessandro Roncaglia 1981, Translation ©
The Macmillan Press Ltd 1981

All rights reserved. No part of this publication may be
reproduced or transmitted, in any form or by any means,
without permission

*First published 1981 by*
THE MACMILLAN PRESS LTD
*London and Basingstoke*
*Published in the U.S.A.*
*by Halsted Press, a Division*
*of John Wiley & Sons, Inc.*

*Printed in Hong Kong*

---

**Library of Congress Cataloging in Publication Data**

---

Main entry under title:

Twelve contemporary economists.

"A Halsted Press Book."
Includes index.
Contents: Introduction—Gary S. Becker, the
economist as empire-builder/J. R. Shackleton—Individuals, contracts, and constitutions, the political
economy of James M. Buchanan/Gareth Locksley
—[etc.]
    1. Economics—History—20th century—Addresses,
essays, lectures. 2. Economists—Addresses, essays,
lectures.   I. Shackleton, J. R.   II. Locksley, Gareth
HB87.T93          330'.092'2          81–2403
ISBN 0–470–27168–X          AACR2

---

# Contents

# Notes on the Contributors

GARETH LOCKSLEY is a Senior Lecturer in Economics at the Polytechnic of Central London and has also taught at the University of Southern California. He has contributed to books and journals including *Public Choice*, *Cambridge Journal of Economics* and *Political Quarterly*. His current preoccupations are big business and computers, about which he has written *A Study of the Evolution of Concentration in the Data Processing Industry* (Commission of the European Communities).

J. R. SHACKLETON was educated at King's College, Cambridge, and the School of Oriental and African Studies, London University. He has taught at Queen Mary College and is currently Senior Lecturer in Economics at the Polytechnic of Central London. He has published various articles in the fields of labour economics, the economics of politics and education.

NORMAN P. BARRY is Senior Lecturer in Government at the City of Birmingham Polytechnic. He is a graduate of the University of Exeter, where he also lectured in Politics. He has also taught at the Queen's University, Belfast. He is the author of *Hayek's Social and Economic Philosophy*, *An Introduction to Modern Political Theory* (both Macmillan) and a number of articles on libertarian political philosophy and public policy.

JOHN BURTON has taught economics at the University of Southampton, Kingston Polytechnic and the University of Birmingham, where he is currently a Lecturer in the Department of Industrial Economics and Business Studies. He has held consultancy posts with the National Board for Prices and Incomes, the Office of Manpower Economics and the OECD. His publications include *Wage Inflation* (Macmillan), *The Consequences of Mr. Keynes* (with J. M. Buchanan and R. E. Wagner, IEA), *The Job-Support Machine: a Critique of the Subsidy Morass* (Centre for Policy Studies) and articles in academic journals.

MARTIN CAVE is a Lecturer in Economics at Brunel University and has been a Research Fellow at the Centre for Russian and East European Studies at Birmingham University. His research interests are planning in the French and East European economies, about which he has published numerous articles and books including *Computers and Economic Planning: the Soviet Experience* (Cambridge University Press). He is also the editor of *Matekon*.

ADRIAN KENDRY is a Senior Lecturer in Economics at Bristol Polytechnic, where he has worked since his graduate student days at Queen Mary College, University of London. During the academic year 1978/9 he was a Visiting Lecturer at Illinois State University. His publications include articles on the economics of imperfect information and the statistical uncertainty of macro-economic policy.

BRIAN MORGAN studied at the London School of Economics and has taught at North East London and Middlesex Polytechnics. He is currently a Senior Lecturer at the Polytechnic of Central London. His publications include *Monetarists and Keynesians: their Contribution to Monetary Theory* (Macmillan). His research interests include monetary economics.

MAURICE PESTON was a student and taught at the London School of Economics. He has been Professor of Economics at Queen Mary College for several years and has frequently served as an adviser to British Governments. He has published widely in the fields of macroeconomics and the economics of education, and is editor of *Applied Economics*.

JOSEF POSCHL studied economics at the University of Vienna. He is an Assistant Professor in the Institute of Economic Theory and Policy at the University of Linz, Austria. His research interests are the dynamics of advanced capitalist economies, about which he has co authored books and had articles published in *Empirica* and *Wirtschaft und Gesellschaft*.

DAVID REISMAN is a Lecturer in Economics at the University of Surrey. His numerous publications include *Adam Smith's Sociological Economics* (Barnes and Noble) and *Galbraith and*

*Market Capitalism* and *States and Welfare* (both Macmillan). His area of research interest is social economics.

ALESSANDRO RONCAGLIA is a graduate of the University of Rome and spent a period of research at Cambridge University. He has taught at Rutgers University, and is currently the Director of the Institute of Political Economy and Public Finance at the University of Perugia, Italy. He is the author of *Sraffa and the Theory of Prices* (Wiley), of a book (in Italian) on William Petty and the birth of political economy, and of a number of essays on the theory of value and distribution contributed to English, French and Italian journals.

THANOS SKOURAS has taught economics at the Architectural Association School, Cambridge University, and Middlesex, Thames and North East London Polytechnics. He is currently head of the Applied Economics Department at NELP. His publications include *Land and its Taxation in Recent Economic Theory* (Papazissis) and numerous journal articles. He is editor of the *British Review of Economic Issues* and his current research interest is the role of the state in the economy.

# 1 Introduction

The idea for this volume emerged one morning on the Northern Line of the London Underground, when we were stuck as usual somewhere between Mornington Crescent and Euston. Having exhausted the slender resources of *The Sporting Life* and *The Times Higher Education Supplement*, our conversation returned to a familiar theme, namely the way in which we economists are misunderstood by our fellow academics, our students and the general public. There were, we agreed, two popular stereotypes of economists which, while probably contradictory, were frequently adhered to simultaneously by our critics. On the one hand, economists are seen as a bunch of blinkered reactionaries whose only concern is to assert the primacy of pecuniary motives in the determination of people's behaviour. All practitioners of the discipline are thought of as holding a commitment to the view that human possibilities are narrowly constrained within the limits of a particular institutional form – an idealised private enterprise capitalism – deviations from which can rarely be justified or even considered. Despite the general concurrence on this position, however, it is equally firmly held on the other hand that, when practical advice is required, economists immediately dissolve into a babble of conflicting assertions and assessments. Five economists in a room can easily produce half-a-dozen opinions on the matter in hand.

Although we could see why these stereotypes persisted, our feeling was – and is – that economists get a bad press, and deserve a better one. Certainly a great many economists would assent to a few key propositions about the way in which economic systems operate. But this does not by any means imply the rigid conformity in approach which some have inferred from a hasty perusal of the financial press or some of the more pedestrian introductory textbooks. Even in a world where the economics

1

profession communicates as never before across frontiers, languages and cultures, there are major differences of approach which make the subject as exciting and stimulating an area of study and practice as anyone could wish for. But our assertion and celebration of this diversity should not lay us open to the alternative criticism, that the economics scene is just a confusion of idiosyncratic academics, each with his or her own pet theory to peddle. Economists cannot avoid working within a tradition, a framework, and the cleavages of opinion tend to be around those problems which have been central to the discipline; they are not simply random deviations. More of this later.

In an attempt to bring this out, we hit on the idea of producing a book which looked at the different views of economics espoused by some of the leading economists of the post-war period. One way to do this, of course, would have been for us to have attempted a major survey of developments in economic thought over the last 35 or more years. We felt that we lacked the qualifications for this; but, more importantly, we felt that such an undertaking would inevitably reflect our own prejudices and predilections rather than providing an introduction to the wide range of thinking which we wished to publicise.

We therefore decided to commission a collection of essays on leading contemporary economists, each of which would attempt to summarise the contributions the subjects have made, and the criticisms which have been levelled at them.

This concentration on individuals might be queried. In an age which increasingly stresses systems, schools, movements, aggregates of all kinds, it may be thought rather quaint – or perhaps ideologically unsound – to look at personalities in isolation. It probably is; nevertheless, we felt that few of our subjects could be easily lumped together under one heading, except perhaps some such category as 'bourgeois economists', which conceals more than it clarifies. And then again, perhaps we ought to confess to a methodological bias; despite the increasingly 'hard' quantitative nature of economic science, most of the really interesting questions in economics remain questions of interpretation and advocacy. And here individuals remain as important as ever.

The question of which economists to include then came up. We settled on an arbitrary number of twelve. On reflection this still seems about right. It is rather like that perennial school-boy game of selecting your world soccer team to play Coventry City, Tottenham Hotspur and Mars in the Intergalactic Cup; somebody always has to be left out. If you start trying to include everyone who somebody thinks should be in the team you will never get anywhere. Inevitably the management must decide.

Our squad was selected on the basis of three criteria. First, their most important work should have been done over the last 40 years or so, which meant that they were living or recently dead. This was, to be candid, to exclude certain characters who would otherwise dominate the book. Clearly Keynes, for instance, has been a major force in shaping economic thinking over our period of consideration, and has been exhaustively written of and about in works too numerous to mention. Equally Marx is one of the main pillars of economic thought – though not, some may say, of the same temple; further, his class analysis might tend to make our focus on individuals inappropriate. There are other illustrious figures from economics's past – Adam Smith or David Ricardo, for instance – who would clearly make an 'all-time' squad; but we wished to emphasise the contemporary character of economics rather than the history of its development. Although the Past Masters have, as you will see, profoundly influenced most of our subjects, our team has taken the story further to embrace the preoccupations of the post-war years – growth, inflation, the role of the state, the giant corporations, economic planning and other contemporary issues.

Our second criterion for inclusion was that our subjects were to be economists who had made genuinely original contributions to the discipline, rather than simply synthesising or refining the ideas of others. Of course absolute originality is something very rare, but we could defend our choices in detail. In some cases we chose individuals who had been awarded the Nobel Prize for Economics, which is one measure of the worth of their contribution; in all cases informal soundings amongst colleagues in seminar rooms and saloon bars have confirmed that we were on the right track.

The third criterion is more debatable; we argue that all our subjects should have had a major *influence* on their fellow economists. One measure of this might be citations in other people's work: another may be conscious or unconscious adoption of the same framework, the same method of analysis, by new generations of economists. We feel that this is controversial because by this criterion we have had to exclude a number of extremely distinguished and original economists who for one reason or another have not 'caught on' in quite the same way. Inevitably fashion and the spirit of the times influence our choice here; at another date our selection might have been rather different. It will be interesting to see, if we live that long, what future historians of economic thought will make of the contributions of these writers to the development of the discipline.

THE SUBJECTS

Running briefly down our list of subjects – in alphabetical order only – we can get some impression of the diversity of interests of contemporary economists. *Gary Becker* is notable for his analysis of the importance of human capital (resources invested in increasing the productivity of the work force) and more generally for his interest in the way in which economic concepts can be usefully applied in a surprising variety of areas of life. *James Buchanan*'s work has centred on the economic analysis of political choice, and in particular on the profound way in which the choice of political constitutions can structure the possibilities for economic advance and personal freedom. Although this is also an element in the work of Nobel Prize winner *Milton Friedman*, the latter is probably more celebrated for his work in macroeconomics, and especially for his revival of interest in the vital role which monetary aggregates play in the economy. A friendly rival of Friedman for many years has been the elegant Harvard iconoclast *John Kenneth Galbraith*, who has consistently rejected abstract economic reasoning in favour of a close examination of the institutions of the modern economy – big business, big trade unions and big government. Another who has rejected orthodoxy – though for very different reasons – is that other Nobel Laureate *Friedrich Hayek*, whose austere strictures on the responsibility of the state for most of our current problems have been listened to with greatly increased respect in recent years. *Sir John Hicks*, too, is a Nobel Prize winner; before the war he laid the foundations for the kind of analysis which dominates teaching in the Western academic world. In the last 20 years he has turned his prodigious intellectual resources to the issues of capital and growth, and to theorising about economic history and methodology.

The late *Michal Kalecki* was a Polish economist who developed, independently of Keynes, many of the central propositions of macroeconomics, though in the context of a dynamic analysis which recalls Marxian notions in its emphasis on power and the distribution of income between classes. *Wassily Leontief*, a Russian emigré who developed the important planning technique of input–output analysis, is yet another Nobel Prize winner whose influence has been felt world-wide. His work, though strikingly modern in many ways, relates back to several elements of eighteenth-century political economy. *Lionel Robbins*, too, is a man with an interest in the history of economics. Although his most important theoretical contributions – particularly in economic methodology – were probably made prior to the last war, he has been such a major influence on public policy and on the London School of Economics in the post-war period that he probably deserves inclusion on this account alone. *Joan Robinson*, the only woman economist featured here, was a close collaborator of Keynes, and has for many years been a leading proponent and populariser of Keynesian ideas. She has also made major contributions to growth theory, capital theory and the theory of the firm.

*Paul Samuelson*, the author of the Western world's most popular economics textbook, will need no introduction to anybody who has ever studied economics at all. His Nobel Prize was a fitting tribute to his outstanding work in almost every possible branch of economic theory. Although his early work involved the rigorous application of mathematics to microeconomics, his later papers and books have spread far beyond this: macroeconomics, international trade, Marxist economics and even physics. *Piero Sraffa*, on the other hand, will not be as familiar. A far less prolific writer, he devoted his career to the rediscovery and refinement of classical political economy. The importance of his work, as a means of providing a critique of economic orthodoxy, should not, however, be underestimated. For many economists, Sraffa is increasingly seen as a very important figure in the development of economic thought.

COMPARISONS

These, then, are our Twelve Contemporary Economists: a 'team' which, to continue our metaphor, wears odd shirts in a variety of colours and styles. But we spoke earlier of the way in which this diversity was structured around certain key themes. So we ought now to turn to a brief consideration of ways in which we might look for comparisons and differences between these individuals.

Firstly there is the issue of the nature of the actors in the economic system. We can distinguish three broad categorisations; households and firms, classes, and governments. Among those who opt for the first group, often termed 'methodological individualists', we would have to place Becker, Buchanan, Friedman, Hayek, Hicks, Robbins and Samuelson, though there are significant differences within this camp. For writers such as Friedman the individual plays a curiously passive role; he or she simply reacts mechanically to changes in income or prices on the basis of a given set of tastes or preferences. By contrast Hayek sees individuals as creative and capable of doing the unexpected; this links with his view that planning can never satisfy human aspirations in the way which dynamic, organic, uncontrolled markets can. Amongst the other writers Kalecki, Sraffa and Robinson discuss classes – capitalists (or entrepreneurs) and workers – to the virtual exclusion of individuals. Others are more ambivalent. Galbraith, for instance, occupies an intermediate position. His analysis of the modern industrial state, while denying the type of individualism inherent in the notion of consumer sovereignty, nevertheless draws attention to differences of interest between owners and managers of firms, between competing groups within firms, between trade unions, between politicians and bureaucrats. It is certainly not simply a crude class analysis.

None of our economists, of course, would deny the existence of governments as economic actors. However, they differ widely on the degree to which they accept the extent and pattern of government intervention. This may be surprising to those who characterise economists as straightforward advocates of *laissez-faire*. But is it really all that startling? After all, governments are major employers of economists in modern conditions!

A view commonly held in the economics profession is that there are cases of 'market failure' where, even in an otherwise free enterprise economy, the government has a duty to step in to remedy the deficiencies of the market. This may involve regulation of various types, it may involve the exercise of what Galbraith called 'countervailing power' against strong sectional interests, it may involve income redistribution, it may involve the provision of 'public goods' (those goods which, because, as Samuelson noted, they are 'non-rival' and 'non-excludable', will not normally be provided in sufficient quantity by the private sector), or it may involve, on Keynesian lines, 'pump-priming' expenditures to remedy deficiencies of aggregate demand. Clearly this offers a lot of scope for government involvement in the economy. Some of our subjects – notably Buchanan, Hayek and Friedman – argue against this open-ended conception of the government's role. If it is possible for markets to fail, they claim, it is at least as possible for *governments* to fail, and they claim the consequences are usually even worse.

Clearly these differences over the appropriate role of the government in the economy have a great deal to do with the views which economists have about what sort of entity the government actually *is*.

For many economists the government seems to be seen as some kind of benevolent and unprejudiced body which simply needs good advice (naturally, to be provided by economists) in order to solve all our difficulties. Much of the work of, say, Samuelson, Robbins and Galbraith can be seen in this light. Others, however, are rather different in their approach. Buchanan, for instance, applies economic analysis to the process of government itself. He sees political parties, interest groups and bureaucrats pursuing their own interest rather than any common conception of the popular good. A similar view leads Hayek and Friedman to advocate constitutional constraints on the power of governments. Other writers take a different line, but one which is equally critical of the view that government action is basically benign. It may be argued, for instance, that 'the government' is the wrong thing to discuss; it is more appropriate to analyse 'the state' a wider category which embraces the military, the police, the judiciary, the education system and so forth, rather than simply the political system, narrowly defined. In this view the state is seen as essentially the preserve of the dominant – capitalist – class. This being the case, there are very real limits to the type of benevolent intervention in the economy which the state will undertake in a capitalist system. This, for example, would be the view of Kalecki.

These differences over the nature of the actors also influence the perspectives held on the nature of economic relations and the goals of economic activity. Broadly, those who emphasise households and firms see economic relations as essentially harmonious and the goal of activity as the maximisation of global welfare. Conversely, those operating within a class-based framework view economic relations as conflictual and the goal of the actors as the optimisation of a class interest. Where the nation state or a government is conceived as holding the primary position, the object of activity is the pursuit of national interest and so relations (between states) are seen as largely conflictual.

Finally, on these fundamental issues, we should mention the differing views of the relation between economics and politics, often referred to as political economy. Within the individualist framework of Buchanan and Hayek it is held that economics *should* determine the political structure so allowing individuals the maximum freedom of choice. But if classes are held to be the dominant actors, as with Kalecki, it is believed that the economic base *does* determine the political structure. When governments and nation states are raised to the primary position politics will obviously determine the economic arena.

Another area for comparison concerns the notion of *equilibrium*, which has been called 'the central organising principle in economics'. The idea that market economies, left to themselves, tend towards some kind of equilibrium state, is a central feature of Adam Smith's *Wealth of Nations*, and it has attracted continuous debate ever since. Some writers – most notably, in our collection, the younger John Hicks – have explored the mathematical properties of a set of equations summarising demand and supply factors in each individual market in an economy, and concluded that on certain assumptions the economy might move to a 'general equilibrium' where buyers and sellers are matched by a set of market-clearing prices, an outcome which is claimed to be optimal in the sense that no conceivable reallocation of resources could make one individual better off without making some other worse off. Other economists – such as Gary Becker or Milton Friedman – prefer to adopt the 'partial equilibrium' approach favoured by Alfred Marshall in the late nineteenth century. This approach involves considering equilibrium in one market at a time, and confines its predictions accordingly. Other writers again – such as Friedrich Hayek – are suspicious of an overly mechanistic view of equilibrium, which is both irrelevant and seems to them to imply that an omnipotent government possessed of complete technical information could move straight to equilibrium (through state planning of the kind favoured for example by Wassily Leontief) without the need for a market mechanism. Hayek and other 'Austrian' economists are very dubious of such claims; they believe that no planner could ever possess the necessary information. While they recognise the same tendency that Smith discerned in his notion of the 'invisible hand', they prefer to think of an equilibrating *process* – by which decisions based on partial and imperfect information are gradually coordinated – rather than a static equilibrium position (or steady growth path). Finally, amongst our subjects there are some, like Piero Sraffa and Joan Robinson, who interpret equilibrium very differently. For them the notion of equilibrium is simply a heuristic device. Joan Robinson discusses the properties of equilibria primarily to indicate the difficulties of ever achieving such desirable positions under a capitalist dispensation, while Sraffa uses the properties of market equilibria to provide the basis for an immanent critique of certain propositions of mainstream, neoclassical economics.

Another basis for comparison between our subjects is their attitude towards empirical work and the role of testing and measurement. Economists are often seen by other social scientists as very much more concerned with empirical verification of hypotheses than, say, sociologists or political scientists. While it is certainly true that a tremendous amount of quantitative work is done by economists, we would suggest that its importance can be exaggerated. Certainly an examination of the work of our subjects does not suggest an overwhelming emphasis on empiricism.

The strongest advocate of the testing of hypotheses – which he has proclaimed as the only true basis for progress in 'positive' economics – is Milton Friedman. His empirical research on the association of changes in the money supply and rates of inflation has been very influential. Similarly the work of Leontief depends heavily on empirical research to obtain quantified technical relationships between sectors. But our other writers are certainly not best known for this kind of work. Hayek and Robbins, for instance, have asserted that most of the important propositions in economics are incapable of refutation, and that fact-finding, though useful in itself, can contribute little or nothing to our understanding of economic phenomena. In fact the strictest adherents to methodological individualism deny the possibility of measurement by any outside observer since they assert the subjective nature of costs and benefits. Again, though for different reasons, the work of Sraffa, Robinson and Kalecki towards a critical understanding of capitalism has produced few propositions which could ever be rejected by recourse to 'evidence'.

A final comparison we might make between our writers is in their attitude to the scope of their subject. Although many of them would pay lip service to Robbins's famous definition of economics as being concerned with the allocation of scarce resources which have competing uses – a very general definition – in practice most have confined themselves to the much narrower field of production, distribution and exchange of marketed commodities. Samuelson, Friedman, Hicks, Sraffa, Robinson have done most of their work in the 'economy', strictly defined. However, some economists have spread their net much wider. The bulk of Hayek's work in the postwar period has been concerned with the notion of a legal order in which 'economic' transactions take place. Buchanan's work has been concerned to apply economic reasoning to the political arena. Kalecki, from a very different perspective, discussed the concept of a 'political business cycle', which emphasises the way in which 'economic' and 'political' factors are intertwined. Becker has applied economic reasoning to various forms of purposive human action which are normally considered the prerogative of other disciplines – marriage, fertility, crime and punishment etc.

We see, then, that from our small sample of economists, few generalisations will hold; but, as we have suggested, this may be all to the good. By comparing and contrasting the work of the economists surveyed in this book, we hope that readers will be able to clarify and develop their own ideas on some of the themes we have touched on.

Finally, we should say a word or two about our contributors and the way they have gone about their tasks. Our authors were all recruited because of their previous interest in the work of their subject, or because they have done considerable work in the same field. In several cases the subjects have provided some assistance in producing bibliographies, offering advice or reading drafts, and we would like to take this opportunity of thanking them on behalf of our contributors. But we have been at pains to remind our writers to try to take as detached a view as possible of their subjects, and to try to present both sides of the coin rather than being excessively partisan. By and large, on rereading these chapters, we feel that our contributors have made a valiant effort to achieve this, although inevitably sometimes their obvious enthusiasm for their subjects shines through. They were also asked to write their essays with the interests of non-specialists in mind. Given that our Twelve Contemporary Economists have spent their professional careers operating on the frontiers of economic theory, it is perhaps unreasonable to expect their ideas to be immediately comprehensible to the layman. Nevertheless, our contributors have tried to pitch their chapters at a level where they should be understood by second- or third-year undergraduates or specialists in other disciplines. Mathematics is eschewed in favour of diagrammatic or verbal presentation, and difficult or unfamiliar concepts are explained in the text or in footnotes and appendices.

Now read on!

# 2 Gary S. Becker: the Economist as Empire-builder

## J. R. Shackleton

Few contemporary economists have done as much to extend the generality and range of economic theorising as Professor Gary S. Becker of the University of Chicago. With the exception of one or two papers written as a graduate student, all Becker's publications have applied economic reasoning to aspects of human behaviour which have usually been classified as outside the scope of economics, at least since the discipline started to give itself scientific airs in the latter years of the nineteenth century.

These scientific pretensions were associated with the introduction of mathematical techniques from the fields of physics and mechanics, often by professionals trained in those disciplines; many economists then, and not a few since, resented the intrusion of these alien elements. Similarly, Becker's intrepid expeditions into the jealously-guarded territories of sociology, political science, demography, criminology and biology have encountered considerable resistance. While it is too early to forecast the ultimate outcome of these imperialistic excursions, the increasing numbers of economists eager to join Becker in search of plunder have already forced some of the initially-scandalised natives to come to a *modus vivendi* with the intruding barbarians. Areas for co-operation rather than conflict are earnestly being sought, as we shall note later.

In this essay, major contributions Becker has made to the study of a range of social phenomena are briefly surveyed. We then discuss and try to evaluate the methodology Becker employs, a methodology he has been increasingly concerned to articulate and refine recently, and which forms the subject matter of several of his publications.

12

BACKGROUND

Initially, however, it is appropriate to make some observations about our subject's background and training. After undergraduate studies at Princeton, Becker undertook graduate work at the University of Chicago, with which (apart from a short spell at Columbia and a continuing involvement with the National Bureau of Economic Research) he has been associated ever since. This link with Chicago is not of course a purely geographical one. In many ways Becker's thinking is a logical development of the Chicago economics of such figures as Frank Knight, and certainly he has much in common with modern Chicagoans such as Milton Friedman, H. Gregg Lewis, Theodore Schultz and George J. Stigler. Like them he rejects the idea of a macroeconomics divorced from the microeconomics on which the discipline is based, and builds his theoretical structure on the foundations of methodological individualism and market equilibrium. Like Knight and Schultz he insists on the catholicity of the concept of capital; like Friedman he denies the necessity for valid theory to be a literal depiction of reality, so long as it generates useful 'predictions'; like Stigler he emphasizes the role of information and search in the labour market. Like most Chicago economists (though less stridently than some) he is sceptical of the wisdom of governments. Yet Becker's ideas are more than simply a distillation of that 'oral tradition' of Chicago economics of which Friedman has written. Becker has taken these ideas further than his contemporaries, and has added new dimensions to their application which give him a genuine claim to fame as a theoretical innovator.

DISCRIMINATION

Although Becker's writings range far and wide, we can trace a logical development and a methodological consistency in his work. The signs are there in his first major publication, *The Economics of Discrimination* (Becker, 1957, 1971). This monograph, based on his doctoral thesis, appeared when Becker was 27. By his own account, it was 'greeted with indifference or hostility' by fellow economists. Given the intellectual atmosphere of the mid-1950s this is probably explicable. Exercises in microeconomic reasoning of this kind may have seemed unattractive to an economics profession still heady with enthusiasm for the apparent achievements of Keynesianism, particularly since the work hints at some of those characteristically Chicagoan reservations about the benignity of government action.

The book starts from the position that economic inequality between two groups – blacks and whites, women and men or whatever – is not of itself evidence of discrimination in a market economy. In such an economy, variations in earnings, for instance, can be expected to occur between individuals or groups on a systematic basis, reflecting variations in marginal productivity and hours worked. What is needed is to separate out differentials due to variations in such factors as education, skills and job experience, in order to leave a residual due to 'pure' discrimination, Becker's primary concern.[1] To this end, Becker defines a 'market discrimination coefficient',[2] which in principle would measure the extent of this residual. What Becker is attempting to show is that 'pure' discrimination is simply a special kind of *taste* which, like the taste for apples or (Becker's pre-Women's Lib example) Hollywood actresses, can be analysed in economic terms. As with these other commodities, 'pure' discrimination's consumption is conditional upon variables such as income and price.

The – highly controversial – point that Becker is making is that discrimination in this sense is not, as is usually assumed, a means of raising the discriminator's money income, but actually imposes costs on the discriminator as well as the party discriminated against. Where discrimination exists, then, the discriminator is evidently willing to pay these costs in exchange for the benefit of indulging a taste.

The argument rests on a clever analogy with international trade. Suppose there are two economies, Whiteland and Blackland, which initially do not engage in trade. Within each country, however, perfect competition is the rule. This means, as the neoclassical textbooks tell us, that the incomes of owners of factors of production will reflect relative factor scarcities. Thus in Whiteland, where labour is assumed to be scarce and capital abundant, wages will be relatively high and rates of profit will be relatively low. By contrast, Blackland (where labour is abundant and capital scarce) is characterised by low wages and high rates of profit.

If trade and factor mobility are now permitted, theory predicts that labour and capital movements will occur, so that the long-run result is that profit rates and wage rates will each be equalised in the two economies. As a result of resources moving from areas where their marginal productivity is low to those where it is high, total 'world' output is increased.

The analogy is obvious, and the conclusion important: just as both of these 'countries' can in principle gain from trade and mobility, so can (for example) both blacks and whites in an economy gain from the absence of discrimination, which in this context seems equivalent to some form of trade barrier;[3] or, to put it differently, both blacks *and* whites can lose from discrimination.

Lack of space precludes the detailed examination of the implications of Becker's argument, and indeed of the many objections which have been raised to it. Most of these objections have centred on the assumption of perfect competition in his model: if such a condition is dropped, optimal tariff theory suggests that in some cases discrimination (while reducing total output) could increase the income of the discriminating group, which would undermine Becker's whole analysis. Becker, however, is clearly aware of this criticism, and it is instructive to see why he must reject it.[4] He believes that so pervasive a phenomenon as discrimination cannot be adequately explained by market imperfections – for market imperfections, most Chicago economists agree, disappear in the long run.[5]

We already see, then, in Becker's first important publication, two central features of his work: the insistence on using given preferences, costs and incomes to define a situation where individuals make decisions, and the concern with long-run equilibrium.

FERTILITY

Becker's next important foray into sociological country was to be a paper on the economics of fertility written for the National Bureau of Economic Research (1960b). Although political economy was once closely involved with demography (witness Malthus's famous essay), for much of this century the study of population was firmly in the hands of sociologists and un-theoretical number-crunchers. A few tentative attempts had been made to relate birth rates to economic variables, but Becker's paper went way beyond this. Here the decision to have children is firmly incorporated within the familiar framework of neoclassical economics. More particularly, Becker adopts the startling and controversial position that children are in important respects analogous to consumer durables such as automobiles, TV sets and dishwashers; thus the economic theory which has proved fruitful in relation to these commodities can be applied equally to human beings.

He argues that, at least under modern conditions,[6] the raising of children involves a net cost to their parents. Yet people do continue to have children, despite the availability of effective contraception. Thus if people choose to have children it is because they obtain sufficient utility to compensate for the costs involved.[7] These costs include such obvious things as food, clothing and schooling. Perhaps more importantly, however, they also include costs in terms of parental time, a scarce commodity which has alternative uses. Indeed, if one alternative is to use this time in the labour market, a value (its 'opportunity cost' in the jargon) can be put on it which will indicate that a very large proportion of the total costs of childrearing is accounted for by parental time.

The existence of these net costs indicates that children are some form of consumer good; their spread over time indicates we are dealing with a consumer durable. They therefore have to compete with other consumer durables for a limited share of the household budget: more children means less hi-fi equipment or a smaller car.

Once this rather bizarre comparison is admitted, it opens up the likelihood that decisions to have children will be affected by such variables as their 'price' (in terms of alternatives foregone) and the size of the household budget. As we have indicated, Becker accepts Friedman's view that the usefulness of a hypothesis depends on its ability to explain or predict. So how does Becker's approach fare in this respect?

Straightaway we are confronted with a problem. Broadly speaking, the demand for consumer durables tends to rise with income; on Becker's reasoning we might expect the demand for children to follow a similar pattern. Yet there is much evidence to suggest that family size declines with income. How does Becker handle this apparent refutation of his approach? Are babies inferior goods?!

One argument Becker offers in order to resolve this difficulty is interesting in the light of his later work. This is the argument that the cost of rearing children tends to rise with family income, largely as a result of the higher opportunity cost of parental time. At any particular moment better-off families tend to be better educated and thus to have greater earning power; over time, all earnings tend to rise as income rises. The argument can be illustrated diagrammatically. In Figure 2.1, an increase in income – illustrated by a parallel outward shift of the budget constraint – leads to increases in the 'consumption' of both competing consumer durables and babies, *if the relative price of these commodities remains constant.* At the point of tangency between a new (higher) indifference curve and the new budget constraint, more babies ($B_2$) are chosen. If, however, the increased income results largely from higher wages paid to family members (a highly plausible assumption), this will raise the opportunity cost of time spent on rearing children, and thus increase their relative price. The budget constraint *pivots*, as in Figure 2.2, and the new preferred combination of babies and other consumer durables may involve a smaller desired family size.

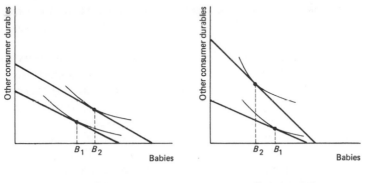

FIGURE 2.1                    FIGURE 2.2

It is ingenious, if not altogether convincing.[8] There is a suspicion that evidence Becker uses to support his arguments is highly selective, and moreover some of the generalisations he makes are amenable to alternative interpretations: for instance the observed inverse relation between education and family size could have nothing to do with the opportunity cost of parental time, but a lot to do with the different values and attitudes education might be expected to inculcate. However Becker's approach is more plausible in relation to short-term variations in fertility; economic factors seem far more significant here than *ad hoc* changes of tastes. In his approach empirical generalisations are linked to a broader theoretical framework; this is why, like it or not, it has stimulated so much further work in this field.

HUMAN CAPITAL

Consumer durables and investment goods are overlapping categories: consider the case of a motor car owned by a travelling salesman. Unsurprisingly, therefore, Becker's interest in fertility was only part of a wider consideration of investment in people. He is, indeed, best known within the economics profession for his work on the concept of human capital.

Although economists ever since Adam Smith have recognised that expenditure on education or training can be considered as an investment, this insight was not systematically used to explain labour-market behaviour until the early 1960s. Prior to this it was often assumed that individuals lacked the information or the foresight to make rational investment decisions in this area. A corollary of this seemed to be that governments should subsidise education.

A number of econometric studies in the 1950s suggested that education was an important element in the explanation of a country's growth performance; in addition the US Government became increasingly worried that its educational system might be lagging behind that of the USSR. As a consequence a good deal of attention was directed towards the analysis of the economics of education. Already Becker had prepared a discussion paper (1960a) which expressed scepticism of the view that there was a shortage of American college places. At the time, however, the theoretical framework for such a discussion was sketchy. It was not until Becker, Theodore Schultz, Jacob Mincer and others had contributed to a special issue of the *Journal of Political Economy* on Investment in Human Beings, in 1962, that the debate really took off.

Becker's contribution to this symposium was subsequently expanded into a book, *Human Capital* (1964, 1975), which was soon recognised as a classic and which made his reputation. In this book Becker's starting point is the assumption that people spend on themselves or their children not just for present gratification, but also with the future in mind. Future gratification may be of a monetary or non-monetary kind, though Becker concentrates on the former. Future-oriented expenditures will normally only be undertaken, he argues, if the present value of expected benefits (discounted by an interest rate reflecting the opportunity cost of capital) at least equals the present value of the costs of the expenditure.[9] Such expenditure includes overt costs such as fees and equipment, but a major element, he argues, is the value of earnings foregone during the period of training.

This category of investment includes far more than the formal systems of education and training which the debate was centred on. In Becker's hands, the concept of human capital embraces such activities as the purchase of health care, time spent searching for the best pay offer rather than taking the first available job, migration, and the acceptance of low-paying jobs which have a large element of learning on the job.[10] In Becker's model, in the long run, all such human capital formation is taken to the point where the marginal returns to such activities are equal to the marginal cost of investment funds. In other words, in equilibrium (always Becker's concern) the rate of return on all investment activities – human and non-human – is equalised. From this, Becker deduces propositions which shed new light on a great many economic activities. Patterns of income distribution, the shape of age-earnings profiles, the duration of unemployment and the existence of male–female educational inequalities are all examples of issues which the approach illuminates.

To some writers, human capital theory also suggests a guide to policy; if the marginal rate of return on some form of training exceeds the cost of capital, for instance, this may be taken to provide a justification for the state to expand the provision of the training. Becker, however, has doubts about this; he points out that such variations may simply reflect underlying variations in the non-monetary benefits and costs of particular activities.

Despite the acclaim which greeted *Human Capital*, Becker's work in this field is by no means universally accepted. Blaug (1975), for instance, has attacked the weak empirical basis of much human capital theorising. Studies indicate major variations in rates of return on different kinds of human capital, he claims, and attacks Becker's attempts to explain this away by reference to auxiliary hypotheses about non-monetary factors as being the same kind of ad hocery Becker deplores in others. We are again struck by the curious way in which Becker tends to use evidence to support or illustrate a hypothesis rather than genuinely to test it.

Another criticism relates to possible alternative explanations of some of Becker's empirical generalisations. For example critics have argued that the positive correlation between the married female participation rate and the level of education achieved can be attributed as much to attitude changes as to Becker's explanation in terms of the high market value of educated women's time. Again, however, as in the case of fertility which we discussed in the last section, it is doubtful whether such alternative explanations are as generally applicable.[11]

Another whole set of criticisms which deserves more space than we can afford it here argues that Becker asks essentially the wrong questions. Educational systems are seen as devices for reinforcing social control. Thus Marxist critics emphasize in particular the supposed structural necessity to maintain the divisions inherent in a complex society. Capitalism creates and maintains educational systems which fulfil its objectives; Becker's individualistic account of human capital investment cannot hope to deal with this. Criticisms on these lines are part of a wider critique of microeconomic reasoning to which we shall return later.

THE ALLOCATION OF TIME

We have seen something of the emphasis which Becker places on the value of time in his analysis of economic behaviour. This concern led to an important article which generalised the question of time allocation and simultaneously provided a basis for the reformulation of standard consumer theory (Becker, 1965).

Before Becker, the established way to deal with time in the context of consumer theory was to concentrate on a simple dichotomy between work and leisure. Work meant paid work in the labour market, by means of which individuals were able to obtain market-produced goods and services, which were the objectives of economic activity. In this context, leisure clearly has an opportunity cost, the goods and services foregone by not working. If individuals choose not to work all the hours they could, this must be because leisure itself is a 'good', some of which is consumed in preference to other goods. Thus leisure can be incorporated into standard analysis very easily, and from the time spent on leisure, we can deduce its complement, the time spent working. Thus the supply of labour is linked to the demand for goods.

Becker however takes the view that time has more than two uses. Certainly, as in the traditional approach, time can be used in the labour market. It can also, however, be used in many types of non-paid work (housework, do-it-yourself etc.). Furthermore all *consumption* takes time too. He suggests therefore that we abandon leisure as a separate category: all 'leisure' involves some 'consumption' and all 'consumption' involves some 'leisure'. Instead of a choice between consumer goods and leisure, the relevant choice is taken to be that between various 'consumption activities' which use different combinations of market-produced goods and services (which have to be purchased with funds largely acquired through the sale of labour time in the market) and time spent in 'household production'.[12]

Becker argues that instead of a choice between paid work and leisure we should analyse a choice between 'high time' activities (like a home-prepared meal) and 'low time' activities (like the purchase and consumption of a hamburger). The choice set is ultimately constrained by the limited time we have available, and the productivity of this time in its various uses. If all our available time were to be allocated to paid work, the value of the time in this use is termed (on Friedman's suggestion) 'full income'. *Some* of the 'full income', however, will normally be used for consumption and domestic production, using as complementary inputs in the domestic production process goods which are purchased with the proceeds of paid work.

All the predictions obtained from the standard theory can be obtained in this framework as well; for instance changes in the wage rate alter the slope of the full income budget constraint, while increases in non-work income shift the constraint outwards – in each case we would expect the allocation of time to be affected whether we apply the Becker analysis or the traditional approach. But in addition Becker's method allows further influences to be incorporated. Thus changes in the technology of household production – the development of labour-saving gadgets – economises on time spent in domestic work. People buy more gadgets and 'spend' less time on housework; the gadgets can of course be purchased by 'spending' some of the time saved working in the labour market. The relevance of this analysis to such phenomena as the rising labour-force participation of married women should be clear. Similarly transport improvements economise on time and can be expected to affect labour supply. The approach also has the incidental benefit of providing a theoretical basis for the classification of goods as substitutes or complements: when goods are no longer seen as the final sources of utility but rather as inputs in a household production process, it is rather easier to see why the consumption of certain commodities is linked.

CRIME AND PUNISHMENT

Becker's analysis of time allocation is by no means confined to legal activities; it includes various forms of crime. In a seminal paper (Becker, 1968) it was argued that crime is not an aberration outside the scope of rational analysis, but rather the predictable outcome of opportunities for gain.

He argues that a decision to engage in illegal activity is the outcome of an individualistic calculus; benefits and costs (both monetary and non-monetary) are weighed up, and the individual makes a decision which reflects the expected balance of them. One way to conceptualise decisions of this kind is as a rather special kind of investment activity. Many of the crucial decision variables – probability of apprehension and conviction, likely punishment, alternative earnings possibilities in legitimate occupations – are empirically observable, and hence their effect on observed crime rates can in principle be tested. As usual Becker's contribution has mainly been to analyse and suggest possibilities for hypothesis testing, but his graduate students and other interested economists have been quick to pick up the challenge. In the last decade a good deal of evidence has been accumulated to support the plausibility of Becker's contention that criminal behaviour responds to changes in costs and benefits.[13]

Unusually for Becker, the argument is couched throughout in normative terms. The model of criminal behaviour put forward is devised to be used in conjunction with cost functions for law enforcement and a simple social welfare function in order to generate conclusions about the optimal levels of policy variables such as the extent of enforcement, type of punishment and perhaps even what should be a crime. Becker is not, however, arguing for major policy changes. Given the behavioural responses to legal and illegal incentives which he discerns, and given the costs and benefits of enforcement and punishment programmes, he suspects that the authorities, at least in the USA, get things roughly right – perhaps a surprising conclusion, given his scepticism of the efficacy of government action in other spheres.[14]

There seem to be two main weaknesses to Becker's arguments. The first is the assumption of social homogeneity implicit in the notion of a social welfare function, when it is widely held (not least among economists) that some groups of the population have greater political power than others, leading to legislation and enforcement patterns which reflect the influence of sectional interests. Secondly, it is difficult not to feel that Becker's enthusiasm for the economic approach does tend at times to run away with him.[15] Although differences in incomes and assets, alternative earnings possibilities, probabilities of conviction and so forth are much more important in determining behaviour than they are often given credit for, there are surely variations in attitudes and degrees of honesty which affect the propensity to commit crimes even among individuals facing similar economic circumstances. While Becker would accept this, by implication he regards them as not particularly significant, possibly assuming that such variations in 'tastes' are randomly distributed.

Nevertheless, Becker's achievement is substantial. This one paper has stimulated a mushrooming literature on the economics of crime which it would be foolish for criminologists to ignore. The debate about deterrence, for instance, has been raised to a new level of sophistication by the introduction of econometric techniques by followers of Becker such as Isaac Ehrlich.[16]

## MARRIAGE

Another of Becker's pathbreaking ventures is his development of an economic theory of marriage (1973, 1974), part of a growing literature on the economics of the family stimulated by his work –

and that of Theodore Schultz – on fertility and human capital.

Once Becker's method is understood, the relevance of his approach to the institution of marriage becomes apparent. Here is a major and persistent phenomenon with ramifications in every economy. Whatever the precise legal arrangements, the majority of adult humans have 'married' throughout recorded history. Individuals (or their parents in some cultures) choose amongst competing potential spouses in an attempt to maximise utility, measured in Becker's terms by the consumption of household-produced commodities of the kind discussed earlier. The ubiquity of marriage suggests to Becker that male and female labour is complementary in certain types of household production, notably the rearing of the partners' own children.

An individual marries when the expected gain from a partnership exceeds the expected cost of marriage in terms of the alternatives foregone (staying single or marrying the next best alternative spouse). Because of imperfect information, individuals engage in search. This is costly, and therefore individuals may eventually settle for spouses with less than ideal characteristics. Or they may engage in bargaining to achieve compensatory concessions; these may include sums of money (dowries etc.) or behavioural commitments (promises to give up fishing). In Becker's view, however, there is sufficient freedom of choice and sufficient information to ensure an equilibrium where there is a Pareto-optimal sorting of partners (any rearrangement of couples could only increase some individuals' utility at the cost of reducing that of other individuals).

The use of the household production approach as an analytical framework may seem simply an economist's joke, an intellectual game; certainly some of its conclusions seem banal. But it does throw up interesting predictions which other methodologies do not. For instance the approach predicts that gains from marriage – and therefore, presumably, the probability of marriage – will be greater for couples between whom there is a considerable variation in earning power, basically because there are greater 'gains from trade' within such a marriage if one partner specialises in paid work and the other in household production.

The analysis is developed further to incorporate non-selfish motives for entering marriage. 'Caring' for the partner is introduced: in the model this means that the individual's utility function includes the partner's consumption as well as his or her own. This is shown to affect the allocation of output produced by the marriage and increase the potential gains from it. The analysis is also linked to earlier work Becker produced on charity and social interaction.

Again the model is not tested in a systematic way and we occasionally get the impression that the anecdotal 'evidence' adduced is of slight value. However Becker has produced another paper (Becker, Landes and Michael 1977), which tests some of the ancillary predictions of the theory with reference to data on marital instability. For instance, the approach suggests that major changes in the variables on which potential spouses make their decisions to marry will make them reconsider their decisions; if divorce is cheap, marital dissolution may follow. This appears to be the case. For example, where earnings are unexpectedly higher or lower than originally anticipated, the probability of divorce increases. The amount of time spent in search is also related to marital instability; those marrying young, on the basis of limited information about the characteristics of their partner and available alternatives, are particularly liable to divorce. There is, then, something to be said for the approach. While it cannot explain all aspects of marriage, it does at least suggest that human mating behaviour is less tightly constrained by biological and institutional factors than is often suggested.

THE METHODOLOGY

From the material surveyed so far it is possible to infer the common elements of Becker's methodological programme. He has however provided us with an essay (Becker, 1976b) which spells out his approach and offers a vigorous defence of it.

In his view, his method is applicable to all human behaviour; its core is 'the combined assumptions of maximising behaviour, market equilibrium and stable preferences, used relentlessly and unflinchingly' (Becker, 1976b, p. 5). Consider these assumptions in turn.

*Maximisation*

The individual, we have seen, is assumed to maximise utility subject to a budget constraint which, although taking a different form to the traditional one, is nevertheless closely related to it – indeed, subsumes it as a special case. It is important to note that this is not necessarily 'rationality' in the everyday sense of the term: it is not necessarily self-interest, nor are the sources of utility necessarily market goods and services. Becker has suggested that social distinction can be a source of utility, and he has gone so far as to claim (Becker, 1962) that even apparently random behaviour by individuals can lead to the basic prediction of downward-sloping demand curves which is at the heart of economic reasoning.

Behind the maximising impulse, Becker has suggested, there ultimately lies the principle of natural selection. In a paper (Becker, 1976a) concerned with the origins of altruism he has expressed approval of the new science of sociobiology, arguing that a synthesis of economic reasoning and natural selection can explain the dominance of maximising behaviour. He also suggests that the basic tastes which determine preference patterns can be attributed to natural selection.

The principle of maximisation must be maintained as a central analytical device. 'When an apparently profitable opportunity . . . is not exploited' we should not 'take refuge in assertions about irrationality, contentment . . . or convenient ad hoc shifts in values' (Becker, 1976b, p. 7). Instead we should look for hidden costs – such as transaction costs, or costs of acquiring information – which render such opportunities unprofitable. This seems dangerously close to tautology, but the test, as good Chicago economists always tell us, is the predictive power of the hypotheses generated – and Becker is optimistic on this score.

*Market Equilibrium*

We have already seen the importance of this in Becker's approach. Even where explicit markets do not exist – as in the case of marriage – Becker insists that we operate on Chicago 'as if' principles.

Note that Becker's approach throughout is to use *partial* equilibrium analysis. He has written with approval of Marshall's development of this apparatus for taking one problem at a time for analysis. This is revealing when we consider his usual reluctance to enter the arena of normative economics. The tradition of *general* equilibrium analysis instigated by Walras is associated with the normative position that unfettered competitive capitalism tends to produce an optimal allocation of resources. To do this it paints a grossly oversimplified picture of an economy without any of the subtleties of Becker's approach. Once we admit Becker's contention that preferences are based on home-produced commodities which are not sold in a market of the normal kind, it is less obvious that the traditional prescription of generalised *laissez-faire* is the appropriate one. The implications of Becker's approach for general equilibrium remain to be determined.[17]

*Stable Preferences*

We have seen how fixed 'tastes' play an important role in Becker's analysis. Such tastes are tastes for consumption activities rather than goods themselves, however, and this is a considerable step forward from the traditional view. Becker has, though, gone further than this, and in a paper written with George Stigler (Becker and Stigler, 1977) has tentatively sketched a theory of taste formation. As already suggested, some basic 'tastes' are probably biologically determined, but the behavioural form they take in a complex society needs further explanation. Becker and Stigler introduce an interesting model where tastes are learnt by exposure to new experiences – a special form of 'learning by doing'. Individuals repeatedly exposed to a stimulus acquire, as it were, 'consumption capital', a body of knowledge and attitudes which raises the 'marginal productivity' of consumption of the good in question, thus increasing demand for it.

Within this framework the success of advertising can be rationalised and some kind of explanation can be offered for the increasing stability of tastes as people get older – they are 'locked into' their accumulated consumption capital, and their reduced 'pay-off period' (life expectancy) discourages further 'investment'. Again, this is all rather fanciful, but it illustrates once more the tenacity of Becker's commitment to the economic approach and his refusal to concede that economics might not have anything to say about some social phenomenon.

CONCLUSION

Becker's ambitions for economics, then, appear boundless. His programme is, he admits, virtually one of colonisation of the other social sciences. Although he has written that the contributions of other disciplines have a role to play he does not spell out what that role might be. One sociologist who has attempted to do this for his own discipline is Duncan MacRae (1978). Impressed by the methodology, the main weakness he sees is the difficulty of measuring some of Becker's variables, such as the non-material costs of crime, or 'caring'. MacRae suggests that sociologists might devote their time to the task of devising appropriate indicators for these variables. An odd reversal of roles; sociology is usually thought of as a theoretical discipline, while economists are considered dull empiricists. Perhaps a less impressionable sociologist might wish rather to emphasize such topics as inequality of status and political power, the formation and maintenance of norms and the latent functions of, for instance the educational system, to suggest just a few areas where Becker's analysis is not conspicuously illuminating.

One critical approach to take to Becker's approach is that adopted by a number of Marxists. This is to argue that Becker is dealing with essentially trivial and irrelevant questions, providing an updated version of the 'vulgar economy' that Marx scorned. While it may be admitted that the variables Becker distinguishes (notably the opportunity cost of time) can be significant determinants of behaviour within a given social structure, it is argued that he can contribute little to our understanding of broad differences between societies at different stages of development, or societies with different political and economic systems.

To take an example, Marxist discussions of the role of women under capitalism have usually summarily dismissed Becker's analysis, insisting that women's specialisation in domestic production is not simply determined by their comparative advantage in housework, but is rather a reflection of a male-centred ideology with specific historical roots and which reflects the interests of the ruling class. Similarly, Becker's analysis of crime, while probably correct in emphasizing the responsiveness of individuals to opportunities for gain, does not deal adequately with the question of how laws come to be enacted to protect particular interests.

The validity of this type of criticism is outside the scope of this paper. But it should be noted that it is not only Marxists who have their doubts about Becker's approach. There seems to be a feeling amongst many commentators that the method Becker adopts is clever but ultimately empty. Certainly the approach lends itself to parody, but surely this is the price of taking any theoretical approach seriously? It is equally possible to construct a Marxist analysis of Winnie the Pooh. In the 1960s the neoclassical paradigm was under attack from all sides for its unrealism and its apparent inability to cope with the interaction of social and political factors with narrowly economic considerations. One response to this was a resurgence of interest in Marxism; another was to abandon conventional economics for a less rigorous and more discursive form of analysis best exemplified in the work of Galbraith. Becker, clearly, took a different route. His insight was that neoclassical economics is essentially metaphorical in nature, and that metaphors can be applied in different contexts; his strategy was to modify and extend the neoclassical framework, and it has paid dividends. His approach may have a tautological flavour; it seems difficult to see what kind of behaviour could *not* be rationalised within it. But, as Lakatos has made clear, a scientific research programme is necessarily a closed system. What marks a 'progressive' from a 'degenerating' programme is its ability to react creatively to new information and problems, to generate new hypotheses which are capable of shedding light on a range of hitherto unconsidered issues. By this test Becker's approach must surely be considered a success, certainly in relation to its rivals. Whatever may be thought of his wilder flights of fancy, there is evidence of solid research achievements in the fields of human capital, the economics of the family and the economics of crime and punishment.

Becker's critics may point to the relatively small amount of genuine empirical research he has himself conducted, and perhaps even to the relatively unsophisticated technical apparatus he uses – it is noteworthy for instance that the difficult mathematical bits are usually provided in an appendix a colleague has written for him. But Gary Becker's approach has added new words to the economist's lexicon. His work illustrates above all a singularly imaginative approach to the possibilities of the discipline. In a field particularly obsessed with scarcity, such imagination is the scarcest of resources.

NOTES

1. This is not to deny that there may be discrimination in the access of different groups to education and training opportunities. Becker has made useful contributions to this question. See, in particular, Becker (1967).

2. The MDC is defined as

$$\text{MDC} = \frac{Y(W)}{Y(N)} - \frac{Y_O(W)}{Y_O(N)}$$

where $Y(W)$ and $Y(N)$ are the actual incomes obtained by members of a dominant group $(W)$ and an oppressed group $(N)$, while $Y_O(W)$ and $Y_O(N)$ are their incomes in the absence of discrimination.
3. Though Becker in fact claims that discrimination resembles a kind of exogeneously given cost, like a transport cost.
4. This is the author's interpretation.
5. Of course, where imperfections exist, a tendency to discrimination may be intensified. Thus governments, as in South Africa, monopolies and trade unions (see Becker, 1959) are responsible for some discrimination.
6. In pre-modern societies things may be different; children may be capable of producing their subsistence from an early age in the context of family farming. Any surplus would be a return on a parental 'investment'.
7. It is not implied here that children are equivalent to consumer durables in any sense other than that outlined. The moral outrage which Becker's analogy often provokes in non-economists is unnecessary.
8. For a critical discussion, see Leibenstein (1974).
9. Benefits and costs arising in the future do not have the same value as similar sums of money available today. This is basically because money available today could be invested to return a larger sum in the future. One way of taking this into account is to compare costs and benefits in present value terms. The present value of a sum of money $£A$ to be received $t$ years from now is

$$PV = \frac{A}{(1 + i)^t}$$

where $i$ is a discount rate measuring the opportunity cost of capital (that is, the rate of return available on other investments elsewhere in the economy).
10. Becker makes an important distinction here between *general* and *specific* training. The former involves the acquisition of skills useful in a variety of jobs with different firms, while the latter produces skills having value only to the particular employer providing the training. Becker argues that while general training will have to be financed by individuals – either through paying fees or by accepting low pay during training – firms will be willing to finance specific training as their 'investment' is safer, specifically-trained workers having no incentive to leave. The distinction leads to further predictions, such as that specifically-trained labour will not be as subject to cyclical unemployment as other types of employee.
11. We should note in passing that the so-called 'Screening Hypothesis' – the view that schooling merely selects trainable individuals for top jobs, rather than genuinely increases their productivity – cannot be used to criticise Becker. As we have indicated, he has not committed himself to the view that education should be expanded or is valuable in itself.

12. Note that the abandonment of a separate category of 'leisure' also involves the abandonment of 'work' as a clearly defined concept. Work is now linked with consumption as well as activity in the labour market. A further consequence is that this opens up discussion of elements of consumption in *paid* work; the well-established concept of the 'net advantage' of a particular occupation is given a greater generality.
13. For a recent review of the field see Heineke (1978).
14. It does seem rather odd; quite how the Invisible Hand is supposed to operate in the absence of a market is not spelt out. To be sure, it could be claimed that a 'political market' existed, with vote-maximising politicians responding to public preferences, but Becker is known (see Becker, 1958) to share Chicagoan doubts about this.
15. For instance, where he argues that 'a useful theory of criminal behaviour can dispense with special theories of anomie, psychological inadequacies, or inheritance of special traits and simply extend the economist's usual analysis of choice' (Becker, 1968, p. 170).
16. See, for example, Ehrlich (1973, 1975).
17. Work by Gintis and Katzner (1979), for instance, suggests that neoclassical propositions about the optimality of competitive capitalism are undermined when a rigid demarcation between work and leisure is dropped.

REFERENCES

Becker, G. S., 1957 (1st edn), 1971 (2nd edn) *The Economics of Discrimination* (University of Chicago Press).
—— 1958 'Competition and Democracy', *Journal of Law and Economics*, vol. I, pp. 105–9.
—— 1959 'Union Restrictions on Entry' in P. D. Bradley (ed.), *The Public Stake in Union Power* (University of Virginia Press).
—— 1960a 'Underinvestment in College Education?', *American Economic Review*, vol. 50, no. 2.
—— 1960b 'An Economic Analysis of Fertility' in *Demographic and Economic Change in Developed Countries* (National Bureau of Economic Research).
—— 1962 'Irrational Behaviour and Economic Theory', *Journal of Political Economy*, no. 70, pp. 1–13.
—— 1964 (1st edn), 1975 (2nd edn) *Human Capital: a Theoretical and Empirical Analysis* (Columbia University Press).
—— 1965 'A Theory of the Allocation of Time', *Economic Journal*, Sep 1965.
—— 1967 *Human Capital and the Personal Distribution of Income: an Analytical Approach* (University of Michigan).
—— 1968 'Crime and Punishment: an Economic Approach', *Journal of Political Economy*, no. 80, pp. 169–217.
—— 1973 'A Theory of Marriage, Part I', *Journal of Political Economy*, no. 81, pp. 813–46.
—— 1974 'A Theory of Marriage, Part II', *Journal of Political Economy*, no. 82, pp. 11–26.
—— 1976a 'Altruism, Egoism and Genetic Fitness: Economics and

Sociobiology', *Journal of Economic Literature*, vol. XIV, no. 3.

—— 1976b *The Economic Approach to Human Behaviour* (University of Chicago Press).

Becker, G. S., Landes, E. M. and Michael, R. T., 1977 'An Economic Analysis of Marital Instability', *Journal of Political Economy*, no. 85, pp. 1141–87.

Becker, G. S. and Stigler, G. J., 1977 'De Gustibus non est Disputandum', *American Economic Review*, vol. 67, no. 2.

Blaug, M., 1975 'The Empirical Status of Human Capital Theory', *Journal of Economic Literature*, vol. XIII, no. 4.

Ehrlich, I., 1973 'Participation in Illegitimate Activities: a Theoretical and Empirical Investigation', *Journal of Political Economy*, no. 81, pp. 521–66.

—— 1975 'The Deterrent Effect of Capital Punishment: a Question of Life or Death', *American Economic Review*, vol. 65, no. 3.

Gintis, H. and Katzner D. W., 1979 'Profits, Optimality and the Social Division of Labor in the Firm' in L. Levy-Garboua (ed.), *Sociological Economics* (Sage).

Heineke, J. M. (ed.), 1978 *Economic Models of Criminal Behaviour* (North-Holland).

Leibenstein, H., 1974 'An Interpretation of the Economic Theory of Fertility: Promising Path or Blind Alley?', *Journal of Economic Literature*, vol. XII, no. 2.

MacRae, D., 1978 'The Sociological Economics of Gary S. Becker', *American Journal of Sociology*, vol. 83, pp. 5.

# 3 Individuals, Contracts and Constitutions: the Political Economy of James M. Buchanan

Gareth Locksley

James Buchanan began his distinguished academic career in 1948 at the University of Tennessee. At the time of writing he is General Director of the influential Center for Study of Public Choice at Virginia Polytechnic Institute and State University, a post he has held since 1969. He has taught at many seats of learning in both the US and Europe including UCLA, UC Santa Barbara, LSE and Cambridge. During his career Professor Buchanan has picked up numerous awards and honours, served on very many important boards and undertaken a sizeable amount of consultancy work. Within this packed working life he has also managed to produce an almost frighteningly large volume of publications, only a fraction of which are referred to here.

Like many important economists of our time, Buchanan studied at the University of Chicago, where he was influenced by the legendary Frank H. Knight. He also lists Knut Wicksell's work on public finance (which he translated) and the importance Wicksell placed on unanimity among his influences. But the factor that gives Buchanan's work its distinctive flavour is his familiarity with the Italian School of Public Finance. In 1955/6 Buchanan was Fulbright Research Scholar in Italy where he was exposed to a perspective entirely different to that which informs the Anglo-Saxon tradition. The most significant single influence of his Italian experience was the contrast between our essentially pluralist view of the state and the Italian denial of the democratic process and insistence that decisions for the collectivity are always made by a small group (Buchanan, 1960).

Buchanan's major contribution to economics has been in the mistakenly neglected realm of Public Choice or the Economics of Politics. He was driven to this field because of his dissatisfaction with public finance theory (Buchanan, 1949). His approach to the subject has been to integrate, (*i*) the structure of taxes, (*ii*) the various activities the taxes finance, and (*iii*) the political process within which decisions on what goods are provided collectively, and how output and costs are shared (Buchanan, 1966). This leads quite naturally to the study of individuals' responses to different decision rules and collective institutions, i.e. Public Choice. Recently the literature on Public Choice has blossomed and many approaches, ranging from the narrowly empirical to exercises in abstract logic, have gained a wide audience and made a significant impact on our interpretation of government and the political process.[1]

Buchanan has been the dominant figure in these developments. Eschewing empty theorising he has sought to construct and indicate forms of political order that channel individuals' self-interested behaviour towards the common good. Here there is a clear affinity between Buchanan's analysis and Adam Smith's vigorous attack on the straitjacket of mercantilism. In fact, Buchanan acknowledges his rediscovery of the conventional wisdom of the classical political economists. His starting point is a deep mistrust of the government process and its predilection to generate an ever increasing set of constraints on individual actions. His conclusion is to point to the urgent necessity for constitutional constraints on government and its multifarious agencies.

METHODOLOGY

Buchanan's methodology is of crucial importance to an understanding of his work for it both indicates the questions to be asked and influences the answers that are found. He is a self-declared adherent to methodological individualism. This is far more than the application of a mere tool kit for it also embodies a set of beliefs. Within this framework 'Choice . . . cannot be predetermined and remain choice' (Buchanan, 1969b) and only an individual can identify his 'goods' and 'bads'. Further an individual does not know his complete personal ordering for his utility function; if he did then he could communicate this to some external machine that would perform the act of selection. But this would not be choice. Thus, reasoning, purposeful individuals are perceived as the ultimate decision makers in both private and collective action. This being the case, individuals require the maximum freedom of choice, i.e. of the arbitrary will of another. Buchanan explicitly recognises that individuals are unequal (1971). They differ as to tastes, capacities and their environmental setting. Further, they will have non-uniform expectations, knowledge and interpretations of the course of events. From this emerges another basic block in Buchanan's methodology, the subjective nature of costs, benefits and thus choice. Unequal individuals will appraise the value and cost of any activity very differently and importantly these subjectively derived sums will be unpredictable to an external observer (Buchanan and Thirlby, 1973).

Since individuals are concerned with freedoms generally, these will enter their personal utility functions which now contain both economic and non-economic arguments. A choosing individual is thus concerned with trade-offs between goods and between goods and non-economic arguments. So an individual's utility is influenced both by the goods and services he receives and supplies and by the institutional setting. Changes in this setting, or the rules of the game, affect someone's utility just as changes in the quantity of goods he receives would. In Buchanan's schema individuals are neither solely hedonistic nor materialistic, they can espouse any motivation as long as it does not take into account the other participant in an exchange.

Through exchange individuals can achieve improvements in their position. This may involve private or joint actions. But for Buchanan that which emerges from exchange is merely that which emerges. From his individualistic viewpoint the definition of 'good', 'bad' and 'better' relate to how an outcome emerges rather than to what the outcome is. No outcome is 'bad'; rather the process used to achieve it may be 'bad'. Any reduction in an individual's freedom of choice is regarded as 'bad' and any increase 'better'. But this does not mean there should be no restrictions on individuals. Buchanan recognises that society cannot exist without some minimum set of rules: the problem for

Buchanan is to keep the minimum from creeping up. But at the very least individuals must accept each others' property rights. Involved here is another important feature of Buchanan's analysis, the concept of mutual agreement and society's search for it.

Exchange can only be effective if individuals acknowledge the mutual existence of others and admit their property rights. If mutual agreement on this point is not reached exchange will break down and society will degenerate into the anarchy of all against all. Private exchange proceeds under implicit unanimity. If any individual objects to a particular transaction he can always offer better terms to one of the participants. To the extent that third parties do not interfere, implicit unanimity is reached. Mutual agreement is of great importance in Buchanan's analysis of collective decisions. Clearly if a particular proposal is carried unanimously no one feels damaged by it and somebody, if not everybody, rates it an improvement. Palpably, at this collective level, explicit unanimity provides a criterion for 'better' and satisfies the Pareto principle[2] (Buchanan, 1962b).

Altogether, Buchanan's emphasis on unequal individuals who evaluate possibilities subjectively within the context of changing rules of the game, denies the existence of a 'truth' or a 'public interest' which awaits discovery. It also negates any notion of an organic state. His concept of the state is purely individualist. Collective action is taken when individuals choose to use government to achieve some purpose jointly rather than acting individually. This position brings Buchanan into conflict with many economists for in effect he is questioning the role of the political economist (1964).

Economists have a predilection for giving advice. Advisory posts with governments are keenly sought after and in this capacity the maximisation of social utility is a universally accepted goal. But there are many ways of achieving and of conceiving this state of affairs. Utilitarians, using measurable and comparable utility functions, found no difficulty in advisory posts. However the positivist revolution, with its emphasis on scientific hypotheses testing, arrested the progress of those operating within the utilitarian perspective. The upheaval this caused and the debates it generated were eventually resolved for some in the 'new' welfare economics.

By accepting the Bergson–Samuelson formulation of the social welfare function (SWF) many economists were once again in a position to give advice. Within this framework the notion of Pareto Optimality[3] is used to define optimal and sub-optimal states of the economy. The purpose of the SWF is to order all possible states of the economy and from this list a best or Pareto Optimum State is chosen (or rather, recommended). The most important assumption here is that the SWF has conceptual and operational meaning.

The ordering of the SWF is carried out by some external observer who performs this operation on the basis of his objective pay-off matrix for all possible movements. He can perform this task because he assumes all individual choices are fairly predictable. So there are two further assumptions; omniscience (on the part of the observer) and 'economic' man.

Both the SWF and the condition of Pareto Optimality, with its associated 'market failure', has provided many economists with a wide scope for the identification and improvement of 'imperfection'. Generally this has involved a shift of activities from the market to a political agency and some restriction on private behaviour, i.e. a loss of choice. To help in their work, economists have developed a range of scientific techniques in which some objective function is maximised subject to a set of constraints. The solution to the calculus is then proposed to government as the best course of action.

Given Buchanan's individualist standpoint he naturally rejects the above outline as an appropriate role for a political economist (1959); 'this is a bridge that should never have been crossed' (1975b). Subjectivism flatly denies the ability of any external observer to order states since only individuals themselves can know their own utility. For Buchanan, the whole approach is erroneously centred on a materialist viewpoint of unmeasurable private and social costs and benefits. The behaviouralist assumption of 'economic man' embodied in the economist-as-predictor is for Buchanan a complete rebuttal of the concept of choice (1969a), and he denies that shifting activities from the market to the public sector ensures improvements (1962a).

Besides these methodological and theoretical assaults Buchanan raises a very practical issue. He notes that, in the above role, political economists are acting without regard to politics and the political process. They are making recommendations to a benevolent despot. This is one of his criticisms of Keynes

(Buchanan and Wagner, 1977) and interestingly Kalecki searched all his life for a new Prince to whom he could play a Machiavelli.[4]

What then is Buchanan's perspective on the role of the Political Economist? He denies the existence of one decision-maker who can choose and maximise for society. He does not accept the notion of a known society utility function or that an aggregation of differing individuals' utility functions can be ordered into an SWF. It was thus no surprise to Buchanan when Arrow discovered the Impossibility Theorem[5] (Buchanan, 1954a). In his schema the role of the political economist revolves around individuals not a super-individual being.

Individuals hold various property rights which allow them to do certain things and exclude others from certain actions. With these property rights individuals engage in exchange whenever they perceive the possibility of gains. In doing so, they make implicit and explicit contracts. If the outcome of the multifarious contracts is identified as being sub-optimal or inefficient Buchanan's political economist would not recommend some course that constrains individuals. Buchanan's response is to examine the rules of the game, searching for organisational–institutional changes and modifications to the structure of property rights. The purpose is to discover prospective opportunities for enlarging the scope for potential trades. This approach has had a considerable influence on proposed remedies to the problem of pollution.[6]

The criterion used to decide whether to introduce a proposal on rule changes is of course whether it achieves a consensus (Buchanan, 1962a). Any unanimously and deliberately chosen modification is clearly an improvement, for everyone expects to be in a better position after its enactment. Even in the case where someone feels harmed by the proposed changes, mutual agreements can be attained if the individual is compensated. And compensation need not be pecuniary, it can also take the form of further modifications in the structure of rights. In this way individuals enter into contracts with one another either explicitly or implicitly.

Buchanan thus sees the role of the political economist as someone probing for changes in the rules of the game that will provide mutual gains from trade. He is crucially concerned with how property rights emerge (between individuals and between individuals and the state) and how they are modified. Within the realm of collective action he focuses on individuals' responses to different collective institutions, fiscal structures and decision rules. His subject matter is positive Public Choice, inhabited by individuals holding property rights and with a propensity to trade who enter into voluntary contracts to their mutual benefit.

## THE NEED FOR CONSTITUTIONS

Buchanan's ideal is ordered anarchy, the archetype of which is voluntary exchange. Ordered anarchy pervades many areas of human interaction. One has only to think of the ethics of the queue where mutual tolerance exists without formal rules. Though Buchanan considers movements away from this ideal a 'bad' he does recognise the necessity for some laws and rules, even though his overriding concern is with individual freedom. Liberty cannot be unbounded due to the necessities of social interdependence. Without some mutually agreed set of rules the fruitful association between Crusoe and Friday would have broken down into open conflict. Society exists when property rights are defined and boundaries are drawn. 'Good fences make good neighbours.' Property rights place limits on the set of activities an individual can carry out and exclude others from certain actions. These rights will differ between individuals and so provide the incentive to make contracts and enter into exchange. When conflicts arise between individuals institutions will emerge to resolve them. But of paramount importance in Buchanan's framework is reciprocal respect for individuals' property rights, i.e. a contractual relationship. Individuals must therefore search for and maintain agreement amongst themselves. How do they do this? How does law emerge? How are laws modified and enforced? What can go wrong? These questions are the subject matter of one of Buchanan's major books *The Limits of Liberty* (Buchanan, 1975a) and of a collection of his essays *Freedom in Constitutional Contract* (Buchanan, 1977).

In the beginning Buchanan sees an initial distribution of rights emerging as individuals fight over scarce resources. This 'natural' distribution is achieved by individuals' investments in defence and attack capabilities to secure the supply of the scarce resources. No matter what the characteristics of the natural distribution, there will exist the possibility of mutual gains from trade. By agreeing to a set of behavioural limits, i.e. making a contract, individuals can benefit from disarmament. This first step is, in Buchanan's terminology, the formation of a 'constitutional contract'. It represents the transition from anarchy to ordered anarchy. The constitution will define, as carefully as possible, individuals' rights within the existing state of knowledge. It may include some procedure for the redistribution of income (Buchanan and Bush, 1974) and will certainly cover rules for the enforcement of contracts.

As already noted, individuals differ as to tastes, capabilities, knowledge and now property rights. This acts as an incentive for them to trade i.e. they enter into 'postconstitutional contracts'. This is the subject matter of economics where individuals trade in private and public goods, the latter involving social contracts.

Private contracts require that a set of rules for interpersonal behaviour is established. They also need enforcing i.e. a government. Private contracts between two individuals reduce transactions costs to a minimum and, because of the wide variety of possible alternatives, reduce the possibility of conflicts. The outcome of these contracts is directly dependent upon the actions of the participants. But public goods require social contracts which have high transactions costs and a severely limited range of possible alternatives. Further, individuals in this context may expect their own behaviour to be independent of that of other participants. This acts as an incentive to become a 'free rider' taking the benefits of public goods but avoiding the costs. Public choice on constitutions must therefore establish the following: (*i*) private property rights; (*ii*) an enforcement agency; (*iii*) a list of what goods will fall within the public domain; (*iv*) how these goods will be provided; (*v*) how they will be financed. What rule should be used to make these decisions? Buchanan naturally suggests the rule of unanimity but here there is a problem if any one individual stubbornly refused to agree. If he is coerced into agreement this is clearly a 'bad'. Alternatively, the individual could be excluded from any collectively provided benefits. Thus the constitution will define the generalised right of citizenship which will be limited to the extent that an individual will be excluded from public benefits when he is unwilling to contribute to their costs. This will act as an incentive for every individual to join and maintain the voluntaristic character of contracts.

A constitution can be conceived of as a set of rules developed to enable individuals to achieve the gains from trade. The formation of a constitution is not a once and for all event; as the environment evolves so will the constitution. The status quo is not rigid; what is important is that the constitution provides a basis for predictions, allowing individuals to formulate expectations concerning the unfolding of events. Clearly a demand for a revised constitution will arise, particularly from future generations who were not party to the original constitutional contract. Conceptually they could compare their existing property rights with those they might expect if they returned to the underlying 'natural' distribution. If this is significantly different from their current position they will wish to renegotiate the constitutional contract.[7] Again, unanimity can be achieved for a new contract. Those who might reasonably expect to have their rights reduced may accept current reductions to forestall even larger reductions in the future. Also the hand of those wanting constitutional change may be strengthened by the attitude of the enforcement agency which may become increasingly unwilling to uphold property rights so divergent from the 'natural' distribution.

But public choice under the unanimity rule will be costly and may retard the development of exchange. Is there then a case for operating under less than unanimity rules (LUR) and how generally do different rules for decision making emerge? These questions were tackled by Buchanan and Tullock in their influential book *The Calculus of Consent* (1962).

CHOOSING RULES

We have seen why Buchanan perceives the necessity of laws, how social order emerges from the contracts individuals make at the constitutional level, thereby allowing them to engage in trade. What needs to be explained is an individual's considerations when faced with the constitutional choices that will crucially influence all his subsequent conduct.

At the ultimate constitutional level when property rights are assigned, we have seen Buchanan argue for consensus. This represents a minimal collectivisation. However, there may exist a demand for an extension of collective action. The source of this demand may be either to eliminate the external costs of private action on the individual or to secure an external benefit that cannot be achieved through private action. It is in dealing with these decisions that LUR may emerge.

Buchanan and Tullock's approach is 'cost' as opposed to 'cost-benefit' based. Two costs are identified. First, 'external costs', which represent the expected cost to an individual imposed upon him by the action of others. Secondly, 'decision-making costs' being the cost to an individual of his participation in an organised activity. Decision-making costs can also be viewed as the costs of two or more individuals reaching agreement. The sum of these two costs is termed 'interdependence costs'. For purely private actions interdependence costs are zero. Clearly there are many areas where these costs are positive and collective action is a possible means of reducing them. However there are alternative means involving voluntary associations. Buchanan has made a significant contribution to the theory of clubs (1965) which offers a solution to positive interdependence costs without an extension of collectivisation.

The existence of non-zero interdependence costs may induce individuals to consider constitutional changes bringing an activity within the realm of social choice. His decision will depend on his relative evaluation of private, voluntary and collective action.

The cost of collective action can be explained with the help of Figure 3.1. Curve $E$ is the present value of external cost function. It relates the expected cost to an individual of action taken by others to the number of individuals who must agree before a collection decision is made for the group. Under dictatorship external costs are at a maximum whilst if unanimity prevails external costs are zero as the individual can exercise his veto on any potentially damaging action.

When two or more individuals must agree, decision making costs are positive. When the proportion of individuals needed to make a decision is low there are many potential replacements if one individual refuses, so decision-making costs are small. As the proportion needed to make an agreement rises so do decision-making costs. As unanimity is approached the number of alternative individuals is very small; people will invest time and resources in bargaining and decision-making costs rise rapidly. With unanimity every individual has a monopoly over a valuable resource, his agreement, and decision-making costs are very high indeed. This movement of the decision-making cost function is

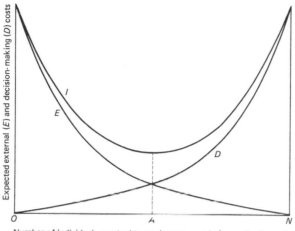

Number of individuals required to reach agreement before collective action can be taken

FIGURE 3.1

represented in Figure 3.1 by the curve D. The curve I is the vertical summation of C and D and is the interdependence costs. By assuming that each individual seeks to minimise interdependence costs the optimal decision-making rule for the individual is at A.

Figure 3.2 helps to explain whether an individual will support the movement of an activity into the collective realm. The curve I is as above. X is the cost of the activity when carried out privately or voluntarily, whichever is the cheaper. Since X is greater than Z, the individual's assessment of the costs of his preferred decision rule, he will support the activity's shift into the realm of collective action. If however the cost of private or voluntary action is Y he would not support any shift.

There are several important implications to be drawn from the above analysis. First, under collective action interdependence costs are never zero, collectivisation always imposes a cost on the individual. Further the existence of the external costs of private behaviour is neither a necessary nor a sufficient condition for an activity to be collectivised. Finally, there is nothing special about simple majority rules. Buchanan feels these implications are frequently ignored by many social scientists.

The calculus of consent is, like the rest of Buchanan's work, based on the individualist postulate. Obviously, individuals may

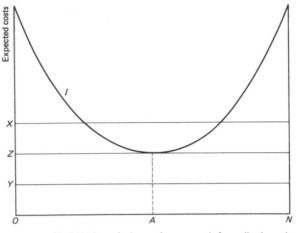

Number of individuals required to reach agreement before collective action can be taken

FIGURE 3.2

have different optimal voting rules for any given activity. How are these reconciled? Individuals will be involved in a continual process of decision-making on whether activities should be collectivised and then on how any collective activity will be operated. This opens up the possibility of gains from trade, i.e. log-rolling on an explicit or implicit basis. Further, though individuals will be guided by self-interest in their decisions this will be tempered by additional characteristics. Social contracts differ from private contracts with respect to the degrees of social participation, responsibility, coercion (collective choices bind everyone) and certainty. They also differ with respect to the nature of alternatives being considered and the power relations between people (Buchanan, 1954b). It is perhaps the associated degree of uncertainty that brings about the movement of individuals towards a consensus on rules. Each individual, not knowing where he will be in the future, will be interested in generating a 'fair' set of rules – one that will make the 'most interesting game'. There is a similarity here with John Rawls' (1971) concept of 'justice and fairness' (Buchanan, 1971). It is the weakest element in Buchanan's analysis, though doubtless individuals could act in this way.

The outcome of the calculus of consent is a set of rules, a constitution. Where these rules deal with property rights, unanimity is likely to be used. When the rules deal with the operation of a collective activity less than unanimity rules (LUR) will be introduced. In accepting LUR the individual expects to incur some external costs as decisions go against him. But on balance he is willing to endure these as he expects them to be less than if the activity were run on a private or voluntary basis. The external costs he bears are the price he pays in the social contract just as law abiding is the cost he pays in the constitutional contract.

## A STATE OF BIAS?

From the formation of a social contract two distinct types of government emerge. Self-interest leads an individual to default on contractual agreements when he believes that this can be achieved unilaterally. Consequently, at the constitutional stage an agency is created to perform the function of enforcing contractual agreements. Buchanan terms this agency the 'Protective State'. At the post constitutional stage we have seen that individuals may choose to provide a good collectively rather than through private or voluntary organisations. So a 'Productive State' is devised to provide public goods.

The most important features of the protective state are that it is external to the parties it is protecting and that it has no potential for operating in its own interests. Unfortunately, Superman is a comic book character so individuals must select some internal candidate to act as enforcer and treat him as if he were external. The protective state does not make law, rather, given a specification of law and penalties, it acts in a scientific manner to determine whether contracts have been violated and metes out the appropriate punishment when it finds that they have.

Given the individualist postulate the productive state must be internal and respond to individuals' desires. The productive state determines the quantities and cost-sharing arrangements for those goods within its domain, where these decisions are derived from individuals' values this is not a scientific operation. The productive state is a mechanism enabling individuals to achieve the benefits of public goods.

Given Buchanan's perspective of government and his view that the status quo is not rigid, is everything in the garden rosy?

Buchanan's answer is an emphatic 'no'; instead of 'ordered anarchy' he sees 'constitutional anarchy'.

It is not necessary to locate some malignant cause for this corruption of the ideal. Adopting LUR, on a rational basis, may be a source of undesirable outcomes even when there are a set of procedural limits on the use of LUR. Such a limit might be that, in all proposals for collective action, gross benefits must exceed gross costs. A series of collective decisions on proposals that meet this criterion can easily produce an over-expanded budget. Though each proposal taken separately with LUR appears to create benefits in excess of costs this overlooks the spillover effects. For as the budget expands so the resistance to paying tax and enforcement costs rise. The increase in enforcement costs influences not only the current decisions but all previous decisions as well, thereby reducing net benefits.

But frequently such criteria are not institutionalised. We can examine the possible outcome in the absence of such criteria with the aid of Table 3.1. It represents a three-person group where taxes are equal for each individual. Three proposals are considered, separately. Each costs £9 so that tax is £3 per head. The benefits are distributed unevenly as illustrated in Table 3.1. With a simple majority rule Project 1 will receive the support of both *A* and *B* for whom benefits exceed tax. Similarly projects 2 and 3 will be adopted. However, in total, each person will have paid £9 in tax but received only £8 in benefits. Again the acceptance of LUR has produced the undesirable outcome of an over-extended budget.

TABLE 3.1

| Person | Benefits (£) | | |
| --- | --- | --- | --- |
| | Project 1 | Project 2 | Project 3 |
| *A* | 4 | 4 | 0 |
| *B* | 4 | 0 | 4 |
| *C* | 0 | 4 | 4 |

This is not the only source of budgetary bias. Politicians, government employees and bureaucrats can also affect budgetary outcomes. Politicians are unlikely to be drawn from those who prefer a minimal role for government but rather from those interested in social engineering and the concomitant budgets. Politicians who derive utility from making decisions for large numbers of people are interested in big budgets and projects with differential impacts. And that small proportion of politicians who are motivated by the possibility of pecuniary rewards of government and corruption will probably prefer large budgets. Consequently, there exists a preference amongst politicians for larger budgets that will find expression when the control mechanism of voters over politicians is less than absolute. Equally bureaucrats and government employees have a preference, based on self-interest, for large budgets, for their own welfare is directly related to budget size. Further, as budget size and the number of active programmes grows, politicians will find it increasingly difficult to control their employees who, in turn, will express their preference for large budgets. Finally, growing budgets will make public employees a significant voice in the political process. Thus within the productive state there is an inherent bias towards very substantial budgets, and thereby a loss of freedom of choice.

There are also problems within the protective state. Enforcement of contractual agreements is costly and defaults are certain to occur unless individuals decide to uphold the law at any cost. In this sense individuals' property rights are related to the cost incurred in enforcing them and exogenous changes in these costs clearly determine the extent to which laws can remain socially viable. Any law is only as good as the policeman.

Further the enforcement agency's view of what rights can be justifiably guaranteed may alter in time. But the costs of enforcement do not relate purely to those taxes necessary to cover the discovery and punishment of law-breakers, they also contain a subjective element.

Choosing and handing out punishment, either directly or indirectly, is for most people a 'bad', something that imposes a utility loss and something they will wish to avoid or pay to be reduced. This attitude does not reflect just charity, self-interest is also present. The individual may conceivably become a law-breaker himself, or be erroneously found guilty. The benefit of punishment is in its function as a deterrent, whilst the cost of the punishment has to be met after it has failed and will not restore the original position. Taken together these factors are an incentive to relax the enforcement of laws which in turn may promote further law-breaking. An increased frequency of such behaviour normally leads to a higher level of discoveries and potential punishment. And so the circle continues. Obviously a Samaritan is in danger of being exploited (Buchanan, 1975c). This general reluctance to punish Buchanan terms the 'Punishment Dilemma' and it has a debilitating effect on the functioning and the notion of enforcement.

But these general biases within the productive and protective states are not the real source of 'Constitutional Anarchy'. An individual might reasonably expect them and take them into account and a political economist might fruitfully be employed in suggesting beneficial institutional changes. For Buchanan the source of the problem is the inter-penetration of the two states and the violation of the constitutional contract by the state itself.

Due to rising decision-making costs a system of representatives for political decisions has evolved. In turn the representatives have established a bureaucracy in the interests of 'efficiency'. However the bureaucrats, lacking any criteria or popular control, have departed from the voluntaristic nature of the social contract. Experts (economists) have been recruited to advise on social goals. The experts, instead of searching for possible institutional changes, have identified 'market failures' and recommend an ever expanding role for government.

The outcome has been policies with differential rather than general beneficial effects. Naturally, those who are damaged by specific policies agitate to gain their own preferential proposals and the circle starts again. Buchanan comments 'collectivized governmental attempts to do more and more have been demonstrably revealed to accomplish less and less' (1975a).

Buchanan's view is that individuals, locked into this impersonal system, have found little succour from the protective state. The productive state having decided on provision and cost sharing, has utilised the protective state to enforce its decisions. The protective state has failed to distinguish between 'constitutionality' and 'the public interest'. It has made law, it has not recognised the limits to the use of LUR and has supported arbitrary and uncompensated shifts in property rights. In behaving in this manner the protective state has failed to punish violations of the constitutional contract by the state.

This breaking of fundamental rules is for Buchanan no more apparent than in the dropping of the balanced-budget rule (Buchanan and Wagner, 1977). Budget deficits are in politicians' interests, enabling them to win electoral support and express their preferences for large budgets. But the costs of such actions in terms of inflation and the dysfunctional impact on economic co-ordination could be ruinous to the whole economy. Buchanan bluntly states 'Sober assessment suggests that, politically, Keynesianism represents a substantial disease that over the long run can prove fatal for the survival of democracy'. (Buchanan, Burton and Wagner, 1978).

The state has become too powerful and persuasive; it has acted unlawfully. This has induced the citizency to behave in a similar manner so that disorder characterises many areas where pre-viously ordered anarchy prevailed (Buchanan and Devletoglou, 1970).

The most poignant aspect of Buchanan's analysis is that it is *government* that has failed not just markets.

EXIT OR WAY OUT ?

Unless some dramatic action is taken, Buchanan believes the spectre of the Hobbesian jungle will become concrete very shortly. He rejects any piecemeal approach for that is largely how we raised the ghost. His valuable insight into the punishment dilemma indicates that greater enforcement will not be sufficient. But this is not the crucial issue, as state violations of the constitutional contract are the fundamental cause of the problems. Buchanan's solution is a 'constitutional revolution' in which individuals engage in a major reassessment of their constitutional rights and freedoms (Buchanan and de Pierro, 1969). But being a methodological individualist he is unable to predict the outcome of such a renegotiation of the constitutional contract; certainly he expects a rolling-back of state intervention. This is not the bugle call for the return of *laissez-faire* doctrines and their implied support of the status quo because he also expects that the question of income distribution to be on the agenda. But in the cases of 'market failure' and 'externalities' Buchanan forsees the emergence of new institutional arrange-ments rather than state intervention.

However, Buchanan's constitutional revolution can only come about if the contractarian perspective is adopted by citizens, legislators, the judiciary, social philosophers and economics professors. The intellectual climate appears conducive to such a conversion given the confidence of the 'radical right' and the growing ascendancy of monetarism. But the problem remains of constructing a political machine whose function is to dismantle and modify the state apparatus without itself being corrupted. Further, those who currently benefit from the existing machine will resist any changes whilst changes in technology (e.g. the coming 'chip'-based-information society) and in the international economic order (e.g. increasing dominance of the global corporation) may induce an increased desire for state intervention. The growing ground swell of tax payers' revolts, the success of California's Proposition 13 (which surfaced in a fairly unusual constitutional setting) and the general dissatisfaction with government, testify to the possibility of a renegotiation and the importance of public choice. Buchanan gloomily sees the alternatives as either an intensification of the social dilemma of being governed or violent revolution.

Buchanan's analysis of the emergence of law; of constitutions as a process; of the pervasiveness of contracts; and of the problems of the day, are not exactly historically descriptive. They provide a framework for discussion and study and one that is at variance with many more popular perspectives. Within the framework the focus of attention is the state which is deemed to have failed. His economics of politics examines head-on an apparatus that impinges on everyone's life, apparently without limit. Of course Buchanan attracts many detractors who can criticise his rejection of an organic state, class, the public interest and his view that economics is about markets not allocation. But ultimately all criticisms can be reduced to an attack on Buchanan's methodology which embodies his beliefs. Thus, finally there is only one question: do Buchanan's beliefs offer us an exit from our current problems – or are they just too way out?

NOTES

1. For recent surveys of the Public Choice literature see Mayston (1974) and Mueller (1976).
2. In its weakest form this holds that if everyone in a constituency prefers state $x$ to state $z$ then a social ordering will also rank $x$ above $z$.
3. Pareto Optimality is achieved when various marginal rates (of substitution, transformation and technical substitution) are simultaneously equivalent,

the implication being that no movement whatsoever can improve welfare under the current technological constraint. See Rowley and Peacock (1975) for a vigorous attack on this concept.

4. 'One of the few dreams he ever permitted himself was for a socialist *Il Principe Nouvo*, who would be prepared to listen carefully to the advice of his counsellors, and to value their independence of mind and devotion to society above devotion to his own person. Kalecki looked for such a prince from Havana to Delhi' Lipinski (1977).

5. Arrow (1951) attempted to devise a constitution for making choices amongst three or more alternatives which would satisfy five reasonable conditions. He found it logically impossible to construct such a constitution without breaking one or more of the conditions. The impossibility theorem has attracted a great deal more attention than the impossibility of Pareto Optimality.

6. There is considerable debate concerning the appropriate response to externalities stressing property rights – institutional setting, various forms of pricing and direct government regulation. Buchanan and Stubblebine (1962) favour a shift in the institutional setting.

7. This notion of frequent renegotiations clearly characterises the experience of the European Economic Community.

REFERENCES

Arrow, K. J., 1951 *Social Choice and Individual Values* (John Wiley).
Buchanan, J. M., 1949 'The Pure Theory of Public Choice: a Suggested Approach', *Journal of Political Economy*, vol. 57, pp. 496–505.
—— 1954a 'Social Choice, Democracy and Free Markets', *Journal of Political Economy*, vol. 62, pp. 114–23.
—— 1954b 'Individual Choice in Voting and the Market', *Journal of Political Economy*, vol. 62, pp. 334–43.
—— 1959 'Positive Economics, Welfare Economics, and Political Economy', *Journal of Law and Economics*, vol. 2, pp. 124–38.
—— 1960 *Fiscal Theory and Political Economy* (University of North Carolina Press).
—— 1962a 'Politics, Policy and Pigovian Margins', *Economica*, vol. 29, pp. 17–28.
—— 1962b 'The Relevance of Pareto Optimality', *Journal of Conflict Resolution*, vol. 6, pp. 341–54.
—— 1964 'What Should Economists Do?', *Southern Economic Journal*, vol. 30, pp. 213–22.
—— 1965 'An Economic Theory of Clubs', *Economica*, vol. 32, pp. 1–14.
—— 1966 *Public Finance in Democratic Process* (University of North Carolina Press).
—— 1969a *Cost and Choice: an Inquiry in Economic Theory* (Markham Publishing Co.).
—— 1969b 'Is Economics the Science of Choice ?', in E. Streissler (ed.) *Roads to Freedom* (Routledge and Kegan Paul).

—— 1971 'Equity as Fact and Norm', *Ethics*, vol. 81 pp. 228–40.
—— 1975a *The Limits of Liberty: Between Anarchy and the Leviathan* (University of Chicago Press).
—— 1975b 'A Contractarian Paradigm for Applying Economic Theory', *American Economic Review*, vol. 65, pp. 225–30.
—— 1975c 'The Samaritan's Dilemma', in E. S. Phelps (ed:) *Altruism, Morality and Economic Theory* (the Russel Sage Foundation).
—— 1977 *Freedom in Constitutional Contract: Perspectives of a Political Economist*. (Texas A and M University Press).
Buchanan, J. M. Burton, J. and Wagner, R. E., 1978 *The Consequences of Mr Keynes* (Institute of Economic Affairs).
Buchanan, J. M. and Bush, W., 1974 'Political Constraints on Contractual Redistribution', *American Economic Review*, vol. 64, pp. 153–7.
Buchanan, J. M. and Devletoglou, N., 1970 *Academia in Anarchy: An Economic Diagnosis* (Basic Books).
Buchanan, J. M. and de Pierro, A., 1969 'Pragmatic Reform and Constitutional Revolution', *Ethics*, vol. 79 pp. 95–104.
Buchanan, J. M. and Stubblebine, W., 1962, 'Externality', *Economica*, vol. 29, pp. 371–84.
Buchanan, J. M. and Thirlby, G. F. (eds), 1973 *LSE Essays on Cost* (Wiedenfeld and Nicholson).
Buchanan, J. M. and Tullock, G., 1962 *The Calculus of Consent: Logical Foundation of Constitutional Democracy* (University of Michigan Press).
Buchanan, J. M. and Wagner, R. E., 1977 *Democracy in Deficit: The Political Legacy of Lord Keynes* (Academic Press).
Lipinski, E., 1977 'Michal Kalecki', *Oxford Bulletin of Economics and Statistics*, vol. 39, pp. 69–77.
Mayston, D. J., 1974 *The Idea of Social Choice* (Macmillan).
Mueller, D. C., 1976 'Public Choice: A Survey', *Journal of Economic Literature*, vol. 14, pp. 395–433.
Rawls, J., 1971 *A Theory of Justice* (Harvard University Press).
Rowley, K. R. and Peacock, A. T., 1975 *Welfare Economics: A Liberal Restatement* (Martin Robertson).

# 4 Positively Milton Friedman

John Burton

Attempting to portray the work of Milton Friedman in 5000 words is an impossible assignment. It is like trying to catch the Niagara Falls in a pint pot. A diminutive man in physical stature (5 ft 3 in), Friedman is also one of the intellectual giants of twentieth-century economics – the source of a cascade of ideas, papers and books, of a highly diverse, original and (nearly always!) provocative nature.

A journal article written to assess Friedman's scientific contributions to economics (Thygesen, 1977), to occasion his achievement of the 1976 Nobel Prize in Economics, lists some 245 Friedman publications, including 26 books; Friedman has also contributed a regular – and regularly effervescent – economics column to *Newsweek* for many years.[1] Nor was this to be any valedictory assessment. Although now 'retired' from the University of Chicago, where he rose to international prominence as the leader of the so-called 'Chicago School' of economics, Friedman continues his work in a variety of forms. Now at the Hoover Institute, he is currently engaged upon a major research project (with Anna J. Schwarz) on international price-level and monetary linkages from an historical perspective. Over the past two years he has also worked on a TV documentary series entitled *Free to Choose*.

Friedman's work is hallmarked by its diversity as much as by its quantity. His theoretical and empirical contributions to economic analysis have ranged over such varied topics as utility theory, income distribution theory, the aggregate consumption function, tax theory, and many other topics, although his central concern has proved to be that of monetary economics. His contributions to the discussion of public policy have been even more varied, covering virtually the entire gamut of major economic and social issues of contemporary concern.[2]

A third hallmark of Friedman's work has been his originality – and talent for controversy. Both in his 'technical' economic writings and his more 'populist' writings on public policy, Friedman has exhibited a persistent flair for attacking established orthodoxy. As Dolan (1977, p. 206) has remarked, when Friedman got the 1976 Nobel Prize in Economics:

> Few were surprised. The main surprise was that this most original and influential of economists had had to wait in line so long! The explanation is that Friedman has built his career outside the economics establishment – built in, in fact, by challenging virtually every major establishment doctrine.

It says much for the penetrating lucidity of Friedman's writing, let alone the sheer tenacity of the man himself, that his attacks upon the establishment thinking of the post-war years have them-selves – at least as regards certain topics – gradually, if grud-gingly, become accepted as a sort of new orthodoxy. There are, for example, now few governments which would not pay at least lip-service to Friedman's insistence upon the need for monetary control in the fight against inflation.

Finally, it needs to be noted that Friedman's work has not been confined to economic analysis and policy. He has also contributed to statistical theory and its applications, to the study of economic history – particularly as regards the monetary history of the USA, to the discussion of the methodology of science, and to the political philosophy of a free society.

How *does* one summarise this kaleidoscopic thinker in 5000 words?

## ON MILTON AND MAYNARD, MONETARISM AND KEYNESIANISM

The other giant of twentieth-century economics with whom Friedman invites close comparison is, inevitably, John Maynard Keynes.

There are in fact fascinating similarities between the two: their prodigious output, their wide range of concerns combined with a central interest in monetary theory; their talents for controversy and antiestablishmentarianism; their international status; their exceptional mental acuity and agility in debate; their noted personal charm.

A second matter that compels comparison is the 'monetarism *v* Keynesianism' debate that has raged in economics over the past two decades. Keynes gave birth to the 'Keynesian revolution' in macro-economic thought and policy via his *General Theory* (1936). One of Friedman's intellectual crusades has been to replace that revolution with a 'monetarist counter-revolution' (Friedman, 1970c) as the ruling paradigm in macro-economics.

The intensity of the monetarist-Keynesian 'war' in economics has propagated a belief, prevalent among Ministers of Finance, let alone students of economics, that Keynes and Friedman are to be seen as completely opposed, both scientifically and ideologically. An underlying theme of this essay is such a belief is in many ways erroneous, if not misguided in its entire general thrust.

Given the size of the task, this essay confines itself to a critical appreciation of but a few aspects of Friedman's large and diverse work: his methodological approach, his macro/monetary economics, and to a general consideration of Milton Friedman *qua* normative political economist.

FRIEDMAN'S VIEWS ON THE METHODOLOGY OF ECONOMICS

Friedman's methodological position was to be elaborated at a relatively early stage in his work. It was to provide a vital underpinning for much of his major theoretical and empirical research to follow.

According to Friedman (1953b), the appropriate criterion for establishing the 'fruitfulness' of a theory is not the 'realism' of its assumptions, but the degree of empirical corroboration attained by its predictions. His argument bases itself on the proposition that the assumptions of any theory are inevitably – if it is to be scientifically fruitful – 'unreal' in some degree. This is so because the purpose of science is not to *replicate* the 'real world', in all its manifold complexity, but to provide simple models which abstract from the inessentials, and allow us to predict its behaviour.

This stress on the role of abstraction and predictive power leads to an important corollary implication. Friedman rejects both large-scale theoretical (e.g. general equilibrium) and econometric models, in favour of small-scale empirical models derived from relatively simple but predictively powerful theories. This approach has been much evident in his own empirical work (e.g. Friedman, 1957, 1959; Friedman and Meiselman, 1963).

Friedman's approach to the methodology of positive economics has given rise, as so commonly with his work, to controversy (e.g. Samuelson, 1963, Wong, 1973). Simply put, much of this argument boils down to the proposition that Friedman's stress upon scientific prediction leads him to ignore the importance of scientific *explanation*, in the sense defined by the classic statement of the concept of causal explanation provided by Hempel and Oppenheim (1948).

I would, however, argue that Friedman's methodological prescriptions have had a generally beneficial effect upon the orientation of subsequent economic research. First, the Hempel–Oppenheim conditions for the adequacy of a causal scientific explanation of the deductive-nomological variety are so stringent that it is difficult to visualize how, if ever, theories that meet these conditions can be generated in economics. Friedman's emphasis upon predictive power would thus seem the more realistic criterion for economists to utilize for the foreseeable future. Secondly, in the current state of econometric 'technology' and data availability, an emphasis upon empirically-fruitful small-scale models would likewise seem the more realistic research strategy. You have to be able to walk before you can run. Friedman has at least provided us with a reminder of that pertinent fact, and a reasoned rationale for doing so, in the context of economic research.

THE NATURE AND SIGNIFICANCE OF FRIEDMAN'S MACRO-ECONOMIC ANALYSIS

Friedman's work on the role of money in the economy – his 'major professional interest for many years' (Friedman, 1975, p. 56) – and macro-economics generally, has touched on so many topics, and is so central to contemporary debates in macro-economic analysis and policy, that it is exceedingly difficult to encapsulate even this one aspect of his work in the space available. I therefore confine myself to a discussion of Friedman's contributions to the positive side of macro-economics, ignoring his (closely-related) work on the implications for macro-economic policy.

A central 'strategem' which Friedman has employed in founding an alternative framework for macro-economic analysis to that of the prevailing textbook Keynesianism (epitomised by the income–expenditure and IS–LM models) has been that of, in fact, *building upon* the Keynesian revolution, in order to erect a more theoretically-sophisticated alternative. A second 'strategem', closely related to his methodological perspective, has been that of developing simplified specifications of his own alternative hypotheses that make them eminently suitable for empirical testing against large bodies of data relating to a wide variety of contexts.[3]

These two talents were to be displayed most impressively in Friedman's (1957) presentation of his permanent income hypothesis of consumption. Note that in this work Friedman did not *reject* the concept of an aggregate consumption function – which is the central strut of Keynesian analysis because it underpins the multiplier process – but rather sought to provide a more theoretically-sophisticated analysis of it. On the basis of Fisherian capital theory, Friedman argued that neither the dependent variable (current consumer expenditure) nor the independent variable (current income) were specified properly in the Keynesian consumption function. Friedman's alternative hypothesis was that only the *permanent* component of current consumption is functionally related to the *permanent* component of income, where the qualifying adjective 'permanent' is taken to refer to the magnitudes of these variables viewed in a long-term, intertemporal choice context. Expressed at its simplest, the underlying idea is that choices about consumption 'now' are influenced not only by current (e.g. today's, this year's) income, but also by longer-term income expectations.

This simple idea proved to be empirically powerful, because it enabled Friedman (1957) to explain much wider classes of consumption phenomena than the Keynesian hypothesis – such as the apparent paradox in the form of the estimated secular and cyclical consumption functions, and observed differences in the savings behaviour of such groups as business entrepreneurs, farmers, and wage earners.

Friedman's contributions to this particular branch of macroeconomics were largely to lapse after this seminal publication, but the permanent income hypothesis has exerted a profound influence on the later direction of research in this area.[4]

Friedman's own attentions have been drawn the more heavily to the monetary aspects of macro-economics. A major step in the evolution of his work in this area came with his restatement of the quantity theory (Friedman, 1956). Over the two previous decades, the quantity theory of money had been jettisoned, as a result of the effective demolition job done on it by Keynes and his disciples. Their central argument was that the relationship between the demand for money and nominal income is not one of proportionality (as assumed by the textbook 'straw-man' version of the quantity theory) – that the 'Cambridge $k$' in the formulation $M_d = k\,PY$, is not a constant but a variable, influenced by the level of interest rates.

Friedman re-established the acceptability of the quantity theory by the simple device of taking these Keynesian criticisms on board in his re-statement of it. Friedman, in essence, *re-defined* the quantity theory as a theory of the demand for money – as a theory of the determinants of $k$, in other words. Furthermore, by once again turning to Fisherian capital theory, Friedman derived a (supposedly quantity-theoretic) analysis of the demand for money which is far more sophisticated than the original Keynesian hypothesis, setting the demand for money decision in a much broader portfolio choice context. There is thus clear justice in Patinkin's (1969, p. 47) contention that:

> what Friedman . . . actually presented [in his 'restatement' of the quantity theory] is a statement of the modern portfolio approach to the demand for money which . . . can only be seen as a continuation of the Keynesian theory of liquidity preference.[5]

In his 'restatement' paper, Friedman derives a (real) demand-for-money function, the arguments of which include not only the yield on bonds (as in the original Keynesian liquidity preference function), but also the yield on equities, physical capital and human capital, and the expected rate of inflation – a theoretically-relevant variable (as inflation acts as a tax on money holdings) which Keynes had ignored. Friedman's theoretical treatment of the demand for money is further differentiated from its Keynesian predecessor by assuming that permanent income, and not current income, is the relevant income constraint variable in the money-demand function. Finally, the Friedman specification does not, as in the Keynesian treatment, partition the demand for money function into a demand for 'active' balances and a (money-illusioned) demand for 'idle' balances.

In his later empirical work on the demand for money, however, this elaborate theoretical model is considerably pared down. Friedman (1959) found that the demand for money over a long span of time in the US is primarily explained by permanent income, and that alone. Subsequent research has confirmed generally that permanent income (or some similar proxy for wealth) performs better than current income in estimated demand-for-money functions. The same body of research, however, has generally corroborated the postulate that the level of interest rates does have an independent and significant effect on the demand for money, contrary to Friedman's (1959) own findings. In the light of the gathering evidence, Friedman has subsequently reformulated his stated position on this issue, now accepting that no fundamental significance attaches to the matter of the actual interest-elasticity of the demand for money, provided that it is not minus infinity (i.e. a Keynesian 'liquidity trap' situation – the existence of which he denies). It is, in any case, quite in accordance with Friedman's (1956) theoretical specification that the (real) return on bonds affects the demand for money.

## THE SUPPLY OF MONEY

In the early Sixties Friedman's writings on money shifted from the demand to the supply side, or rather to the influence of changes in the money supply. In a herculean effort, Friedman and Schwarz (1963a) constructed a series of money-supply statistics for the US ranging as far back in time as 1775 (although concentrating in particular on the period from 1867 onwards). A primary purpose of this *magnum opus* of historical-monetary research was to express and corroborate Friedman's often-expressed thesis that changes in the stock of money exert a powerful effect on the level of economic activity, albeit with a long and variable lag.

Interest in the Friedman–Schwarz findings centred, inevitably, on their interpretation of the 'Great Contraction' of 1929–33 in the US. This is a crucial test case in the dispute between Friedman and Keynesian orthodoxy, because the standard Keynesian interpretation is that this episode demonstrated the impotency of monetary policy under the supposed conditions of a depression-fired liquidity trap. Friedman's argument, to the contrary, is that the Great Contraction was the very consequence of the potency of monetary changes, (mis-)engineered by the FRB (the central bank of the US). Friedman and Schwarz (1963a) documented, in great detail, the factors which led the FRB to create or allow almost a one-third *reduction* in the US money stock in this short period – causing what might otherwise have been a mild recession to escalate into a major economic catastrophe. As Friedman (1970b, p. 97) himself puts the point:

> The Great Contraction is tragic testimony to the power of monetary policy – not, as Keynes and so many of his contemporaries believed, evidence of its impotence.

Conflict over the monetarist and Keynesian interpretations of history was further sharpened with the publication of a highly influential but controversial study by Friedman and Meiselman (1963). This assessed the comparative predictive performance of a simple Keynesian (multiplier) model and a simple money stock determination hypothesis of the level of 'induced' expenditures (*i.e.* private consumption in the main). Both hypotheses were estimated in linear form (for both levels and changes in the dependent variable) using data for the period 1897–1958. They found that, with the exception of the Thirties, the results were 'strikingly one-sided': the money stock clearly outperformed the autonomous expenditures variable. Critics fastened upon the potential simultaneous-equations bias implicit in such a one-equation estimation approach. Thus, Ando and Modigliani (1965) were able to demonstrate that if purportedly endogenous components were removed from the specification of the money supply, the balance of evidence on the predictive power of the two hypotheses was less one-sided than Friedman and Meiselman had claimed.

The same theme of money-stock endogeneity runs through criticisms of the use of the observed lead relationship between fluctuations in money and economic activity which Friedman and his collaborators (e.g. Friedman, 1958; Friedman and Schwarz, 1963b) have utilised to argue their hypothesis of the impulse dominance of money. The critics (e.g. Tobin, 1970) argue that to rely on such evidence is to fall foul of the *post hoc ergo propter hoc* fallacy, and that it is possible to generate the observed lead of money over economic activity in Keynesian-type models with an endogenous money supply. In the critics' view – most trenchantly expressed by the 'Old Cambridge' disciples of Keynes, Professor Lord Kaldor and Ms Joan Robinson – causation runs from income to money stock (the so-called 'reverse causation' hypothesis). Friedman has accepted that the lead of money does not demonstrate in itself the direction of causality, which must be inferred from an examination of the determinants of the money supply. However, Friedman and Schwarz (1963a) had in fact provided just such a detailed examination of this matter. Their historical evidence, and Cagan's (1965) associated study, provides very substantial empirical support to the contention that (at least for the US, over the long time-period examined) the money supply is not primarily endogenously determined. The further research conducted on this matter to date also supports this position. It suggests that while there is a 'reverse causation' running from income to money, it is of relatively minor significance, and that the primary line of causation runs from money to income.

The transmission process underlying this monetary impulse-propagation mechanism is visualized by Friedman and his collaborators (e.g. Friedman and Meiselman, 1963; Friedman and Schwarz, 1963b) to be a general portfolio adjustment process affecting the entire balance-sheet of decision makers. This is a logical complement of Friedman's (1956) theoretical treatment of the demand for money – and thus is simultaneously to be seen as but a generalization of the Keynesian view of the monetary transmission process, which concentrates on a narrower range of asset adjustments in 'credit' markets.

On this point, as with many others, Friedman's 'monetarist' treatment is to be seen properly as an outgrowth, or sophistication of Keynes's own basic theoretical framework, and not as some radical, fundamentally antithetical departure. On the analysis of inflation, however, Friedman's work does represent a break with the Keynesian heritage. In the *General Theory* Keynes was primarily concerned with a depression scenario and gave little (clear) scrutiny to the determination of the money wage and price level. Friedman's macro-economics, on the other hand, makes the price level an explicit endogenous variable. An analysis of the inflation–unemployment nexus, incorporating an explicit treatment of short-run dynamics of the inflation process was presented in Friedman's (1967) highly influential presidential address to the American Economics Association. This re-introduced the role of price expectations in inflation theory,[6] and presented a taut verbal statement of Friedman's 'natural rate' (of unemployment) hypothesis. As the very titling suggests, this hypothesis lies in the tradition of Wicksell's quantity theory rather than Keynes *General Theory*.

The natural rate hypothesis was presented by Friedman as a challenge to the concept of a stable, negatively-sloped Phillips curve – a concept which itself may be seen as a 'curved' generalization of Keynes's (1936) apparent dichotomisation of wage-price determination into less than/greater than full employment states. Friedman's argument was that monetary policy could not be used to reduce unemployment below its equilibrium ('natural') level permanently (as the Phillips curve idea suggested) unless an *ever-accelerating* inflation was to be engineered by the monetary authorities. His argument rests upon the premise that decision-makers will seek to set the prices they 'command' (or negotiate) with a view to their *real* value over the future transaction period – that is, with a view to the expected future course of the price level. Consequently, 'the' Phillips curve will shift according to the state of inflationary expectations. Furthermore, if (as seems plausible) people come to fully anticipate – and thus compensate for – any stable inflation rate, unemployment will move back to its equilibrium level. Thus the long-run full-equilibrium Phillips curve is vertical.

Friedman's re-introduction of price expectations to inflation analysis was greatly to affect the subsequent direction of empirical research in this area.[7] To summarize the matter briefly, a very large body of evidence now corroborates the hypothesis that inflationary expectations are a significant factor in the inflationary process, but that whether the long-run Phillips curve is strictly vertical – or just more steeply sloped than 'the' short-run Phillips curve – is still a matter of econometric dispute.

In his Nobel lecture, Friedman (1977) was to offer a further 'modest elaboration' of his earlier natural rate hypothesis, in order to account for the apparent, long-term *positive* association of rising inflation and rising unemployment witnessed in the western economies from the mid-Sixties onwards (a 'positively-sloped', very long-term 'Phillips curve'). His explanation is that higher secular rates of inflation are likely to be accompanied (due to political forces) by greater instability in the inflation rate and thus greater uncertainty. Friedman sees this greater volatility as leading directly (in the economic arena) and indirectly (via adjustments in the entire politico-institutional framework) to a higher equilibrium rate of unemployment, at least during the present 'adjustment phase' (which might be decades long) to the current era of volatile inflation. This hypothesis would seem to warrant entitling as a significant generalisation rather than a 'modest elaboration', dealing as it does with a very long-run perspective, and adjustment processes to inflation lying outside the narrow area of pecuniary markets (Burton, 1980). Research, stimulated by Friedman's conjecture, into the connection between the secular inflation rate, its volatility, and politico-economic consequences, is now beginning to open up.

To conclude, what should be said about Friedman's contribution to macro-economics in general? I shall first try to define the underlying general themes of his work, and then point out the 'loose ends' that exist in it.

SOME GENERAL THEMES IN FRIEDMAN'S MACRO-ECONOMICS

Three themes are of central importance to a general understanding of Friedman's contribution to macro-economics:

(*i*) 'Money matters'. That is, variations in the rate of growth of the money supply are a primary determinant of the rate of growth of nominal national income. This is the basic proposition of 'monetarism'. Be it noted, however, that what Friedman has opposed himself to, in taking this position, is not Keynes's basic theoretical framework per se, but rather the 'vulgar Keynesianism' of the introductory texts, epitomized by the income–expenditure and fixprice IS–LM models.

(*ii*) 'Inflation is always and everywhere a monetary phenomenon'. Friedman does not deny that 'real' factors (e.g. union monopoly power) may sometimes affect the course of money wage/price movements. It is the positive burden of his contention, however, that the primary *proximate* determinant of inflation is the rate of growth of the money supply relative to the rate of growth of real aggregate output.

(*iii*) The long-term horizon of decision-making. Themes (*i*) and (*ii*) are well-known components of Friedman's intellectual brand-image (the catch-phrases summarizing them are in fact of his own coining). A less recognised, but fundamental, theme of Friedman's work in macro-economics is the importance that he accords to the influence of both past experience and future expectations upon behaviour in the present. This underscores his use of the concept of permanent income in his analysis of the demand for money and the consumption function, and his stress upon the role of price expectations in the explanation of inflation. On this point there is again a fundamental correspondence and continuity between Keynes' and Friedman's work, as the *General Theory* may be seen as a (short-run) model 'of an economy in which behaviour is governed by expectations about the future' (Johnson, 1961). However, Keynes provided no formal analysis of the formation of expectations, whereas Friedman has been concerned centrally throughout his work to formalize the systematic influence of past experience upon anticipations of the future, and the manner in which the latter thereby influences behaviour in the present.

SOME 'LOOSE ENDS'

Friedman's work in this area represents a deeply impressive contribution to the explication of macro-economic processes. There are, however, some loose ends in the macro-economic 'paradigm' which Friedman has provided us with.

First, in his attempts to provide an overall theoretical perspective in which to view his work Friedman (1970a, 1971) erects a theory of nominal income movements, which ignores the important question of the division of this magnitude into price and output responses in the short-run. Many (e.g. Johnson, 1971) would see this as a significant lacuna in Friedman's macro-economic framework.

Secondly, there are difficulties in reconciling Friedman's thesis of the long lead of money over nominal income with his permanent income analysis of the demand for money. The problem here, as Thygesen (1977) has noted, is that the latter hypothesis implies that the impact effect of monetary change on nominal income is large, which seems inconsistent with the 'long lead' hypothesis.

Thirdly, Friedman's whole work is open to the charge that, far from being 'anti-Keynesian' in inspiration, it is in fact of the same *genre* and suffers accordingly from the same basic defect of being too aggregative in nature, and of ignoring the micro-economic impacts of monetary change, as analysed by Hayek and other 'Austrian' economists. The connection between movements in the general price level and the distribution of relative prices is certainly something of a loose end in Friedman's (1977) analysis of the positively-sloped Phillips curve (Burton, 1980).

Fourthly, Friedman's work on inflation is concerned primarily with the proximate causes of that phenomenon, and leaves open the question of the identity of the so-called fundamental de-terminants of inflation – the causes of monetary growth.[8] On this latter question Friedman is apparently an eclectic, arguing that the political forces causing monetary growth vary widely from circumstance to circumstance (Friedman, 1970c, p. 24). Reading between the lines of his Nobel lecture, it is also apparent that Friedman (1977) himself feels the identity of the fundamental determinants of inflation to be an important and unanswered question, for he there records the view that the application of public choice theory will constitute the next major stage in the evolution of inflation theory.

Loose ends certainly remain in Milton Friedman's macro-economic framework, as it currently stands. Such is the import-ance of the questions that these lacunae give rise to, however, that it might be said that he has provided us with an agenda for the future of macro-economic research.

## MILTON FRIEDMAN THE POLITICAL ECONOMIST

It is in the area of debate on government policy that Friedman has become most well-known publicly, and established himself as the most controversial – and influential – economist of his times. As noted earlier, Friedman's writings on these matters cover a vast variety of issues. He is perhaps best well-known for his redoubtable advocacy of the cases for educational vouchers, the negative income tax, flexible exchange-rates, a volunteer army, a fixed money supply growth rate, and for general indexation as an anti-inflation measure. Each of these issues warrant lengthy and serious treatment: here I must confine myself to an evaluation of Friedman's general position as a normative political economist. A common characterization of Friedman by the media is that he is an intellectual father-figure of something called the 'extreme or far right'. Some Marxists go further and label Friedman as a 'fascist', or as a tool of the ruling (capitalist) class. Thus, for example, the noted writer on the political economy of development, André Gunder Frank, has openly accused Friedman (and his Chicago colleague, Arnold Harberger) of supporting policies of 'economic genocide' in ('fascist') Chile:

> . . . for the glory and benefit of the bourgeoisie in the USA, whom you so faithfully serve as paid executors and executioners (Frank, 1976, p. 48).

Both of these characterizations in fact involve gross – indeed grotesque, in Frank's case – misunderstanding or misrepresentation of the spectrum of ideological debate, and of Friedman's position in it. Underlying them both is a misconception that the array of ideological positions can be adequately represented by a one-dimensional political issue space, as shown in Figure 4.1 below, a continuum whose ends are defined as 'Left' and 'Right'. At the 'Centre' lay the advocates of the 'mixed economy', among

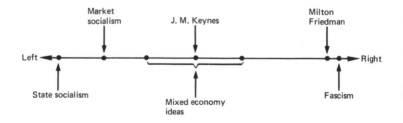

FIGURE 4.1   *The spectrum of economic philosophies: the conventional portrayal*

which Keynes is often supposed to number. Friedman is pictured as being over on the 'far' right, close up against fascism.

I seriously doubt that a one-dimensional space can adequately represent the spectrum of ideological positions; and if one such must be chosen, it is not the one portrayed in Figure 4.1. It is also certainly not one that Friedman would accept, for a number of reasons.

First, the left–right spectrum confuses the distinction between means and ends. Friedman does not see himself divorced primarily from socialists on the question of goals or ends:

> I would venture the judgement . . . that currently in the Western world . . . differences about economic policy among disinterested citizens derive predominantly from different predictions about the economic consequences of taking action – differences that in principle can be eliminated by the progress of positive economics – rather than from fundamental differences in basic values . . . (Friedman, 1953b, p. 5).

Where Friedman differs radically from socialist economists is on the issue of the likely effects of the means or actions that the latter advocate to tackle social problems such as poverty. Thus, for example, Friedman (1975, p. 9) argues that 'the actual outcome of almost all programs that are sold in the name of helping the poor (such as the minimum wage rate) is to make the poor worse off'. He himself advocates the replacement of the whole collection of welfare state programmes by a negative income tax – a supplement to the incomes of the poor, which is some fraction of their unused income tax exemptions/deductions.

Secondly, it is quite incongruous to position Friedman, in Figure 4.1, as next to fascism in his ideological position. Friedman is a staunch and consistent exponent of classical liberal philosophy – an advocate of a system of free enterprise and the free society. The non-individualistic, *dirigiste* economic philosophy of fascism – corporatism – is utterly alien to Friedman.

A more reasonable representation of Friedman's ideological position in terms of one-dimensional issue space is shown in Figure 4.2. This is cast in terms of the nature of the *solutions* advocated by different thinkers or systems of thought, as regards the balance they adopt as between the principles of voluntary exchange and state actions in co-ordinating the economy. At one

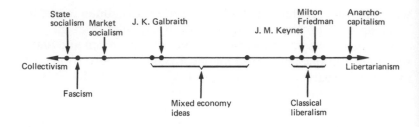

FIGURE 4.2    *Friedman's position on the collectivist–libertarian spectrum*

end we have the totally state-controlled economy, or pure collectivism; at the other end we have zero government – anarchism or libertarianism.

There are a number of points to be emphasized in this more adequate characterization of Friedman's position in the ideological spectrum. First, note that Keynes and Friedman are in the same general camp of classical liberalism; they are basically ideological fellow-travellers, not opponents, differing only on the issue of the advisability of aggregate demand management by the State.[9] Both reject state control of the supply side of the economy, except in the case of public goods, such as defence.[10] Secondly, even on this redefined spectrum, Friedman is by no means 'as far right as you can go'. Friedman is a classical liberal in the tradition of Adam Smith, John Stuart Mill and Henry C. Simons: a believer in limited, but not zero, government. As Friedman (1962, p. 34) himself expresses it: 'the consistent liberal is not an anarchist'. There are in fact, a growing number of libertarians who are 'to the right' of Friedman on our redefined spectrum – advocates of zero government and 'anarcho-capitalism'. Milton Friedman's own son, David Friedman (1973) is a leading member of them.

Gunder Frank's misrepresentation of Friedman's ideological position relies upon guilt by association – the fact that a military regime has adopted some of Friedman's advocated economic policies. It is pertinent to remember that one of the first major decisions taken by Mao Tse-tung upon coming to power was fully in line with Friedman's monetarist philosophy: that it is a folly to believe that economic development can be financed by printing money. Should we therefore label Milton Friedman as a Red Guard?

CONCLUSION

What has the 'impish gnome of economics' – as the media love to call him – contributed to the general direction of our subject?

He has provided us with a realistic strategy to follow in theoretical and empirical research. Secondly, he has managed to re-establish an awareness of the importance of monetary forces in generating macro-economic fluctuations and inflation, and added considerably to our understanding of these complex matters. Thirdly, he has with great courage – for a long time being misrepresented and derided as an 'extremist', etc., – challenged the prevailing *dirigisme* in the economic philosophy and political practice of our times, and exposed its flaws. He has done much, with Hayek, to turn the intellectual tide, and to re-establish classical liberalism as a vibrant and influential economic philosophy, of great pertinence to the major issues of our times.

I suspect that, long after the huff-and-puff of the monetarist-Keynesian debate has subsided into a realization that Friedman's monetarism is but a sophisticated elaboration of Keynes' basic macro-economic framework, it will be the last matter for which Friedman will be remembered most of all in the annals of political economy. Milton Friedman is the Adam Smith of this century.

NOTES

1. Some of Friedman's *Newsweek* columns are collected in Friedman (1975).
2. See, for example, Friedman (1962, 1975).
3. An amusing analysis of the strategies employed by Friedman in erecting the monetarist counter-revolution, and their similarity to the devices utilized in prosecuting the Keynesian revolution, is provided by Johnson (1971).
4. Alongside of the (theoretically-related) life-cycle hypothesis of Ando, Modigliani and Brumberg. It is also to be noted that the latter hypothesis has some advantages over the permanent income hypothesis in the explication of aggregate savings behaviour under conditions of a varying age-distribution. See Thygesen (1977, pp. 61–2).
5. Friedman (1970b, p. 73) has admitted in more recent writings that his reformulation of the quantity theory was 'much influenced by Keynesian liquidity analysis'.
6. Earlier emphasized by Mises and Lerner.
7. See Addison and Burton (1980a) for further discussion.
8. See Addison and Burton (1980b) for further discussion of this lacuna in monetarist analyses of inflation.

9. It is Keynes, not Friedman, who might be accused of showing some flirtation with the ideas of the New Order in the Thirties, at least in some of his writings (see Miller, 1979).
10. Even on this issue – defence being the classic public goods case for state intervention – neither Keynes nor Friedman would accept that it constitutes an automatic justification for the State to tamper with the freedom of individuals. Both advocate the principles of a volunteer army.

REFERENCES

Addison, J. T. and Burton, J., 1980a 'The Demise of "Demand-Pull" and "Cost-Push" in Inflation Theory', *Banca Nazionale del Lavoro Quarterly Review*, Jun.

—— 1980b *The Explanation of Inflation: Monetarist or Socio-political Analysis?* (Macmillan).

Ando, A. and Modigliani, F., 1965 'The Relative Stability of Monetary Velocity and the Investment Multiplier', *American Economic Review*, vol. 55, no. 4, Sep, pp. 693–728.

Burton, J., 1980 'Inflation: A Revised Friedman Theory with a Reverse Phillips Twist', University of Birmingham, UK: Faculty of Commerce and Social Science, Discussion Paper, Series A.

Cagan, P., 1965 *Determinants and Effects of Changes in the Stock of Money 1875–1960* (Columbia University Press for the National Bureau of Economic Research).

Dolan, E. G., 1977 *Basic Economics* (Dryden Press).

Frank, A. G., 1976 *Economic Genocide in Chile: Monetarist Theory Versus Humanity – Two Open Letters to Arnold Harberger and Milton Friedman* (Bertrand Russell Press Foundation).

Friedman, D., 1973 *The Machinery of Freedom: Guide to a Radical Capitalism* (Harper and Row).

Friedman, M., 1953a *Essays in Positive Economics* (University of Chicago Press).

—— 1953b 'The Methodology of Positive Economics', in Friedman, M., *Essays in Positive Economics*, (1953a), *op. cit.*, pp. 3–43.

—— 1956 'The Quantity Theory of Money – A Restatement', in Friedman, M., (ed.), *Studies in the Quantity Theory of Money* (University of Chicago Press), pp. 3–21.

—— (ed.), 1956 *Studies in the Quantity Theory of Money* (University of Chicago Press).

—— 1957 *A Theory of the Consumption Function*, (Princeton University Press, National Bureau of Economic Research General Series, No. 63).

—— 1958 'The Supply of Money and Changes in Prices and Output', in *The Relationship of Prices to Economic Stability and Growth*, Washington, D.C.: 85th Congress, Joint Economic Committee, pp. 241–56.

—— 1959 'The Demand for Money: Some Theoretical and Empirical Results', *Journal of Political Economy*, vol. 67, Aug, pp. 327–51.

—— 1962 *Capitalism and Freedom* (University of Chicago Press).

—— 1967 'The Role of Monetary Policy', *American Economic Review*, vol. 58, Mar, pp. 1–17.

—— 1970a 'A Theoretical Framework for Monetary Analysis', *Journal of Political Economy*, vol. 78, Mar–Apr, pp. 193–238.

—— 1970b *The Optimum Quantity of Money and Other Essays* (Aldine).

—— 1970c *The Counter-Revolution in Monetary Theory* Institute of Economic Affairs, Occasional Paper No. 33.

—— 1971 'A Monetary Theory of Nominal Income', *Journal of Political Economy*, vol. 79, Mar–Apr, pp. 323–37.

—— 1975 *There's No Such Thing as a Free Lunch: Essays on Public Policy* (Open Court).

—— 1977 'Nobel Lecture: Inflation and Unemployment', *Journal of Political Economy*, vol. 85, no. 3, June, pp. 451–72.

Friedman, M. and Meiselman, D., 1963 'The Relative Stability of Monetary Velocity and the Investment Multiplier in the United States, 1897–1958', in *Stabilization Policies* (Prentice Hall, for the Commission on Money and Credit) pp. 165–268.

Friedman, M. and Schwarz, A. J., 1963a *A Monetary History of the United States, 1867–1960* (Princeton University Press, National Bureau of Economic Research Studies in Business Cycles, No. 12).

Friedman, M. and Schwarz, A. J., 1963b 'Money and Business Cycles', *Review of Economics and Statistics*, vol. 45, part 2, Suppl, Feb, pp. 32–64.

Hempel, C. G. and Oppenheim, P., 1948 'Studies in the Logic of Explanation', *Philosophy of Science*, vol. 15, pp. 135–75.

Johnson, H. G., 1961 'The General Theory After Twenty-Five Years', *American Economic Review*, vol. LI, no. 2, May, pp. 1–17.

Johnson, H. G., 1971 'The Keynesian Revolution and the Monetarist Counter-Revolution', *American Economic Review*, vol. 61, May, pp. 1–14.

Keynes, J. M., 1936 *The General Theory of Employment, Interest, and Money* (Macmillan).

Miller, R., 1979 'A New Wisdom for a New Age; Keynes, G. E. Moore, and the End of Capitalism – The Origins of the "Presuppositions of Harvey Road" ' (Institute of Economic Affairs, mimeo).

Patinkin, D., 1969 'The Chicago Tradition, The Quantity Theory, and Friedman', *Journal of Money, Credit, and Banking*, vol. I, no. 1, Feb, pp. 46–70.

Samuelson, P. A., 1963 'Problem of Methodology – Discussion', *American Economic Review*, vol. 53, May, pp. 231–6.

Thygesen, N., 1977 'The Scientific Contributions of Milton Friedman', *Scandinavian Journal of Economics*, vol. 79, no. 1, pp. 56–98.

Tobin, J., 1970 'Money and Income: Post Hoc Ergo Propter Hoc?', *Quarterly Journal of Economics*, vol. 84, May, pp. 301–17.

Wong, S., 1973 'The "F-Twist" and the Methodology of Paul Samuelson', *American Economic Review*, vol. 63, June.

# 5 The Dissenting Economist: J. K. Galbraith

David Reisman

John Kenneth Galbraith was born on 15 October, 1908 in Iona Station, Ontario, and spent his childhood in a Scottish–Canadian farming community dominated by the Puritan hostility to luxury and the Calvinist work-ethic. His father was a teacher turned farmer (and in addition an active member of Canada's Liberal Party), and Galbraith originally intended too to follow some sort of agrarian career. He graduated in 1931 with a BSc degree from the Ontario Agricultural College (at the time a part of the University of Toronto) and then departed for the United States (not all that foreign a country to a farm boy from Iona Station, situated as it was less than 100 miles from Detroit: heavily dependent on American markets, local farmers were well informed about economic and social conditions south of the border) to do a PhD in agricultural economics at the University of California, Berkeley. Two years later he arrived at Harvard as an instructor in economics. His starting salary was $2400.

Berkeley in the Depression taught Galbraith about the miseries of unemployment and the tragedy of the Hoovervilles; Harvard in the New Deal convinced him of the necessity for Keynesian-type interventionist policies to combat, via reform rather than revolution, the demonstrated failures of *laissez-faire* capitalism. At Harvard he was exposed to the sophisticated arguments of Paul Samuelson, Seymour Harris, Alvin Hansen (the latter being far more of a heterodox and evolutionary economist than is usually realised, as might indeed be expected from a man who had studied with two of the giants of institutional economics, John R. Commons and Wesley Mitchell) and, of course, to the ideas of Joseph Schumpeter on technological change, the nature of the corporation and the future of economic systems. In 1937/8 he was

72

a Social Sciences Research Fellow at Cambridge, where, although he did not meet Keynes, he deepened his knowledge of economics through wide reading and discussions with Maurice Dobb, Piero Sraffa and Joan Robinson. Meanwhile, he had gained *entrée* to the salons of the moneyed classes in the United States as a result of his marriage to Catherine Atwater, a modern-languages student at Radcliffe.

In the Second World War Galbraith became, at the young age of 33, the Deputy Administrator in the Office of Price Administration; and was, from 1941 until the unpopularity of his policies led to his forced resignation in 1943, in charge of price control for the whole of the United States. From 1943–48 he was on the board of editors of *Fortune* magazine, where he learned from Henry Luce how to write with clarity for a popular audience. In this period he was also involved in the Strategic Bombing Survey, which studied the effects of allied air attacks on the economy of Germany and Japan.

Galbraith returned to Harvard in 1949 and remained there until his retirement in 1975 (from 1959–75 as the Paul M. Warburg Professor of Economics). It was in this later period that he became a celebrity in his own right. Partly this was because of his active participation in the Democratic Party, as chairman of the domestic policy committee of the Democratic Advisory Council, as president of the radical Americans for Democratic Action, as speech-writer for and advisor to Adlai Stevenson, John Kennedy (for whom he served from 1961 to 1963 as an outspoken and forceful Ambassador to India, taking time as well to warn the President against American involvement in Vietnam), Eugene McCarthy and George McGovern. Principally, however, it is by virtue of his position as a leading commentator on the economic, social and political problems of advanced industrial countries that Galbraith has become one of the best-known intellectuals and most influential social critics of our time. A prolific if also a repetitive author, his publications range from historical accounts of the economic problem (*The Great Crash*; *The Age of Uncertainty*) through books of reminiscences (*Ambassador's Journal*; *A China Passage*) and works of fiction (*The Triumph*; *The McLandress Dimension*) to tracts on social and political reform (*How to Control the Military*; *How to Get Out of Vietnam*), and even include an often-ignored attempt to integrate price controls into the body of economic thought (*A Theory of Price Control*);

but it is most of all due to four important and provocative best-sellers (books that stand alongside *The Theory of the Leisure Class, The Lonely Crowd, The Power Elite, The Organization Man* and *The Sane Society* as classics of modern American thought) that his ideas have come to be more widely discussed than those of virtually any other economist of his generation. It is with those four books – *American Capitalism, The Affluent Society, The New Industrial State* and *Economics and The Public Purpose* – that we shall be concerned in the four sections which follow.

COUNTERVAILING POWER?

*American Capitalism* first appeared in 1952 when Galbraith was already 44 years of age. In it he argued that the powerless perfect competitor of textbook economic theory has in sector after sector of economic life been displaced by the powerful organisation (the giant producer, the nation-wide retailing chain, the huge trade union), but that, because power inevitably develops in pairs (because the original power of a corporation, to take an example, inevitably begets the countervailing power of a union, anxious both to defend the interests of the weak and to tap the profits of the strong), the position of the consuming public remains attractive even without the use of restrictive practices legislation to break up large organisations into small. The check on the abuse of economic power, in other words, is no longer to be expected on the same side of the market (for large size of firm, and the associated market concentration, is unavoidable if the producer is to be capable of supporting the risks and costs of technological progress) but rather from organisations on the opposite side of the market; and the State, recognising that one self-stabilising mechanism has now been replaced by another, should confine its intervention beyond the law and order minimum to reinforcement of positions of weakness where countervailing power appears slow to develop unaided.

The concept of checks and balances in economic life reflects an interesting attempt to apply a political model to an economic problem (a model, moreover, which remains implicit in all of Galbraith's later work, even though he made no further mention by name of countervailing power), and is significant for its stress on the importance of power in economic life (since it is truly misleading to assume, as many introductory textbooks tend to do, that economic actors are powerless automatons). At the same time, however, the specific formulation of the theory of counter-vailing power is such as to leave it open to a certain number of criticisms. These include the following.

First, Galbraith seems to argue in places as if the primary function of countervailing power is the promotion of consumer welfare (as where he asserts that retailing chains challenge the dominance of oligopolistic producers by means of the threat to duplicate via own-brands, and then pass the resultant gains on to the shopper), but then declares categorically that the principal service performed is in reality 'the minimization of social tension' (even at the cost of consumer welfare); and the confusion as to the relationship between these two objectives is heightened by doubts as to whether any balance of power (assuming it could in practice be identified as 'correct' or 'optimal' in some objective sense, and is not merely the balance born of stalemate and inertia) will ever be capable of reducing general (in contrast to highly specific) social tensions.

Secondly, Galbraith does not make clear how the consumer interest is to be defended (for if a powerful union confronts a powerful producer, it is to be frank much more likely that it will seek to redistribute existing super-normal profits towards its members than that it will press for their elimination through an expansion in sales and a reduction in prices). In 1952 he suggested that retailing chains would exercise countervailing power on behalf of powerless shoppers; in 1954 he explained that the chains would do this (would, in other words, pass on to the consumer whatever gains they were able to wrest from the producer) because of intensive competition among themselves and on the same side of the market; and in 1973 he recommended that the consumer interest should itself directly acquire power (an argu-ment in favour of Ralph Nader and the consumerist move-ment).

Thirdly, Galbraith argues as if original power typically gene-rates countervailing power; whereas the case of the consumer reminds us that power, historically speaking, simply does not always develop in pairs, and the case of the National Health Service illustrates the proposition that giant organisations often develop for reasons (the desire to acquire genuine economies of large scale, for example, or to attain broadly-defined social and philosophical objectives) totally unconnected with the pre-existence of lucrative bastions to storm. Regarding State support to positions of weakness, moreover, Galbraith himself recognises that the weak must first have some power if they are ever to win the ear of legislators: even political intervention is evidently not automatic, and the social mechanism clearly not therefore self-stabilising.

Fourthly, Galbraith states that whereas unions in a stagnant economy exercise their power against their employers, they in a buoyant economy join their power to that of their bosses, since the corporation does not then resist wage-claims but merely passes the burden of cost-push inflation on to the consumer (in the form of higher prices) or back to the shareholder (in the form of lower dividends). Apart from the controversial diagnosis of cost-push inflation in that sector of the economy dominated by powerful unions and giant firms (Galbraith indeed has next to no policies for the control of demand-pull inflation since he totally rejects monetary policy and, as for fiscal policy, insists that taxation may be increased but that government expenditure must never be cut) and the assertion that the shareholder is powerless (the owners of a low-dividend firm might at the very least sell out, leaving the shares undervalued and the organisation ripe for a take-over bid; and the fact that large blocs of shares are concentrated in the hands of founding families and institutional investors suggests that capitalists may after all be able to influence managers), Galbraith's insistence that countervailing power in the labour market no longer serves the public interest in a period of steadily rising prices paved the way for one of the most controversial of all his conclusions: there is a need in inflationary times for the institution of a permanent and fully-comprehensive prices and incomes policy to plan factor-rewards for all economic actors able to exercise power in the economy.

### PRIVATE AFFLUENCE AND PUBLIC POVERTY

*The Affluent Society* was published in 1958 (one year after the launching of the first Russian sputnik). It had a dual theme: private affluence and public poverty.

Regarding private affluence, Galbraith argued that economics was born into a poor world where wants were authentic to the sovereign consumer and growth and allocation still eminently relevant concerns. Now, however, that basic needs for food, clothing and shelter have been so extensively met, the consumer has become satiated with opulence and confused as to what frivolous trinkets he wants next; and is in this state vulnerable to the artificial insemination of tastes and preferences by means of advertising and salesmanship. Such tastes and preferences are deliberately manufactured via an appeal to the basest of instincts, aspirations and insecurities. They are nonetheless treated by economists as if they originated within the individual consumer; and in this way economists play into the hands of the powerful by unintentionally disguising the replacement of buyer by seller sovereignty. The recognition of this 'revised sequence', of course, calls into question the acceptability of the GNP as an index of felicity, and its rate of growth as an index of social progress.

Regarding public poverty, Galbraith asserted that vital public services (roads, schools, museums, low-cost housing, slum clearance, the police) are today starved of revenue because of factors such as the traditional (if irrational) view that only the private sector is productive of wealth, the truce on inequality (for many reformers who favour a welfare state are nonetheless reluctant to see it financed out of progressive taxation in a way which marries provision of service to redistribution of current income), and the absence of consumer credit and sales promotion in the State sector. Yet it is precisely these services that are increasingly in demand in a rich society where households want clean streets once they have a roof over their heads and where firms want not simply physical inputs but schooled manpower as well. Galbraithian socialism is evidently lame duck socialism, for it stresses that the private sector simply cannot satisfy needs which are today increasingly acute and insists that the alternative to full social provision is no provision at all. Galbraithian socialism postulates that social balance is in a rich society of greater urgency than economic growth, and identifies, as an important reason for this greater urgency, an unambiguous propensity on the part of balance to favour the lower-income groups: thus unemployment benefits help to combat insecurity (whereas it would be highly inflationary to seek the maximum rate of economic growth in order to create jobs for even the most marginal worker, quite apart from the blatant absurdity of having then to engineer artificial wants so as to be able to sell the goods that that worker will produce), and training and retraining schemes help to combat poverty (whereas economic growth by itself does nothing to integrate those unfortunates left outside the mainstream of activity).

Galbraith's theory of private affluence and public poverty is a controversial one, and the following comments may perhaps be made.

Galbraith is being somewhat arrogant in assuming that consumers increasingly choose to purchase baubles and trinkets yielding them *ex* propaganda and want creation zero-marginal utility (it is, to be fair, not the gold-plated mousetrap or the toaster that prints an inspirational message on each piece of toast that enjoys the most significant income-elasticity in real existing affluent societies, but rather commodities such as consumer durables and complements to leisure towards which it is less difficult to be tolerant); that consumers genuinely do not know what they want (for there must always be a presumption in a democratic society that citizens who are deemed able to vote intelligently for their political leaders are also capable of choosing their own brand of toothpaste); and that consumers actually allow themselves to be manipulated by persuaders (although the latter would naturally be foolish not to try) into buying some frivolous new product bearing no relation to existing ways of life and developed purely because of the fact that innovation in its own right yields job-satisfaction to the boffin on a salary and contributes to the growth of his organisation. Given that persuasion is not a free good but has a price, the firm will probably not market new commodities at random, but rather will first conduct intensive research into what most people potentially most want; and it will in any case direct its appeal not towards economic man in isolation but towards social man in general (whereas Galbraith, in contrast to Veblen, underestimates the extent to which status-anxiety, invidious comparison, peer-group pressures, and the rat-race all inhere in the very process of social interaction itself and are exploited rather than inculcated by the forces of advertising and salesmanship).

Next, Galbraith neglects the possible failure of want-creation not simply in his account of consumer preferences but also in his account of corporate behaviour. Specifically, he assumes that corporations do not compete with one another for larger shares in a given market (that they do not, in other words, ever seek to invade each other's territory); and that they actively create wants purely so as to boost total demand for the product as a whole (and for consumption itself, as opposed to savings or leisure), while fraternally keeping their percentage of aggregate sales constant. Yet, if producers have different cost-relations, then it is difficult to see why an efficient firm would or should willingly pass up the opportunity to increase its profits or expand its sales (utilising techniques of price or non-price competition) simply out of courtesy to a less-efficient rival in the industry. Such a strategy (orientated as it is towards mutual security) would serve the firm's protective but not its affirmative purpose; and the very frequency with which market-shares in the real world do alter reinforces the suspicion that a go-ahead organisation will be reluctant to constrain its own growth rate by that of the market for the good as a whole.

Finally, Galbraith never resolves the problem that it is easiest to transfer resources from the private to the social sector at a time when the former is growing rather than stagnating; and that a rapidly-growing GNP may be the precondition (particularly in terms of popular acceptance) for a healthy welfare state. Besides that, the distinction between the two sectors is at least in part an artificial one in Galbraith's model; for many goods and services in the private sector are in strict logic worthy of the approbation particularly of a cultural elitist such as Galbraith (the case of private hospitals, fringe theatres and publishing houses), while many in the social sector are in truth rather organs of social division than architects of social equality (the case of university education, which demonstrably favours the children of the suburb more than it upgrades those of the ghetto). More generally, the very concept of social balance implies a unique point; and since a unique point may be passed as well by the public tortoise as by the private hare, many readers will no doubt regret that Galbraith never suggests when and where a mixed economy is at last properly mixed. Such a point would, of course, be easier for him, as a believer in technological determinism and the residual supplier argument, to specify, than it would be for the social philosopher who assigns a greater importance to values and believes that the welfare state must be consciously chosen rather than being imposed willy nilly upon an advanced industrial society.

THE POWER OF THE TECHNOSTRUCTURE

*The New Industrial State*, published in 1967 and one of the most hotly-debated treatises of the troubled late-Vietnam years which followed, is in some ways Galbraith's most ambitious attempt to construct a theoretical synthesis concerning the role of power in economics. It is about advanced technology and the emancipation of belief, and most of all about the incipient struggle between the 'technostructure' and the 'educational and scientific estate'.

The technostructure in the modern giant ('mature') corporation is that group of highly-trained experts (engineers, scientists, economists, lobbyists, advertising men) who, collectively, have a monopoly of scarce skills and crucial knowledge and who, in committees but in place of nominal managers and functionless shareholders, increasingly make decisions for the large and technologically-advanced organisation. The technostructure has goals of its own; and whereas the old-style textbook capitalist favours that of profit-maximisation (the centrepiece of the private vices, public virtues argument concerning the unexpectedly beneficent outcome of the market mechanism), the new-style technocrat pursues objectives such as job-satisfaction, security (which means not simply the prevention of redundancies – painful for those dismissed and a cause of diminished efficiency for the team left behind – but also the autonomy of the specialist from interference on the part of uninformed outsiders, notably shareholders, unions, financiers and government) and corporate growth (which means expansion of its bureaucracy, and thus more pay, prestige, power and promotion prospects for members of the organisation). These new-style goals it pursues by means of techniques which Galbraith calls 'planning' (a term he uses to indicate the attempt on the part of large organisations first to forecast and then to shape the business future – otherwise a prohibitively risky one due to the expensive commitment of sector-specific capital in technology-intensive industries substantially in advance of marketing the final product – in its desired image). The corporation seeks via advertising and salesmanship to tailor consumer attitudes in such a way as successfully to sell a planned quantity at a planned price; it strives to obtain subsidies (say, for the development of advanced technology in the space exploration field) and guaranteed markets (say, via weapons contracts) from the State; it makes long-term contracts with other firms for inputs and outputs; it integrates backwards (into raw materials) and forwards (into retailing), both at home and abroad; it insulates itself from outside borrowing on the capital market through the expedient of reinvestment of profits; and it copes with uncertainty and disruption stemming from the labour force by policies which replace confrontation by displacement (substituting machines for men since the former input does not go on strike) and pacification (conceding wage-claims and then passing the poisoned chalice to consumer or capitalist). In all of these ways, the technostructure seeks to mould the community to such an extent as to accept organisational objectives (the 'Principle of Consistency' postulating, moreover, that it will succeed in its attempt); and it is unwittingly but effectively served in this exercise by textbook economists, residual utilitarians who conceal the facts of corporate power under the multiplied fictions of perfect markets and who conveniently talk of *whether* the system works efficiently rather than *for whom*.

The educational and scientific estate, fortunately, may be counted upon to challenge the technostructure and to uphold the social interest (which includes a high priority for social welfare schemes, environmental and aesthetic considerations, and even some nationalisation – especially of technostructure-run corporations doing the greater part of their business with the government, as is typically the case in the defence industries). They offer countervailing power on behalf of ideological emancipation and they will win, partly because the present-day premium on trained manpower itself generates an increase in the numbers of educators as a percentage of the population (coupled with an improvement in their social status), partly because all education, even the training of technocrats, develops critical intelligence (an antidote to sophisticated persuasion and to the disciplined conformity of the technostructure) and inculcates socially-responsible attitudes (so that the graduate may be expected to see through the special pleading of the military-industrial complex and demand an end to the war in Vietnam, coupled with an insistence that there is no alternative to prices and incomes policies if inflation is to be contained). The industrial system thus generates its own gravediggers, and these turn out to be the intellectuals, who alone among the groupings in modern society see through the Establishment fictions of vested interests in a way which the classical proletariat (nowadays a pillar of the *status quo*, as its support to the war in Vietnam and its participation in the gains from cost-push inflation abundantly demonstrates) does not.

Galbraith's model has the breathtaking simplicity of the triumph of good over evil. It is, however, precisely its simplicity which leaves it open to criticism.

Concerning the technostructure, there is no reason to conclude that the locus of power has shifted from managers to technocrats; for it remains the managers who select the technostructure, choose the problems it is to solve, and evaluate its recommendations in the light of company policy. Nor would it be fair to say that the objectives of the firm have irrevocably altered; for (and quite apart from the question of shareholder power) the very goals of the technostructure itself are not substitutes for profit-maximisation but complements to it (as where, for instance, growth without outside interference necessitates a sufficient pool of internally-generated investment capital as to obviate the need for borrowing). Galbraith, moreover, tends to exaggerate the extent to which private firms actually succeed in 'planning' the economy, not simply in his attitude to advertising and salesmanship, but also in his insistence that the strike weapon is *passé* and in his underestimation of the significance of corporate growth via the development of the conglomerate form (where expansion involving diversification may also reduce the power of the corporation in each of its individual markets – a case of large aggregate size and power not justified by economies of large scale which might, incidentally, justify a more intensive use of anti-trust laws than Galbraith is prepared to condone).

Concerning the educational and scientific estate, it is important here to remember that not all intellectuals are democratic socialists hostile to conformity and the affluent society; that many intellectuals are close to bureaucracies and dependent on them for research grants; and that most students are not activists and display, at times, an unbelievable fascination with business careers and consumer goods. It is, moreover, somewhat misleading to argue that it is the process of economic change itself which automatically generates a new class uniquely capable of modifying the direction of that change; for even if the new class truly enjoyed a class-consensus, it would still be a misuse of the concept of economic determinism to argue, as Galbraith does, that the sensible views of that élite are not simply an emanation of its own values and ideals but also correspond perfectly and precisely to the silent imperatives of the material environment, of the pre-existent reality which the intellectual merely uncovers and reveals.

## THE PUBLIC PURPOSE

*Economics and the Public Purpose*, published in 1973, completed the Galbraithian system. It restated his basic hypotheses about industrial society and expanded in particular on two themes.

First, it stressed the significance of the dual economy which obtains in modern industrial societies, a dual economy made up of a 'planning system' (the powerful corporate sector able to dominate) but also of a 'market system' (the world of small, passive, competitive buyers and sellers, still operating as if in the textbook model of perfect competition). The two sectors are, in the USA, approximately equal in size (each representing about 50 % of GNP generated in the domestic private sector). They are not, however, approximately equal in power; and to prevent the strong from bullying the weak Galbraith is eager to recommend public support to the small firm (say, in the form of research and development done on its behalf in government laboratories), together with support to positions of weakness located within the market system itself (notably via support to unionisation, including that of migrant workers; via minimum wage laws to defend those unable to unite for mutual protection; and via the imposition of maximum hours of employment so as to prevent self-exploitation, including that of the owner-entrepreneur and his family).

Secondly, it drew attention to 'bureaucratic symbiosis' (the phenomenon whereby the goals, ideology and even personnel of the technostructure interact symbiotically with the goals, ideology and personnel of the civil service; so that, for instance, the expansion of defence ministries results from an expansion of weapons suppliers, and both monoliths collude, in the USA as in the USSR, in order to attain organisational objectives). Arguing that the executive is abnormally dependent on bureaucratic advice, Galbraith emphasized that the check on organisational power must be exercised by the legislative branch of government: it, he contended, is less likely to be the prisoner of bureaucratic truths, pre-digested fictions and organisational inertia, especially after it has come to be dominated by the radical wing of the Democratic Party.

Here once again Galbraith's assertions, with respect to both themes, are subject to challenge. Regarding the dual economy, it is perhaps unhelpful to treat businesses as either weak or strong rather than falling into a continuous spectrum; and it is certainly misleading to lump together, within the market system, both the Harley Street specialist and the Chinese waiter. Also, Galbraith underestimates the dynamism of small business: many important new ideas (despite the advent of the large organisation, with its unquestioned superiority in glamorous areas such as computers, space exploration and atomic energy) in fact originate in the small firm, and are likely increasingly to do so in some future 'post-industrial' service society where the demand for a personal contribution encourages the (flexible) individual rather than the (inflexible) organisation. If, moreover, small business is dynamic, then Galbraith's proposals to buttress positions of weakness within the market system are to be regarded with some caution: neither minimum wage laws (which he admits would lead to the loss of some jobs) nor the imposition of maximum hours of self-employment would assist the weak in their on-going struggle with the strong.

Regarding 'bureaucratic symbiosis', while one welcomes any attempt to prevent bureaucracies public and private from agreeing upon, say, an aggressive foreign policy principally to improve promotion-prospects and enhance their own social status, it is not clear that such a phenomenon will be overcome by an increase in the power of the State. If anything, it suggests a need for more decentralisation and less concentration in both public and private sectors.

EVALUATION

Galbraith is a man of letters in the eighteenth-century mould. Although his hypotheses are loosely formulated, his evidence often intuitive rather than factual, his economic determinism a mask to conceal moral judgements, his presentation theatrical and frequently exaggerated, it would be wrong to underestimate his contribution to economics in particular and to the social sciences in general.

First, his methodology is unusual insofar as he adopts a historical and evolutionary approach to the study of economic phenomena. Galbraith believes that actions and perceptions are to be understood within the situational framework of their cultural and institutional context, and this conviction impels him to proceed in an interdisciplinary and functionalist manner to the construction of a holistic synthesis. He is thus writing rather in the tradition of systems-builders such as Smith and Marx than in that more modern tradition which focuses on the purely purposive, the narrowly rational, the useful, the technological; which takes ends as constants; and which dismisses social institutions and interaction (and the laws governing their development) as more the province of the sociologist and the philosopher than of the economist.

Secondly, he introduces political concepts into economics, both in his theory of the firm (as where he examines the power of the corporation to influence other economic actors and even the State) and in his theory of governmental intervention (as where he argues that the non-market sector should be expanded). He has in this way become the prophet of the mixed economy and a staunch critic of that conventional wisdom in economics which teaches (if not preaches) the valuable function performed by automatically self-stabilising markets and invisible hands. Here he would argue that historical change has made the description of *what once was* into an irrelevant approach to *what is*; and would also no doubt wish to stress the extent to which a heterodox economist who rejects neo-classical ideas of competition, *laissez-faire*, consumer sovereignty, profit maximisation, the existence of scarcity, the importance of growth, and the need efficiently to suit means to random ends, will even today find it difficult to obtain a doctorate or a lectureship, to have his articles accepted by leading scholarly journals, or to secure a grant from a major foundation or research council. Such an economist will quickly discover to his own cost the true nature of social power and vested interest.

Thirdly, he recognises that ideas have consequences, and that there exists a dialectical relationship between mind and matter such that the scholar not merely identifies social change but helps to influence it. Convinced that social theories are themselves social facts both produced by and capable of transforming other social facts, Galbraith has himself sought to formulate a non-Marxist theoretical system aimed at persuading a wider audience than professional economists alone to alter their beliefs and thus their society as well; and he has in great measure succeeded, not only due to the force of his arguments but also because of the articulate, witty and accessible manner in which they are presented. As John Gambs has put it, explaining why Galbraith has succeeded where Veblen failed, in winning the interest and sympathy of an extensive popular audience, 'Veblen was an eccentric scholar; Galbraith is a smoothie and a man of the world'.

REFERENCES

Galbraith, J. K. 1957 *American Capitalism* (Hamish Hamilton).
—— 1958 *The Affluent Society* (Hamish Hamilton).
—— 1967 *The New Industrial State* (Hamish Hamilton).
—— 1974 *Economics and the Public Purpose* (André Deutsch).
Gambs, J. S. 1975 *John Kenneth Galbraith* (Twayne Publishers).
Hession, C. H. 1972 *John Kenneth Galbraith and His Critics* (New American Library).
Reisman, D. A. 1976 'Social Justice and Macroeconomic Policy: The Case of J. K. Galbraith', in Aubrey Jones (ed.), *Economics and Equality* (Philip Allan).
—— 1980 'Galbraith and Social Welfare', in N. Timms (ed.), *Social Welfare: Why and How?* (Routledge & Kegan Paul).
—— 1980 *Galbraith and Market Capitalism* (Macmillan).

# 6 Re-stating the Liberal Order: Hayek's Philosophical Economics

Norman P. Barry

Friedrich August von Hayek was born in Vienna in 1899, the son of a professor of botany at the University. He studied law and political economy at Vienna University, the home of the 'Austrian School' of economics which began with Carl Menger and continued under Wieser, Böhm-Bawerk and Mises. From 1927 to 1931 Hayek was director of the Austrian Institute of Economic Research and from 1929 to 1931 was also lecturer in economics at Vienna University. After delivering some lectures on trade cycle theory at the London School of Economics he was invited to become Tooke Professor of Economic Science and Statistics in 1931, a position he held until 1950. In that year he went to the University of Chicago, not as a professor of economics but to a chair in social and moral science. In 1962 he became Professor of Economic Policy at the University of Freiburg, West Germany. On his retirement in 1969 he returned to his native Austria and was a visiting professor at the University of Salzburg. He has recently left Salzburg to return to Freiburg. However, he has retained his British citizenship, which he acquired in 1938.

In a long and distinguished academic career Hayek has made many significant contributions to knowledge in a wide range of disciplines including economic theory and policy, psychology, law, and political and social philosophy. The early part of his career was entirely devoted to pure economic theory in the areas of money, the trade cycle and capital theory. Throughout the 1930s he was engaged in intellectual battles with Keynes over the theory of money and the causes of industrial fluctuations. He published his most comprehensive treatise on economic theory, *The Pure Theory of Capital*, in 1941 but he was by then already publishing more general work in the social sciences. In fact he ceased to write on money and general economic theory after 1950, although in recent years his interest in the subject has revived and he has made some controversial suggestions for monetary policy. He shared, with Gunnar Myrdal, the Nobel Prize for Economic Science in 1974.

Since the Second World War Hayek has been known primarily as a legal and political philosopher and a trenchant intellectual critic of planning, socialism and all varieties of statism. He found some notoriety in 1944 with the publication of *The Road to Serfdom*, in which he argued that even mild state interference with a spontaneously evolving market economy is likely to set in motion processes that eventually lead to the destruction of liberty and the emergence of a totalitarian state. Since then he has made the original argument much more sophisticated and in a series of books and essays (see References) has produced the most complex and comprehensive defence of traditional liberalism this century.

Despite the great variety of his works Hayek's social philosophy constitutes a 'system' in which the early works in pure economic theory can be integrated into his writings on law, psychology, methodology and the political philosophy of liberalism. This 'system' of political economy is partly a restatement of the eighteenth-century liberal political economy of Smith and Hume, but it also incorporates much of what is valuable in modern social science, most notably the contributions of the 'Austrian School' of economic theory which emerged from the 'marginalist' revolution of the 1870s.

METHODOLOGY

At the centre of Hayek's system of ideas is a profound concern with the key epistemological questions of social science. Most important is his insistence that there are necessary limitations on the amount of knowledge that one mind or institution can acquire; a point that is crucial to his argument that the failures of rational economic planning stem from the mistaken attempt to *centralise* all knowledge (Hayek, 1960, Chapter 2). The social sciences deal with knowledge that is dispersed throughout a social order and the most *efficient* use is made of this decentralised information when individual actors are allowed to pursue their own purposes within general rules. Hayek's social philosophy is specifically addressed to a certain *hubris* in man which leads to successive attempts to reconstruct the social world according to rational principles. These attempts, whether they come from eithteenth-century European rationalism, nineteenth-century British utilitarianism, or the many contemporary versions of collectivism and socialism, all treat economic knowledge (that is, knowledge of consumer tastes, productive resources, inventiveness, costs and so on) as if it could be centralised and made available for the advancement of collective goals.

The kind of knowledge an economic planner has is *engineering* knowledge, the technical knowledge which is limited to one input, process or purpose, whereas a society is characterised by a variety of competing purposes. Hayek, therefore, stresses the importance of the knowledge of 'time and place' that is maximised in free societies; this is the knowledge of merchants and traders in decentralised markets which enables them to respond to ever-changing events more efficiently than a centralised planner could (Hayek, 1955, p. 98).

It follows from this that the methods of explanation appropriate to the physical sciences are inappropriate to the social sciences and the error of 'scientism' (Hayek, 1955, pp. 53–63) consists of the illegitimate transfer of the former to the latter. The physical scientist deals with essentially 'simple' phenomena (Hayek, 1967, Chapter 2), i.e. phenomena that display regularities between elements which can be readily observed; therefore knowledge of a purely physical system can be 'objectified'. This objectification is possible because the physical scientist classifies objects by reference to common properties which they possess. Furthermore, because of the small number of variables involved in the explanation of physical events, the predictions made in the natural sciences are highly precise, in a quantitative sense. In other words, theories in the physical sciences have a high degree of empirical content.

In the social world, however, there are no regularities which can be directly observed, so that a form of explanation that employs *mechanical* laws of cause and effect is inappropriate. It is true that societies and economies are understood in terms of certain kinds of regularities but these are not directly observable: they are reconstructed out of the opinions, attitudes and beliefs of individuals. Thus words like 'society', 'market' and 'legal system' do not stand for real entities which can be observed but are *theoretical* concepts used to explain the behaviour of individuals (Hayek, 1955, pp. 53–8). The 'subjective' element in social science consists of the fact that the social scientist classifies the data and establishes regularities not in virtue of common properties that objects possess but because similar minds react to phenomena in similar ways. There are no 'constants' or regular events in social affairs which constitute the basis of 'empirical laws', there are only individuals; and the 'facts' of the social science are no more than the assumptions that we make about individual behaviour. From these assumptions it is possible to deduce the properties of market economies and legal orders.

It follows therefore that economic 'laws' are not established by the inductive method. The law of demand is not established by repeated observations of the fact that a fall in price is followed by a rise in demand; it is a logical implication of certain axioms of human nature. Again, the familiar properties of monetary theory, including the explanation of inflation, can be deduced from true generalisations about individual behaviour.

The generalisations on which deductive economic theory rests are simple. Hayek says that they include the assumptions that 'most people engage in trade in order to earn an income' and that 'they prefer a larger income to a smaller one' (Hayek, 1967, p. 35). At the heart of this methodology is the concept of man as 'acting' man. This means that individuals are not automatons who obey causal psychological laws but are *choosers* who employ means to realise their ends (although these ends are not always 'economic' in the strict sense of the word). For this reason there will always be a large element of unpredictability in economic affairs so that economic science is concerned with the explanation of human behaviour and not the prediction of discrete events.

It should be clear from this that Hayek is a rigorous defender of methodological individualism against collectivism. For example, 'classes' do not save or invest, only individuals can do those things. Yet it does not follow from this that social science is reducible to psychology. Social science is concerned primarily with the *unintended* consequences of individual action. From the free actions of individuals a market order emerges, even though it was not intended or designed by any one individual (Hayek, 1967, Chapter 6). Hayek argues that many of the most beneficial social institutions were not deliberately created and he is especially critical of social theorists who maintain that the way to social improvement is to rationally plan institutions with specific purposes.

In fact Hayek's methodology has departed a little from the standard Austrian approach since he accepts Sir Karl Popper's argument (1957) that the *logic* of both the physical and social sciences is the same.[1] This is because all science is characterised by deduction and not induction so that the original Austrian argument that economics is unlike physics because there are no empirical regularities in the economic order was misdirected since induction cannot establish the laws of physics either. However, the Popperian approach to science embodies the 'hypothetico-deductive' methodology in which knowledge grows by the constant attempts to *falsify* hypotheses: no theory can be regarded as invulnerable to tests. This contrasts sharply with the Austrian stress on axiomatic reasoning from necessarily true premises (Mises, 1962).

Hayek accepts the doctrine of 'falsifiability' but maintains that falsification is a matter of degree and that well-established economic theories should not be regarded as falsified simply because a very small number of observations appears to refute them. Obviously, Hayek would not say that the central tenet of liberal economics, that *unhampered* market economies tend towards the full employment of all resources, was refuted by the experience of the Great Depression. Hayek also agrees that economics is concerned with prediction but it is prediction of a *general* kind. From certain generalisations about human behaviour we can, for example, predict that if the rents of council houses are subsidised the demand will go up, queues will develop and the authorities will have to allocate the property by political or bureaucratic methods. This is, of course, a theoretical, not an historical, prediction.

An economic order is a competitive order which can be predicted to emerge if individuals are allowed to transact within general rules. Its elements can be understood by contrasting it with orthodox neoclassical theory, especially that which developed from the Walrasian model. While the Walrasian system of economics is subjectivist in regard to the theory of value it is objectivist in its explanation of the competitive market order. This is because it is concerned almost entirely with the conditions that describe a stationary equilibrium. An economy is in equilibrium when it is impossible to switch any resource from one use to another without making one person worse off (the marginal rates of substitution between any two factors of production must be identical in all their different uses). In the Walrasian stable equilibrium all incentives to *change* are therefore removed. In principle, if knowledge of technology, resources and consumer tastes is 'given' to the observing economist, then an equilibrium state could be 'objectified', that is translated into quantitative terms, and economic behaviour made fully predictable (on the assumption, of course, that individuals behave economically in the narrow sense). Hayek's main objections to the notion of a static, timeless equilibrium are that, first, it misdescribes the real world of market economies, which are characterised by repeated movements away from the state of rest described by general equilibrium theory; and secondly, it distorts the nature of competition. This is because it describes the state of affairs competition has brought about rather than analyses the competitive *process* itself.

SOCIALISM VERSUS THE MARKET

These objections appear in his arguments against socialist economics (Hayek, 1935) and in a series of important papers on the competitive order (Hayek 1948). It is significant that Hayek should approach the critique of Walrasian economics via the critique of socialism since socialist economists in the 1930s thought that, because the private market economy was characterised by imperfections, a centrally-planned economy could improve on capitalism in an *efficiency* sense. If the central planner had perfect knowledge then the solution to the allocational problem could be predicted mechanically and an economy deliberately adjusted to bring this about. Thus a socialist economy might be *designed* without a market or decentralised planning by individuals. But it is this objective solution that Hayek denied on the grounds that the requisite knowledge was not given to the central planner. The knowledge of prices and costs required in order to achieve an efficient allocation of resources can only be acquired by the *operation of a market process itself*. In fact, 'cost', in the Austrian model of 'market process', is subjective: it is not the observable money expenditure required to produce a commodity but the value of foregone output from an alternative use of the same resources. But obviously this alternative can be known only to the actors in the economic process.

Since knowledge is dispersed and fragmented throughout an economy and cannot be objectified central planning will always be less efficient than decentralised planning. The best way of serving the interests of all is to allow each individual to make the best use of decentralised knowledge through competition itself. There is a *tendency* towards equilibrium in which the plans of individual transactors are harmonised through the price system.

A competitive market order is an information system which transmits knowledge automatically through the signals sent out by prices. The point about high wages and high profits is that they attract labour and capital to their most productive uses, and in so doing produce a greater net output for society than would otherwise be the case. Competition, then, is a discovery procedure in which individuals learn through a process of trial and error to improve their well-being. The crucial advantage of a decentralised competitive market is that in it each individual has only to be aware of the facts that affect him personally; yet out of private actions emerges an 'order' which was no part of any one person's intentions. The market order is the best example of a social order that emerges without being designed. As a self-regulating order the market requires very little central direction or control. Only in this order can entrepreneurial activity be understood. The entrepreneur's role is to respond quickly to market signals and entrepreneurship illustrates well the unpredictability of human affairs. In the 'perfect competition' model, since all adjustment is instantaneous, there is strictly speaking no role for the entrepreneur. Therefore, it is inappropriate to evaluate a competitive process in accordance with how close it is to perfect competition. The relevant comparison is between those economies that display some competition and the *dirigiste* alternatives.

It follows from this that monopoly and the customary market imperfections are interpreted differently from the conventional analysis. Since we can never know in an objective sense whether an economy is 'efficient' or not it is impossible to calculate the 'welfare loss' caused by monopoly. In fact Hayek thinks that the problems of monopoly have been grossly exaggerated. 'Natural' monopolies are extremely rare and as long as free entry into any economic activity is permitted the monopolist operates under some constraint. The existence of monopoly does not mean the absence of entrepreneurial activity: it may be the case that without the possibility of monopoly gains certain goods would not be produced at all. Certainly Hayek is doubtful if much anti-trust legislation is helpful to the consumer. The role of govern-ment should be limited to guaranteeing free entry and it must refrain from creating monopolies itself (for a discussion of Austrian market theory in relation to Britain see Littlechild, 1978). Hayek argues that the only serious monopoly is that of labour unions, and this is entirely a product of governments conferring legal privileges upon them. The effect of labour-union monopoly power is to keep the price of labour above its market-clearing price, thus creating involuntary unemployment. In Britain labour unions have been responsible for creating those rigidities in the labour market which prevent adjustment to changing circumstances and the co-ordination of disparate plans through competition.

CREDIT AND THE TRADE CYCLE

It is, of course, true that market systems, although they are in principle self-regulating, experience frequent crises and much of Hayek's early career as a pure economic theorist was concerned with the regular ups and downs of capitalist market economies known as the trade cycle. His work here was concerned primarily with the disequilibriating effect of money. Because of the institution of money the signals put out by the market may systematically mislead transactors so that the automatically-adjusting properties of the market are impaired. Hayek (1941, p. 408) has described money as a kind of 'loose joint' in an otherwise automatically-adjusting system and the policy implications of his economic theory have been concerned with the various ways in which the discoordinating effects of money can be mitigated. What is remarkable is that it is only recently that Hayek (1976a) has made his most radical policy suggestion. This is the proposal that, because government control of money has lead to such economic dislocation, this monopoly should be removed and the supply of the money good left to the private market. It is important to trace the steps by which Hayek has reached this dramatic conclusion.

Although Hayek is known today mainly for his refutations of Keynesian macroeconomic policies his early economic theory (1931, 1933 and 1939) was directed at certain versions of the quantity theory of money. While Hayek has always stressed the truth of the basic propositions of the quantity theory, and has insisted that inflation invariably follows if governments forget these, his economics goes beyond 'monetarism'. While the simple quantity theory directs attention only to changes in the *general* price level Hayek's theory concentrates on short-run changes in the structure of relative prices brought about by monetary disturbance.' Money is therefore not 'neutral' in the short-run and policies which are aimed at merely stabilising the general price level are deficient since changes in this macroeconomic magnitude conceal changes in the structure of relative prices (a microeconomic phenomenon).

Changes in relative prices depend upon the particular point in the system at which new money enters. In his trade-cycle theories Hayek demonstrated the disequilibriating effect of extra money created by the banking system. Through their normal operations banks create credit which lowers the 'market' rate of interest below the 'natural' or 'equilibrium' rate. The 'natural' rate of interest is the rate at which the demand for loan capital by entrepreneurs and the supply of savings offered by the public exactly agree. The market rate is simply the price of loans on the money market. In *long-term* equilibrium, of course, the two rates must be identical since here money is neutral, but in the short-run, in a dynamic economy, increased credit from the banking system makes available funds for investment which are not justified by the level of voluntary saving.

Bank credit enables entrepreneurs to 'pre-empt' a disproportionate share of economic resources and invest in longer production processes at the expense of consumption. In the Austrian theory of the trade cycle production is understood as a series of stages with immediate consumption goods at the near end and investment goods at the furthest stages. As an economy becomes more 'capitalistic' it employs more 'roundabout' methods of production: these will lengthen the time it takes to bring goods to the final consumption stage (although they will yield a greater supply of consumer goods in the long-run).

Now if the lengthening of the production occurs because of an increase in the supply of voluntary savings the resulting structure is fundamentally stable since capital will be available for the *completion* of all the stages necessary to bring goods to final consumption. But this is not the case if it comes about through 'forced saving', i.e. when monetary injection makes available credit for a capital expansion not warranted by the current consumption-savings ratio. When this happens the expansion is unstable because people's time-preferences have not changed, so that the higher incomes earned by factors at the longer stages will be spent on consumption goods. The higher prices for consumption goods makes inevitable a switch back to shorter, less capitalistic methods. The 'crisis' comes when the injection of credit ceases, so that the market rate approaches the natural rate, and capital is not available for the completion of the longer processes. The *complementary* capital goods which are required for the completion of these processes are used in the stages nearer consumption so that 'specific' capital goods, those at the furthest stages of production which *cannot* be easily adapted to other uses, lie idle. There must therefore be unemployment at the stages of production furthest from immediate consumption.

The crisis is not characterised by a surplus of capital but by its *scarcity*, since complementary capital goods are required to complete the longer processes. Furthermore, it is not a drop in demand that precipitates unemployment but, in effect, the opposite. The only way unemployment in the longer processes can be alleviated is for demand to fall so that extra savings become available to provide the capital required to bring longer processes back into use.

In fact, the problem of malinvestment can be solved only by the liquidation of those investments which cannot be sustained, given the current level of saving, through the market process. Recessions are therefore an inevitable part of the trade cycle and interventionist policy to end them is to be eschewed since, by keeping in operation businesses that should be liquidated, it must disrupt the tendency towards equilibrium.[3]

The policy of stabilising the price level by monetary methods was consistently opposed by Hayek in the 1930s because a stable price level may conceal an underlying disequilibrium. It is noticeable that the orthodox quantity of money theorists thought that the boom in the late 1920s was harmless precisely because it was accompanied by a stable price level but Hayek (1931, pp. 160–2) argued that prolonging the boom led to a distortion of relative prices which turned a mild recession into a depression. In fact, Hayek has always said that the time to start worrying about the cycle is during the boom itself, yet action is not normally taken until the recession.

Hayek continued to develop his trade-cycle theory throughout the 1930s but a theory that predicted a *rising* price level could have little appeal at that time (see Hicks, 1967). Hayek resolutely opposed attempts to stimulate consumer demand, provide public works and prop up the price level because he maintained that the market was self-correcting and that changes in relative prices would tend to harmonise saving and investment intentions which had been discoordinated by monetary disturbance. He did distinguish between an ordinary recession and a genuine deflation (a contraction in the supply of money which leads to such a fall in demand that there is substantial unemployment of all factors) and implied that different policies apply to these different phenomena. But even in really deep depressions Hayek believed that any corrective measures by government were essentially the actions of a 'desperado' (1939, pp. 63–4). Since money is not neutral in the short-run, stabilisation measures would be self-defeating and a policy of benign neglect, which is of course dependent on something like the Gold Standard or fixed rates of exchange, is likely to be the least harmful.

In the circumstances of the 1930s it is perhaps not surprising that Keynes's new macroeconomic theory should come to dominate the economics profession and that its associated policy prescriptions were seized upon by activist governments. Without going into the details of Keynes's ideas it is easy to see how they differ from Hayek's. The Keynes of the *General Theory* had no faith in the self-adjusting properties of the market and thought that once a depression had set in there was no necessity for a self-reversing process to correct it. Unemployment was not a consequence of microeconomic factors but of a deficiency in *aggregate demand*, therefore, in a depression, government should boost spending by running a deficit in order to create full employment in the short run.[4]

Hayek has always denied that macroeconomic aggregates are significant in the determination of economic events and insisted that theories of unemployment must be micro in origin and must stress the role of relative prices in bringing a tendency towards equilibrium. His theory of unemployment is that there are 'discrepancies between the distribution of demand among the different goods and services and the allocation of labour and other resources among the production of these outputs' (Hayek, 1978, p. 25). The structure of production becomes distorted over time and there has to be a reallocation of resources, via price changes, to bring about a move to a new equilibrium. Spontaneous readjustment is of course slowed down by rigidities in the labour market caused by trade union power. Since an efficient allocation depends upon wage flexibility it is natural that Hayek (1960, pp. 361–2) should be an unrelenting opponent of prices and incomes policies.

Post-war Keynesian economic policy worked longer than Hayek expected but in the last ten years the attempt to sustain virtually full employment by monetary and fiscal methods has produced just what Hayek predicted – inflation *and* unemployment. The great increase in government activity has meant that the effects of monetary expansion are different from those Hayek described in the 1930s; instead of expansion encouraging longer production processes it now directly stimulates consumer-goods industries. Nevertheless, the long-term discoordination is similar because constant stimulus to spending means that businesses that should be liquidated by the market process are allowed to continue, so making the necessary readjustment, if a free economy is to be preserved, all the more painful. In Great Britain the rise of the welfare state, and the power of the trade unions, has made the market more rigid than elsewhere in the west. The attempt, therefore, to mop-up unemployment, caused by these rigidities, by inflation can only lead to economic breakdown and the abandonment of money as an accounting device (Hayek, 1978, Chapter 13). In Hayek's grim prognosis, Keynesianism, with its implicit rejection of the signalling functions of the market, must lead to the direction of labour and a command economy.

The problem is that governments are no longer restrained by rules in economic matters. The end of the Gold Standard and the abandonment of the system of fixed exchange rates between currencies (which Hayek always preferred to 'floating' precisely because it imposed strict limits on government) has meant that governments have great discretion in economic matters. In fact the whole Keynesian system depends on a *fully-informed* economic manager operating macroeconomic variables ('fine-tuning'). Hayek assumes that not only will the market be better-informed in a technical sense but also that it is a necessary, but not a sufficient, condition for individual liberty. It is therefore not really surprising that he should now recommend (Hayek, 1976a) that government must cease to have a monopoly over money and that the banks' own money, and foreign currencies, should be allowed to circulate in the market. Thus natural self-interest will dictate that only sound currencies will survive so that the distortion and discoordination produced by that 'loose joint' will be reduced to a minimum.

POLITICS AND LEGAL ORDER

Of course, Hayek's reputation does not rest solely on his achievements as an economist and since the publication of *The Road to Serfdom* (1944) the bulk of his work has been in political and legal philosophy. Yet there are clearly strong connections between his economics and his politics for it is the case that his theory of how free economies are transformed into directed economies is part of a general social theory.

The evolution of a stable legal order (Hayek, 1973, 1976b) can be explained by principles not unlike those used to explain the economic order. A legal order that survives through time and economises on knowledge is the product of evolution rather than design. It is another example of the phenomenon of unintended consequences of human action proving to be beneficial. While it is true that a legal order could be created by a deliberate act of will this is likely to be less stable and less efficient than an evolutionary system. What Hayek has in mind is the difference between a legal system based upon the *commands* of a sovereign and one based on the common law. Since it is impossible for any one mind or institution to possess the knowledge that exists in a decentralised form in a modern industrial society it is impossible to design a system of statute law which can handle all possible cases; a more complex order will develop if a system of general rules is allowed to evolve in a case by case manner. Since the judiciary in this type of system is engaged in seeking to find an objective solution to a problem within an ongoing set of rules it is not making policy or implementing collective purposes. The system of impersonal rules that emerges in this manner is capable of dealing with future unknown cases and is appropriate for individuals in a 'Great Society' who cannot possibly know the intentions and purposes of more than a minute fraction of the total population.

Nevertheless, Hayek himself concedes that systems of rules do not always spontaneously develop in the desired manner, that of facilitating individual exchanges so as to bring about a more complex social order, and may have to be supplemented by positive legislation. In fact, some thinkers who are friendly towards Hayek's social theory are not as optimistic as he is with regard to the spontaneous development of legal orders and maintain that individualist systems have to be rationally demonstrated and embodied in positive law.

It is recognised by Hayek that there has to be government and that the law by which it operates is different from the rules of just conduct that guide individual action. Since government does exist to implement common purposes its 'rules' will take the form of commands and directions, (Hayek, 1973, Chapter 6). Hayek argues that if the government is limited to supplying 'public goods', i.e. goods such as a police and defence system which cannot be provided adequately by normal market processes, the fact that it acts by command and regulation need not undermine liberty. In fact, Hayek (1960, Chapter 15) even concedes that government may intervene in commerce and welfare as long as it does not claim a monopoly in any field.

Freedom and law are consistent only if law meets the criteria specified by the concept of the 'rule of law' (Hayek, 1960, Chapter 14). This means that laws must be perfectly general, non-discriminatory, and binding on governments as well as on governed. Freedom is not simply a function of the range of choices open to the individual but depends upon whether the law directs the individual to do certain tasks. According to Hayek a perfectly general rule which forbids a certain course of action is consistent with liberty since the individual may plan his life so as to avoid that rule. Other libertarians, however, are deeply unhappy with this account of liberty since Hayek's formulation legitimises restrictions on free exchanges as long as such restrictions are cast in the form of general laws. They maintain that if an exchange is uncoerced the law must not intervene and they have thus been in the forefront of the demand for the removal of restrictions on the sale and consumption of addictive drugs and on various forms of unconventional sexual activity. Also, Hayek is inconsistent with his own definition of liberty when he says that conscription is legitimate, since this is clearly a direct command. Nevertheless, Hayek's argument that the rule of law provisions enable individuals to predict how the law will affect them is essential for the understanding of a free society.

THE ROAD TO SERFDOM

In recent years Hayek has been concerned with describing the threats to a free society and his 'road to serfdom' thesis implies that totalitarianism is the inevitable result of collectivist policies. It is to be noted that this is not the demonstration of an empirical trend but rather the *inference* that, if certain policies are adopted undesirable (and unforeseen) consequences must follow. There are three causes of the transformation of free societies into totalitarian orders which Hayek has highlighted. One, government direction of market economies by inflationary measures, we have already discussed. The other two are policies of social justice, and the practice, common to all western democracies, of entrusting elected legislatures with the making of *both* the rules of just conduct and the rules of government. All three errors are examples of 'constructivistic rationalism', (Hayek, 1973, Chapter 1), i.e. the dogma that the human mind can design institutions which can improve on those that have developed spontaneously.

The idea of *social* justice poses a serious threat to market efficiency and liberal individualism because it 'justifies' the imposition of a particular pattern of income distribution on a self-generating market system (Hayek, 1976b). His argument is that it is illegitimate to describe the outcomes of a market process as 'just' or 'unjust' since they are the results of impersonal forces. The concept of justice can only be used to evaluate individual conduct within general rules. A market is required to draw labour to its most efficient uses and this necessitates inequality of earnings. Now if an efficient allocation is to be achieved without a *market* then labour will have to be *directed* to specific tasks. The replacement of a distribution of income determined by the market with one determined by the subjective opinions of officials can only lead to extreme inefficiency or tyranny. Hayek does concede that it is legitimate for government to make welfare payments to those who cannot earn an adequate income in the market, but this is not owed to them as a consequence of justice since that concept is not relevant to questions of income distribution. Also, Hayek regards the presence of economic inequality as desirable, apart from questions of efficiency, since it provides sources of independence from the state. It is for this reason that he opposes, in general, wealth taxes, or indeed any attempts, by political methods, to equalise access to the market.

The final element in Hayek's 'road to serfdom' thesis is his argument that the operation of unlimited democracy leads to a radical transformation of the legal order. The problem is that in modern democracies the legislature makes both types of law, i.e. the rules of government and the rules of just conduct (Hayek, 1978, Chapters 6–10; 1979). The result is that the area of social life occupied by government tends to expand so that the person and property of the individual come to be used for collective ends.

Hayek does not dispute majority-rule democracy as such but rather *unlimited* government of any kind. In fact, he thinks that majority-rule procedures would be acceptable if the legislature represented genuine majority opinion but says that this does not happen because electoral strategy dictates that a party will put together a *coalition of interests* to win an election. This means that an unlimited legislature can divert the stream of income in an economy to benefit special groups. This happens in Britain where subsidies to politically important industries, uneconomic council rents and inequities in the tax system constitute clear examples of the 'politicisation' of economic life. It is not just the increase in the volume of public spending under a democracy that is the problem, it is the fact that this must be accompanied by a massive increase in government *directions* and the implementation of bogus 'collective' purposes.

Hayek's solution (1979) to the problem is to recommend a new version of the 'separation of powers'. Traditionally this doctrine has meant that the legislature, executive and judiciary should be in separate hands but Hayek argues that, since there are two types of law, the legislature itself should be divided into two parts. The Legislative Assembly should restrict itself to the improvement and modification of the rules of just conduct, while the Governmental Assembly should be concerned only with the despatch of government business. In public finance, for example, the tax rules would be decided by the Legislative Assembly, while how the revenue should be spent would be the responsibility of the Governmental Assembly. To avoid the possibility of party politics dominating the Legislative Assembly Hayek makes the curious suggestion that it should be composed of representatives between their forty-fifth and sixtieth years, who shall sit for 15 years, and be elected by those who reach their forty-fifth birthday. Re-election would be forbidden and voters would vote only once so that the composition of the Assembly would be constantly renewed.

While liberal economists are in general agreement with Hayek that vote-maximising in a competitive-party democracy does not tend to produce the public interest, few have been attracted to his arcane constitutional proposals. Most suggest that the apparently inexorable drive towards inflation, high public spending and the dominance of 'group politics' could be checked by the strict enforcement of more conventional constitutional rules. It has been recommended that governments should be legally obliged to balance their budgets, or that control of the money supply should be taken out of government and given to a body which is independent of politics. In Britain the introduction of proportional representation, which Hayek (1978, p. 161) is against, would go some way towards checking the anti-social activities of government.

Until recently it was thought that Hayek's 'road to serfdom' thesis was a gross exaggeration and had, indeed, been 'refuted' by the co-existence in western countries of macroeconomic planning, welfarism, redistribution *and* the market economy, freedom and the rule of law. However, the recent failures of Keynesian economics, the wastefulness of the welfare state and the threats to the rule of law that have emerged from the relentless politicisation of social and economic life, have all combined to make Hayek's prognosis grimly accurate. Furthermore, those countries that have pursued more market-oriented policies have been economically more successful than others.

## CONSERVATISM AND LIBERTARIANISM

Socialist critics of Hayek have always regarded him as a conservative because he has denied that political action, from centralised authorities, can improve upon the outcomes of a spontaneous market. However, he has stressed that he is not a conservative (1960, pp. 397–406), and indeed his individualism makes him hostile to *all* forms of collective action. His position is, if anything, anti-political. But it is also a position that makes his social philosophy curiously invulnerable to any argument that might derive from 'facts'. For example, market economies and systems of rules may not develop in desirable ways, even from the liberal point of view, yet it is unlikely that the 'evidence' would alter Hayek's belief that the attempt to improve matters is likely to make things worse. This is perhaps less important in relation to the market since the effects of monopoly and other alleged examples of 'market power' have been exaggerated. It is also true that such market power is almost always the product of legal privilege granted by the state. However, all this is much less true of legal orders which rarely *spontaneously* develop in ways that advance individualism. In fact the single institution in Britain which has contributed most to the gradual undermining of the common law and market economy is the *sovereign* Parliament, a product of spontaneous evolution. Indeed, the legal system that is required to service an economic order may, as Hayek concedes in his recent constitutional reform proposals, have to be created *politically*. There is, of course, a difference between the creation and maintenance of those conditions which are required for the evolution of a social order and steering the system in some particular direction.

It is the case that at least a part of Hayek's distrust of intervention derives from his desire to minimise coercion. The only legitimate coercion, he says, is that used by the state to prevent coercion by others (Hayek 1960, Chapter 9). Since coercion, even that 'legitimate' form of compulsion exercised by democratic states, ought not to be used to advance economic and social goals, his system would permit, for example, the persistence of massive inequalities even if the removal of some of them required only a little centralised action. The presence of extreme inequality will, however, make the market order more unacceptable and lead to the charge that it embodies a form of coercion which can only be alleviated by political means. While the latter charge is certainly dubious it will gain plausibility to the extent that Hayek's prohibition on the use of 'politics' to bring about change appears to entrench privilege.

Curiously enough, cogent criticisms of Hayek's doctrines can be made from the market standpoint itself. While Hayek (1960, p. 60) has deliberately rejected anarchy, and even *laissez-faire*, a 'property rights' version of anarchism has been derived from a philosophical position similar to his. The followers of Mises in the USA, led by Murray N. Rothbard (1973), do indeed maintain that the market can satisfy any want, including protection, so that a private enterprise police and jury system is feasible. Also, 'anarchists' say that all cases of external 'bads', such as pollution, could be 'internalised' via a properly-constituted legal code with an extended concept of property. Radical libertarians have been in the forefront of compaigns against narcotics laws, welfare, conscription and income tax, all of which are permitted (logically) by Hayek's account of liberty and law (see Hamowy, 1961). Furthermore, Hayek's market order is not as abstract as it sometimes appears, since he is prepared to countenance restrictions on immigration, for the reason that people of different cultures find it difficult to live under the same rules (1976b, p. 58). This is a statement which has collectivist overtones. Despite Hayek's objections to pragmatism and opportunism in politics his own agenda of government is less strictly libertarian than is often thought (Barry, 1979, Chapter 6). His reasoning permits, for example, subsidies to the arts and the provision of civil amenities.

Despite these problems, however, Hayek has undoubtedly constructed the most coherent defence of traditional liberal political economy this century and many of his warnings of the consequences of collectivist policies have turned out to be well-founded. His major intellectual achievement has been to re-integrate economics into the main body of social science and to remind us that so many of the benefits of civilised living are the product of spontaneous evolution. Now that people are becoming more sceptical of the intellectual foundations of planning and fearful of politicians acting without the restraint of rules, Hayek's social philosophy is, deservedly, reaching a wide audience.

NOTES

1. In my earlier exposition of Hayek's methodology (Barry, 1979, Chapter 2) I suggested that his acceptance of Popper's methodology involved a departure

from his earlier 'subjectivism'. This was a misinterpretation which failed to do justice to the essential unity of his methodology. Also, some of my critical comments were made from a rather unsophisticated 'falsificationist' standpoint. Nevertheless, I still maintain that there is a difference between the Popperian approach to social science and the extreme *a priori* element in some versions of Austrian economics which is not considered by Hayek.

2. It is this that distinguishes Hayek's economic philosophy from that of his fellow warrior against inflation, Milton Friedman. The latter's emphasis on the general price level accords with his positivist methodology.

3. In fact in his later (Hayek, 1939) exposition of the theory of the trade cycle Hayek argued that, irrespective of changes in the market rate of interest, a market economy is self-correcting through the operation of the 'Ricardo Effect'. For an excellent account of this, see O'Driscoll, 1977, Chapter 5.

4. Hayek concedes that, on those rare occasions when there is serious unemployment of all factors, Keynesian methods may be appropriate, but argues that an error was made in interpreting Keynes's theory as a 'general theory'. It was no more than a 'tract for the times'.

## REFERENCES

Barry, N. P., 1979 *Hayek's Social and Economic Philosophy* (Macmillan).

Hamowy, R., 1961 'Hayek's Concept of Freedom', *New Individualist Review*.

Hayek, F. A. 1931 *Prices and Production* (Routledge and Kegan Paul) 2nd edn., 1935.

—— 1933 *Monetary Theory and the Trade Cycle* (Jonathan Cape).

—— 1935 *Collectivist Economic Planning* (Routledge and Kegan Paul).

—— 1939 *Profits, Interest and Investment* (Routledge and Kegan Paul).

—— 1941 *The Pure Theory of Capital* (Routledge and Kegan Paul).

—— 1944 *The Road to Serfdom* (Routledge and Kegan Paul).

—— 1948 *Individualism and Economic Order* (Routledge and Kegan Paul).

—— 1955 *The Counter-revolution of Science* (The Free Press).

—— 1960 *The Constitution of Liberty* (Routledge and Kegan Paul).

—— 1967 *Studies in Philosophy, Politics and Economics* (Routledge and Kegan Paul).

—— 1973 *Law, Legislation and Liberty*, Vol. I, *Rules and Order* (Routledge and Kegan Paul).

—— 1976a *The Denationalisation of Money* (Institute of Economic Affairs).

—— 1976b *Law, Legislation and Liberty*, Vol. II, *The Mirage of Social Justice* (Routledge and Kegan Paul).

—— 1978 *New Studies in Philosophy, Politics, Economics and the History of Ideas* (Routledge and Kegan Paul).

—— 1979 *Law, Legislation and Liberty*, Vol. III, *The Political Order of a Free People* (Routledge and Kegan Paul).

Hicks, J. R., 1967 'The Hayek Story', in *Critical Essays in Monetary Theory* (Oxford University Press).

Littlechild, S. C., 1978 *The Fallacy of the Mixed Economy* (Institute of Economic Affairs).

Mises, L. von, 1962 *The Ultimate Foundation of Economic Science* (Institute for Humane Studies).

O'Driscoll, G. P., 1977 *Economics as a Co-ordination Problem* (Sheed, Andrews and McMeel).

Popper, K. R., 1957 *The Poverty of Historicism* (Routledge and Kegan Paul).

Rothbard, M. N., 1973 *For a New Liberty*, (Collier Macmillan).

# 7 Sir John Hicks's Contributions to Economic Theory

Brian Morgan

The works of Professor Hicks span more than half a century from his earliest published work in *Economica* (1928) to his latest book *Causality in Economics* (1979a). However, so much of his prestigious output has been rapidly absorbed into the main body of economic analysis that the Hicksian origin of much of contemporary theory has become obscured. Therefore, the main purpose of this essay will be to highlight the early contributions of Hicks and to emphasise the revolutionary impact that much of his writings have had on the literature. A curious aspect in this development is that, despite their novelty, Sir John's writings have produced very little controversy. As regards his earlier writings, this lack of controversy can be explained by the almost immediate acceptance by the profession of Hick's pioneering efforts but his later works have stirred little controversy largely because they have been neglected.

Thus in addition to highlighting Hicks's major contributions to theoretical economics, we will also try to account for the apparent asymmetry between his earlier and later works.

J. R. Hicks was born in 1904 in Warwick. At the age of seventeen he won a scholarship to Balliol College, Oxford. He gained a first in mathematical moderation and transferred to PPE in which he graduated in 1925. In 1926 he became an assistant lecturer at the London School of Economics. He remained there until 1935 and during this period he produced some of his best work: the invention of the elasticity of substitution (1932), the distinction of income and substitution effects (Hicks, 1934a with R. G. D. Allen) and the identification of the liquidity spectrum (1935). From

1935–8 he held a fellowship at Cambridge. During this time he completed *Value and Capital* (1939a) and also wrote two influential reviews of Keynes's *General Theory*. He was then appointed to his first chair at Manchester University which he held until 1946. His major contributions at this time were in the area of consumers' surplus and welfare economics (1941). From 1946–52 he was a fellow at Nuffield College, Oxford, and then Drummond Professor of Political Economy at Oxford until his retirement in 1965. In this period he published his *Trade Cycle* (1950) and *Revision of Demand Theory* (1956a).

These works, which complete Hicks's early contributions to economic theory, have recently been referred to as the writings of Hicks the Younger (Leijonhufvud, 1979). However, before retiring Hicks produced two further pieces of analysis that indicate a major change of emphasis in his economic thinking (1956b, 1963) and since then he has produced a further seven major works (1965, 1967, 1969, 1973, 1974a, 1977, 1979a) which have served to highlight the redirection of his thinking. These latter contributions, again following Leijonhufvud, may be referred to as those of the Elder Hicks.

This essay will continue this distinction between the two formative periods in Hicks's work. Consequently we begin by elaborating Hicks's earlier contributions and tracing the extensive developments that these contributions spawned in the 1950s and 1960s. However, it is of interest to note that Hicks took little part in the refinements that were initiated in almost all branches of the subject as a direct result of his pioneering analysis. We attempt to account for this lack of interest and use it to introduce the works of the Elder Hicks.

HICKS THE YOUNGER

The most impressive characteristics of Hicks's earlier writings is their almost overwhelming familiarity to the majority of economists – largely because of the vast literature that subsequently evolved from them. 'Hicks the Younger . . . was supremely successful . . . in constructing the moulds into which 40 years of subsequent theoretical developments were to be cast' (Leijonhufvud 1979). In general it is possible to identify at least five important areas in which Hicks's contribution has been seminal: the elasticity of substitution; ordinal utility theory; money and uncertainty; Keynes versus the Classics; general equilibrium and stability analysis.

## The elasticity of substitution

Hicks introduced this concept in his *Theory of Wages* (1932) in a chapter entitled 'Distribution and Economic Progress'. He noted that although it was generally accepted that an increase in the supply of any factor of production would (as long as the elasticity of demand exceeded unity) increase its *absolute* real income, it was also the case that an

> increase in the supply of any factor will increase its *relative* share (i.e. its *proportion* of the National Dividend) if its 'elasticity of substitution' is greater than unity . . . The 'elasticity of substitution' is a measure of the ease with which the varying factor can be substituted for others (Hicks, 1932, pp. 115–17).

In an appendix Hicks derives the mathematical formula for the elasticity of substitution, $\sigma$, and points out that where $\sigma = 0$ there is no substitution possible and where $\sigma$ is infinite the factors are perfect substitutes. In general $\sigma$ can be shown to be a property of an isoquant,[1] as shown in Figure 7.1.

Thus, $\sigma$ can be seen to be a measure of the curvature of an isoquant – if $\sigma$ is high the isoquant is relatively flat. In addition to the two extreme values of $\sigma$ other interesting special cases occur when $\sigma = 1$ and when $\sigma$ is constant. Much empirical work on production functions make use of these special cases e.g. the Cobb–Douglas function $Q = AL^{\alpha}K^{\beta}$ has unitary elasticity when $\alpha + \beta = 1$ and under this assumption $\alpha$ corresponds to labour's share of national income and $\beta$ to capital's share. In fact Hicks's main purpose in introducing the concept was to demonstrate its usefulness in indicating relative factor shares. However, he also used it to illuminate the various components of Marshall's elasticity of derived demand and to highlight the important consequences that follow from, or are induced by, technical innovations.

For example, Hicks classifies inventions into induced and autonomous inventions in order to demonstrate the biases that

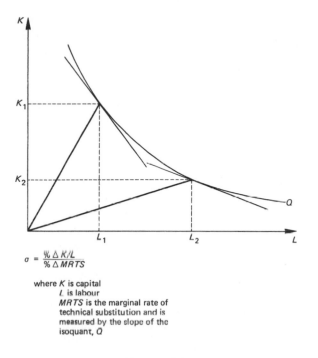

$$\sigma = \frac{\% \, \triangle \, K/L}{\% \, \triangle \, MRTS}$$

where $K$ is capital
  $L$ is labour
  $MRTS$ is the marginal rate of
  technical substitution and is
  measured by the slope of the
  isoquant, $Q$

FIGURE 7.1

might be induced in technical progress by a change in relative factor prices i.e. inventions may be labour-saving, capital-saving or neutral. Autonomous inventions, because of their random nature, are taken to be neutral but induced inventions will be of the labour-saving type if the relative price of labour rises (or the relative price of capital falls). Hicks then points out that labour-saving technical change, *assuming a given capital–labour ratio*, will reduce labour's share of total income. But such an assumption ignores the possibility of factor substitution. Thus, bringing the concept of the elasticity of substitution into the analysis, it is possible for labour-saving technical change to *raise* labour's relative share as long as $\sigma > 1$.

It is also interesting to note that even at this stage in his career it is evident that Hicks's interest lies in *general* equilibrium problems. Thus in addition to comprehensively tracing through the possibilities for product/factor substitution he also alludes to the substitutions that would be induced on the *consumption* side. In this case an increased scarcity of one factor will result in a smaller rise in its price if consumers are able to substitute those goods using a small amount of the factor for goods using a lot of it.

This entirely novel analysis gave rise to a prolonged debate in the journals, beginning with a series of contributions to the new elasticity concept in the *Review of Economic Studies* and the *Economic Journal* from 1933 to 1935, and continuing with the long debate on relative income shares. But Hicks has not contributed much to this debate. He has, as he puts it in the second edition of the *Theory of Wages* (1963), 'left it to others (since my early days) to live in the world of production functions and elasticities of substitution between factors globally defined'.

To some extent Hicks's non-participation in this debate can be traced to the severe criticisms that were made of the whole tenor of his *Wages* book – particularly his almost total acceptance of the doctrine of marginal productivity as the basis for the demand for labour. However, Hicks quickly came to accept these criticisms – '1932 was not a lucky date for the appearance of a book like this. It was the blackest year of the Great Depression; there has been no date in this century to which the theory that I was putting out could have been more inappropriate' (1963). He puts the blame for this on the fact that 'I was entirely the victim of the traditional dichotomy between real and monetary economics' and that 'I wrote my book . . . in a state of monstrous ignorance about everything monetary'.

However, within a year or so of the publication of *The Theory of Wages* Hicks was to rectify this defect in his understanding of economic phenomena by turning his mind specifically to monetary problems (see p. 115 below). We turn now to his contribution to the theory of demand.

## Ordinal Utility Theory

Hicks's work in this area was first published in 1934 in an article he wrote jointly with R. G. D. Allen (1934a), but it is more comprehensively set out in Chapters 1–3 of *Value and Capital* (1939a). Their work in this area was a development of earlier work by Edgeworth, Pareto and Slutsky, and they established that ordinal utility (elaborated in terms of indifference curves and budget lines) could derive the same propositions as cardinal utility (elaborated in terms of measurable marginal utilities) but that the former achieved the same results more clearly and more precisely. However, they accepted that the two theories were saying the same thing, e.g. 'Tangency between the price line and an indifference curve is the expression . . . of the proportionality between marginal utilities and prices' (Hicks, 1939a, p. 17). This can be demonstrated conveniently as in Figure 7.2. The slope of indifference curve, $I$, can be written as $dY/dX$ and measures the marginal rate of substitution ($MRS$) of $X$ for $Y$. However, along an indifference curve the total utility of the consumer is constant. Therefore it is possible to demonstrate that the slope of an indifference curve can also be defined as the ratio of the marginal utilities ($MU$) of $X$ for $Y$.[2] Thus the slope of indifference curve, $I = dY/dX = MUx/MUy = MRS$ of $X$ for $Y$. However, the slope of the budget line, $AB = Px/Py$. Therefore at the point of tangency $MUx/MUy = Px/Py = MRS$ of $X$ for $Y$, i.e. the ordinal and cardinal conditions for a maximum are equivalent.

It is also of interest to note the similarities between this analysis and our previous discussion of isoquants. The elasticity of substitution is a property of an isoquant but the same general principle holds for an indifference curve. Specifically the marginal rate of substitution diminishes along a convex indifference curve and the marginal rate of *technical* substitution ($MRTS$) diminishes along a convex isoquant. Figure 7.2 can then be relabelled to demonstrate the cost minimising output level, i.e. measuring

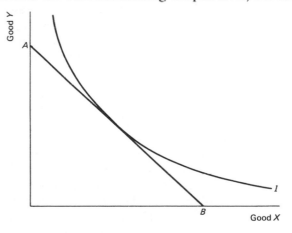

FIGURE 7.2

capital along the $Y$ axis and labour along the $X$ axis, cost minimisation occurs where $P_L/P_k = MRTS$ of $L$ for $K$. In fact, it was the realisation of this symmetry that led Hicks in the direction of the 1934 Hicks–Allen article.[3]

Apart from considerations of presentation and clarity the major advance which indifference curve analysis offered was its ability to distinguish between the income and substitution effects of a price change. Moreover, Hicks and Allen pointed out that the sign of this income effect could not be predicted from the simple assumption that the consumer seeks to maximise utility. However they demonstrated that in the absence of income effects the substitution effects were remarkably regular. For example, they were able to show that not only is the direct substitution effect of a change in the price of $X$ on the quantity demanded of $X$ always negative, but that a number of secondary substitution theorems could also be deduced – the most important being the proposition that the substitution effect of a change in the price of $X$ on the quantity demanded of $Y$ must be exactly equal to the effect of a change in the price of $Y$ on the quantity demanded of $X$.

The latter substitution theorem refers to the cross elasticity of demand and its importance derives from the fact that it successfully cleared up the elasticity problem that had initially prompted the Hicks–Allen article. Specifically, Henry Schultz had estimated some cross elasticities of demand (the demand for $X$ against the price of $Y$ and vice versa) and found them to be non-symmetric whereas Marshallian demand theory suggested they should be symmetric. Hicks and Allen were then able to point out that 'Schultz had left out the income effects which for direct elasticities may indeed be negligible, as Marshall (in effect) supposed them to be; but for cross elasticities there is no reason why they should be negligible' (Hicks, 1974b).

This quotation is important in another respect. Basically, Marshall had ignored the income effect by assuming a constant marginal utility of money. The quotation suggests that from the point of view of ordinary demand analysis Hicks accepted Marshall's neglect of the income effect. Indeed, such a neglect is justifiable as long as the good in question represents a small part of the consumer's budget and Marshall was always careful to make this assumption. Thus in Hicks's view the ordinal approach 'was *not* so clear an advance (on the older marginal utility approach) as is usually supposed' (1976, p. 137). By the same token

Hicks has never accepted the extension of his analysis via Samuelson's revealed preference approach as either necessary or desirable. 'Marshall's consumer who decides on his purchase by comparing the marginal utility of what is to be bought with the marginal utility of the money he will have to pay for it is more like an actual consumer' (Hicks, 1976, p. 138). In fact in his *Revision of Demand Theory* (1956a) Hicks rejects the revealed preference approach even for econometric purposes, stating that for the data to which econometrics is usually applied on ordinal scale of preferences seems the most sensible hypothesis with which to begin the analysis.

However, despite his own reservations, Hicks's ordinal approach in the end met with very little criticism and quickly became a standard part of the economist's tool kit. Moreover, many observers would claim that Hicks has underestimated the step forward that his use of indifference curves entailed, e.g. Blaug explains that European marginal utility doctrine around the First World War proliferated 'in subtle distinctions and metaphysical classifications. [Thus], one is made to realize how much has been swept away by the Hicksian Revolution – all to the good we would say' (Blaug, 1976, p. 388).

*Money and Uncertainty*

Soon after publishing his *Theory of Wages* (1932) Hicks came to feel that his failure to account adequately for monetary phenomena had ruined the greater part of that book, and he soon turned his attention to money. Hicks at this time was still at the LSE lecturing on general equilibrium theory from the viewpoint of Walras and Pareto, and the theory of risk along the lines of Knight and Hayek. The elasticity of substitution and indifference curves were the progeny of the former lectures; the properties of economic probability distributions and stock-flow distinctions, especially in relation to the balance sheet of assets, were the progeny of the latter. Specifically 'It was through Risk that I got to money' (Hicks, 1977).

Hicks's seminal article in this area is his 'Suggestion for Simplifying the Theory of Money' (1935). Characteristically Hicks arrived at his insights into monetary theory by applying marginal utility or value theory to the choice between money and securities *at the margin*. To Hicks the crucial question of monetary theory is why people hold money rather than interest-bearing securities. 'Either we have to give an explanation of the fact that people do hold money when rates of interest are positive or we have to evade the difficulty somehow', and Hicks sees velocities of circulation and natural rates of interest as the great traditional evasions. His own answer to this question is pregnant with insights and in fact it anticipates the monetary developments of Keynes's *General Theory*. But it also does far more than this and in effect laid the foundations of the portfolio theoretic approach to the demand for money by specifically outlining a transactions demand for cash and a risk aversion demand for cash and establishing the permanent income or wealth constraint on the demand for money.

For example, Hicks first notes that whether or not transactions balances are invested in bonds will depend on a comparison of the costs and benefits involved. 'The net advantage to be derived from investing a given quantity of money consists of the interest or profit earned less the cost of investment'. However he further notes that the expected profits from bonds is in general uncertain and therefore a risk factor is involved which means that the *particular* expectation appropriate to riskless situations then has to be replaced by a band of probabilities. 'It is convenient to represent these probabilities . . . by a mean value and some appropriate measure of dispersion'. Thus the whole basis of portfolio theory was set out which allows every asset to be characterised by two parameters: its expected returns (mean value) and the variance of these returns (standard deviation) as a measure of risk. Money is then viewed as one asset in a continuum of assets each differing as regards return and risk. Furthermore money is simply an extreme part of this liquidity spectrum – it is perfectly liquid, it is riskless and it bears no rate of return.

Another novel element in this paper is the discussion of the relevant budget constraint: 'Total wealth in our present problem plays just the same part as total expenditure in the theory of value. In the theory of money . . . the individual's demand for money will respond to a change in his total wealth'. And in a footnote Hicks continues 'Of course [the Classics] say "income". But in this case income can only be strictly interpreted as "expected income".'

This incisive analysis of the central questions of monetary theory obviously foreshadowed the writings of Baumol (1952), Tobin (1958) and Friedman (1956) respectively (although none of these authors make explicit reference to Hicks (1935) – probably because in the fifties it was not a widely read or recommended piece of work). However Keynes at least appreciated the significance of Hicks's analysis and on being sent a proof of the article replied in December 1934: 'I like it very much. I agree with you that what I now call "Liquidity Preference" is the essential concept for Monetary Theory' (Hicks, 1977, p. 142). Perhaps because of this apparent similarity in research interests Hicks was asked to review the *General Theory* for the Economic Journal on its publication in 1936. This turned out to be the first of a number of reviews – in some respects Hicks can be said to have been reviewing the *General Theory* (in the sense of placing it in a modern perspective) ever since – but it was his second review (1937) which became the most famous and to which we now turn.

*Keynes versus the Classics*

In his second review of the *General Theory* (1937) Hicks complained that Keynes, in making his break with the Classics, had not set out a recognisable classical theory. Hicks then proceeds to remedy this defect by setting out a fairer representation of the Classical model in a form in which it can be more effectively contrasted with that of Keynes. Thus he sets out three equations for each model – representing the goods market, the investment sector and the money market – and then performed a comparison. His basic approach was to integrate these three equations into two curves – his famous $SI/LL$ curves (now generally referred to as $IS/LM$).

In contrast to the elaborate four quadrant derivation of these curves which has become popular in the text books, Hicks's derivation can be paraphrased quite simply as follows: The money market equation $M = L(Y, r)$ gives us a relation between income $(Y)$ and the interest rate $(r)$. This can be drawn out as a curve $(LM)$ which will slope upwards since an increase in income tends to raise the demand for money and an increase in the interest rate tends to lower it. The other two equations:

$$I = I(r)$$
$$I(r) = S(Y)$$

can be taken together.

These relate investment (*I*) to savings (*S*) and give us another relation between income and interest. The first equation determines the value of investment at any given rate of interest and the second equation tells what level of income will be necessary to make savings equal to that value of investment. A curve *IS* can therefore be drawn showing the relation between *Y* and *r* which must be maintained in order to make saving equal to investment.

However the *LM* curve is likely to have a peculiar shape (see Figure 7.3). In the first place there will be a limit to how far the interest rate can fall (ensuring a horizontal section to the curve – the liquidity trap). Secondly there will be a maximum to the level of income that a given money supply can finance (giving rise to a vertical section).

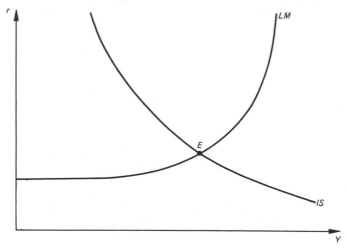

FIGURE 7.3

The novelty of the *IS/LM* framework is that income and the rate of interest are determined simultaneously at point *E*. Thus, Hicks concludes that the quantity theory had tried to determine *Y* without *r* and therefore 'has to give place to a theory recognising a higher degree of interdependence' and accordingly Keynes's real innovation was this explicit recognition of interdependence in the goods, money and labour markets. However, Hicks was not at all convinced that Keynes's model (based on liquidity preference) was saying something completely different from the classical model (based on loanable funds) – except in the extreme situation of the liquidity trap. For example, in Keynes's theory an increase in the inducement to invest is supposed to increase $Y$ (and employment) via the multiplier while in the classical loanable funds theory an increase in investment raises $r$. But Hicks points out (in his reviews of 1936 and 1937) that both approaches are only analysing the short-run impact effects and that when the whole process is traced through the result in each model is an increase in both $Y$ and $r$. In Keynes's model although $Y$ increases initially, there may eventually be an increase in $r$ because the demand for money will rise with the higher level of income. Similarly, in the classical model, although $r$ increases initially, there may eventually be an increase in $Y$ because velocity will rise with the higher rate of interest. Both of these forces are incorporated in the $IS/LM$ model so that an increase in investment shifts the $IS$ curve to the right and thereby raises both $Y$ and $r$—outside the 'trap'.

This analysis highlights again Hick's obvious enthusiasm for *general* equilibrium solutions to even macroeconomic problems—especially where partial equilibrium theory gives rise to spurious results. In this way Hicks demostrated the redundant nature of the liquidity preference versus loanable funds debate on the determination of the rate of interest. Using a general equilibrium approach he was able to show that the two theories are complementary rather than competitive because whether we choose to ignore the bond market (loanable funds) as Keynes did or the money market (liquidity preference) as did the Classics is simply a question of theoretical perspective; but the same results obtain in the end.

Having invented the $IS/LM$ apparatus Hicks then notes 'It does not appear that we have exhausted the uses of that apparatus so let us conclude by giving it a little run on its own'. It is little exaggeration to say that the whole of macroeconomics in the 1950s and 1960s consisted in giving this apparatus some further 'little runs on its own'. Its impact on macro textbooks alone hardly needs elaboration. However, Hicks was more cautious—'it remains a terribly rough and ready affair. In particular, the concept of income is worked monstrously hard; most of our curves are not really determinate unless something is said about the distribution of income . . . and all sorts of questions about the timing of the processes under consideration [have been neglected]' (1937).

Despite these reservations, much of the monetarist versus Keynesian debate of the last twenty years has taken place within this framework and tremendously important policy conclusions have been based upon it. In this respect it is important to note that for purposes of economic analysis or policy discussions Hicks has never been too enamoured of the *IS/LM* model. Indeed he has used it only for purposes of exegesis and it was in this context that Keynes had originally approved of it: for example, referring to the 1937 article Keynes wrote to Hicks, 'I found it very interesting and have next to nothing to say by way of criticism'. Thus Hicks feels justified in claiming that 'Keynes accepted the *IS/LM* diagram as a fair statement of the nucleus of his position. That in any case was what it was meant to be – a means of demonstrating the nature of the difference between Keynes and his predecessors – *not a statement of what I believed myself.* It is much less a statement of my own view than the "Simplifying" article by which I continue to stand' (1977, pp. 144–7). We illustrate some of Hicks's recent contributions to monetary theory below; we turn now to Hicks's contribution to general equilibrium analysis.

*General Equilibrium and Stability Analysis*

Introduction

Hicks began lecturing on the general equilibrium theories of Walras (1934b) and Pareto in 1930 and had written many articles and his *Theory of Wages* from that general perspective but it was not until the publication of *Value and Capital* (1939a) that his ideas were formed into a coherent framework. The book was finished at Cambridge but it was basically an LSE book. Both its title and contents have led many people to suggest that it is a work of bridge-building between micro- and macro-economics – in particular, laying the micro foundations of macro theory. However, Hicks disputes this and sees it instead as *an attempt* to link together static neo-classical theory and the more dynamic theories of capital accumulation. Consequently it may be helpful if we first sketch a plan of this classic work. The analysis proceeds as follows.

(i) First the Hicks–Allen contribution to demand theory is outlined and the *stability* of equilibrium is analysed; first in relation to two goods and then in a multiple exchange system. At this stage Hicks introduces the concepts of 'perfect' and 'imperfect' stability and shows that the instability of exchange arises only from asymmetrical income effects.

(ii) The firm, production and the technical elasticities of substitution are then introduced and a system in which both exchange and production respond to price incentives is analysed and the properties required for the stability of the whole system are then established along the lines of exchange stability.

(iii) The dynamic part of the book begins with an outline of the method of analysis to be employed. The Hicksian '*week*' is introduced and defined as that period during which prices are constant. It was essentially a dynamic concept and it provided the framework for a discussion of equilibrium over time – what Hicks termed *temporary equilibrium*. This represented an heroic attempt to break out of the straitjacket of static theory by specifically analysing the effects of price expectations: i.e. during the 'week' both *current* prices and *expected* prices were allowed to influence production and consumption plans.

(iv) The difficult problems of capital, interest, money and speculation are then preliminarily analysed. At this stage the relationship between long and short rates is introduced and the expectational theory of the term structure of interest rates is formulated for the first time; the loanable funds versus liquidity preference debate is cleared up along general equilibrium lines; the close substitutability between money and other assets is established; the ex ante/ex post distinction between investment and saving is cleared up along with the concept of income; and the elasticity of expectations is introduced for the first time.

(v) The scene is then set for an analysis of the working of the dynamic system. The effect of price expectations on production plans and thereby their influence on the temporary equilibrium of the whole system is then formalised. The stability of the system is shown to be dependent on certain stabilisers – in particular inelastic expectations, normal prices, rigid money wages and contracts.

(vi) Finally, the implications of the analysis for real-world problems such as capital accumulation and the trade cycle are tackled.

The number of novel concepts introduced in this work is remarkable, not to mention older concepts which are rigorously restated and misconceptions cleared up. Thus economists were provided with a far more comprehensive overview of the entire system of production and exchange than had ever been presented before. However, the significance of many of these concepts only became fully appreciated later and this can be illustrated by analysing two of the most important in terms of subsequent developments – Hicks's stability analysis and the concept of temporary equilibrium.

## Stability analysis

Hicksian stability conditions depend on the negative slope of the excess demand function – i.e. stability requires that a *rise* in price makes supply greater than demand. This ensures the stability of equilibrium even in the case where the supply curve is downward sloping as long as it is steeper than the demand curve – this represents stability in the Walrasian sense rather than in the sense of Marshall. In the case of multiple exchange Hicks defined *perfect* stability as occurring when a movement away from equilibrium sets up forces tending to restore equilibrium *both* when other prices are given *and* when other prices are adjusted so as to preserve equilibrium in the other markets. *Imperfect* stability occurs when equilibrium is restored only after all other price repercussions are allowed for.

However, the analysis soon came under attack. Specifically, in the case of multiple exchange the Hicksian stability condition raises problems because it takes no account of *convergence*, i.e. no dynamic adjustment mechanism is incorporated into the system. Samuelson was to point out that for stability – in the sense of convergence towards the equilibrium – one needs the further condition that the rate of change of price in each market is proportional to the excess demand in that market. Otherwise the system might move away from equilibrium once a disturbance occurs (e.g. the cobweb model). Samuelson insisted that an understanding of the dynamics of change was crucial even in comparative static analysis: 'One interested only in fruitful statics must study dynamics' (Samuelson, 1947).

Basically Hicks had defined perfect stability in terms of the cross elasticities of demand as expressed by the *derivatives* of the excess demand functions – the impact on the excess demand for the *i*th good of a change in the price of the *j*th good. However, Samuelson pointed out that stability actually required an analysis of whether the excess demands *got smaller over time*, i.e. whether deviations from equilibrium were gradually eliminated. This involved an analysis of the dynamics of the system. Specifically, what was needed was the *time derivative* of price (its rate of change) with respect to the volume of excess demand in the system. True dynamic stability requires that the roots of this equation (the characteristic equation of the dynamic adjustment process) have negative real parts and Samuelson insisted that this requirement is not equivalent to the Hicks conditions.

Samuelson's criticisms provided the foundations of dynamic analysis and this was unquestionably an important advance. However, although Samuelson's foundations were completely general it was soon pointed out that in practice this generality took the analysis further away from a discussion of *real economic problems*. Samuelson's necessary and sufficient conditions, for example, were based entirely on the *mathematics* of the excess demand functions not on the economics. This is in contrast to Hicks's stability conditions which were specifically derived from his economic model. Later Metzler and Morishima were to prove that the Samuelson and Hicks conditions were equivalent in most cases and that, moreover, the Hicks conditions were *necessary* if useful applications of Samuelson's correspondence principle were to be achieved within a Walrasian price system. Thus although Hicks's method could be criticised, the stability conditions themselves have stood the test of time. As Mundell puts it: 'The stability analysis introduced by Hicks has been one of the most successful failures in economic theory' (in Woolfe, 1968, Chap. 18).

In fact, Hicks' showed characteristic foresight in refusing to accept Samuelson's propositions as an unequivocal step forward. Thus in the 1946 second edition of *Value and Capital* he criticised Samuelson's dynamic analysis for being too *mechanical*. 'I reduced the purely mechanical part of my dynamic theory to the simplest terms . . . But in so doing I did leave myself free to make some progress with the less mechanical parts – expectations and so on. [Thus], I should be sorry to abandon it altogether in favour of pure concentration on mechanism.' The progress with the less mechanical parts refers to the temporary equilibrium concept to which we now turn.

Temporary equilibrium

Equilibrium is temporarily achieved over a Hicksian 'week' by the accommodation of supply and demand to the set of price expectations in force on 'Monday'. If some of these expectations prove to be false they can only be revised on 'Monday week' and then, together with demand and supply, establish an equilibrium path for production and consumption the following week. Obviously this construction is very artificial (indeed the Elder Hicks is very critical of it) but the method did in fact entail an immense step forward because it specifically highlighted those areas in which the future impinges on the present, e.g. the method attempted to take into account stores of value such as money, capital and securities – things which are not wanted for their own sake but as a means to future consumption.

For example, an expectation that prices will fall next week would encourage some individuals to store their wealth until 'Monday week'. This would then influence current prices and future prices and alter the temporary equilibrium. Consumption and production may then converge over time or, of course, they may diverge depending upon people's expectations – specifically on the elasticity of price expectations, defined as the *percentage change in the expected price over the percentage change in the current price*. The stability of temporary equilibrium over time is then shown to depend on the value of this ratio. Convergence requires it to be less than unity, i.e. expectations to be inelastic. Thus Hicks concludes, 'As soon as we take expectations into account (or rather the elasticity of expectations into account) the stability of the system is seriously weakened'.

This analysis can be viewed as an important step forward in the sense that no-one attempted to expand or improve upon this analysis for nearly 30 years. Hicks, it should be noticed, was here attempting to grapple with the difficult problems which arise in general equilibrium analysis whenever explicit account is taken of expectations and stores of value. Because of these difficulties, later researchers progressively limited their analysis and moved away from temporary equilibrium in the direction of proving the existence and stability of a full competitive equilibrium in the absence of complications such as money, uncertainty and expectations. However, even this proved far more difficult to formalise than it appeared in 1946. The existence problem itself was not solved until the 1950s when Arrow and Debreu applied the Brouwer fixed-point theorem (basically a mapping device) to the problem. Then another mathematical technique – the Liapunov method – was introduced in the late 1950s by Arrow, Hurwicz and Hahn to solve the stability problem by taking proper account of the economic properties of the system. Basically they specified a *tâtonnement* process and placed a number of economic restrictions on the actions of the agents of the system in order to produce sufficient conditions for stability.

However, these breakthroughs were much more limited in scope than Hick's original objective because they took no account of expectations or historical time and very little account of false trading, money and other stores of value. It is true that Hicks overlooked some of the problems of existence and stability and this can be regarded as a weakness of his earlier work, but later research became too immersed in rectifying this weakness and did not pay enough attention to the insights into real-world problems that Hicks at the time demonstrated. (These problems were only really being tackled in the latter half of the 1970s). Indeed, the developments by Samuelson, Arrow, Hahn *et al.* did nothing to 'dynamise' the theory in the directions that Hicks (correctly) felt were important – i.e. grounding the analysis in historical time and taking explicit account of expectations and money. (The very concepts, of course, that were the hallmark of Keynes's economics). Thus a distinguished general equilibrium theorist could admit that 'The Arrow–Debreu model describes a world in which *none* of the problems which interested Keynes can occur' (Hahn 1975).

The consensus suggests that the general equilibrium model has not progressed significantly after Hicks's contribution. Thus Morishima (1977) refers to the great tradition of general equilibrium theorists from Walras to Hicks and laments that 'This tradition changed entirely after the Second World War. . . . It seems that general equilibrium theorists are now only interested in proving, reproving or generalising the theorems or laws discovered by their predecessors.' Indeed, there is nothing available in the modern economics literature to match Hicks's grand scheme. *Value and Capital* remains a classic in every sense of the word: 'To this day there have been few works so grand in conception or so pregnant with new ideas about the basic structure of economic theory . . . The identification of temporary equilibrium alone was an intellectual triumph of the first order' (Weintraub 1979).

This completes our discussion of the contribution of Hicks the Younger.[4]

Having made major contributions in the areas detailed above, Hicks took little part in either the debates surrounding his work or in the controversies surrounding the extensions of it by Samuelson, Arrow *et al.* Hicks admits that his work has deeply influenced the work of these economists and that they in turn have sharpened the analysis that he roughed out in *Value and Capital* but basically he remains unsympathetic to their approach, e.g. referring to his non-participation in this debate he writes 'I have felt little sympathy with the theory for theory's sake which has been characteristic of one strand in American economics; nor with the idealisation of the free market which has been character-istic of another; and I have felt little faith in the econometrics on which they have largely relied to make their contact with reality' (1979b).

In some recent correspondence with the author, Professor Hicks has elaborated on this point. He writes, '*Value and Capital* was published in February 1939, six months before the outbreak of war. It was much more of a success in the US than in the UK. But I was nearly cut off from what was happening in the US until 1946. When contact was re-established, I found that what had interested the Americans was the static part of my book, not the "dynamic" part, in which, even in 1939, I had been much more interested. I could not work up much interest in their refinements on the static side. [Thus], I continued, even after 1946, to work in a British milieu. *Trade Cycle* was inspired by Harrod's *Dynamic Economics*. My further work on Keynes is similarly British oriented. The one big attempt I did make to absorb what the Americans were doing was the Survey of Linear Theory (1960). It took me quite a year to write that paper, but in the end I didn't feel that it had much for me. It was still too static.'

After 1950 instead of participating in the debate over *Value and Capital* and his other contributions Hicks, along with his wife Ursula, 'became the servant of applied economics'.[5] Together they advised some of the emerging Commonwealth nations such as India, Jamaica and Nigeria on the economic problems they were experiencing in making the transition to independence. During this period Hicks sees a ten-year gap in his contribution to economic analysis (however, despite this 'gap' he still managed to write between 1950 and 1960 twenty articles, two new books, two revisions of his *Social Framework* (1942), a collection – *Essays in World Economics* (1959) – and four book reviews!) but around 1960 he decided to bring himself up to date and to resume his former work. It is to his recent contributions that we now turn.

## THE ELDER HICKS

In 1972 Hicks received a Nobel prize for his earlier work on 'general equilibrium and welfare economics'. However, Hicks points out that 'it was with mixed feelings that I found myself honoured for that work which I myself found myself to have outgrown' (1977, p. v). The dividing line between his earlier and later writings is not obvious, even to Hicks, but roughly speaking the earlier period ended with the publication of his *Trade Cycle* in 1950 and his more recent work, which he claims was written from a different perspective, begins with *Capital and Growth* (1965). However, two earlier publications (1956b, 1963) are also important and in referring to the 1956 article Hicks acknowledges that it was not until recently that he 'realised how important it is in explaining the development of my thought. It is the beginning of my new work in this field' (1979c).

Taking this as our starting point it is not difficult to demonstrate that there are a number of common themes permeating his later works and that though they may appear superficially different they do on balance hang together and to some extent fortify each other. They offer the reader some penetrating insights into the most controversial areas of current economic theory – capital, growth and money – as well as continuing to shed light on the interpretation, meaning and significance of the Keynesian revolution.

It is both surprising and unfortunate that these later works have not been read with the same spirit of enthusiasm that so obviously greeted his earlier works. Consequently our analysis of these works must inevitably be more limited in scope because this is not the right place to attempt a perspective on largely uncharted areas in economic theory. Therefore this section will attempt only to convey to the reader the method of approach that Hicks now invariably makes use of and to identify the challenge that he so openly presents to current economic theorists.

In pursuing these themes we will concentrate the analysis in five related areas: historical processes; flexprice/fixprice markets; liquidity theory; growth theory; causality.

## Historical Processes

In developing these new themes the Elder Hicks did not start from scratch. Rather he used parts of his earlier works (particularly 1932, 1935, 1939a and 1950) to develop new analytical techniques. The direction of his thinking can be clearly discerned from three recent publications (1976, 1977, 1979b). In these he points out that the basic fault of his earlier works was the essentially static nature of even those processes that claimed to be dynamic, e.g. in *Value and Capital* the concept of the 'week' was only partially dynamic; it did have a past (embedded in the inherited capital stock) and an unknown future (about which expectations were formed) but on 'Monday' both price expectations and current transactions were all wrapped up in an equilibrium and simultaneously solved.

In order to avoid this relapse into statics Hicks's analysis is now grounded in historical processes which are 'in time'. The thing to note about 'time' is that it is *irreversible*; the past is unalterable (but we do have knowledge of it) while the future is unknowable (though it will eventually become known in the sense that the future eventually becomes the present). In analysing the past economists often ignore this very obvious fact and tend to analyse the relationship between (say) 1974 and 1975 in the same way as the relationship between 1974 and 1973 even though transactions in 1974 were based upon *knowledge* of 1973 but only on *expectations* about 1975.

The trouble with *Value and Capital* was that it was not 'in time' in this sense; the artificiality of its constructions did 'deliberate violence to the *order* in which in the real world events occur'. (*Capital and Growth*, 1965, p. 73) There were three aspects of that analysis that were particularly defective. In the first place since prices were determined in an equilibrium manner on 'Monday' the analysis contained no real theory of *markets*. Secondly, the failure to adequately account for the effects of uncertainty on the postponement of decision-making meant that the analysis lacked a theory of *liquidity*. Finally, the relationship between 'Monday' and 'Monday week' was never explored so that the weeks were never effectively linked together i.e. the analysis also contained no real theory of *growth*. Thus, the analysis of market structures, liquidity and growth, with the emphasis on historical processes, forms the basis of Hicks's latest contributions to economic theory.

## *Market Structures: Flexprice/Fixprice distinction*

In *Capital and Growth* (1965) Hicks notes that the fundamental weakness of the temporary equilibrium method was the assumption that prices change rapidly enough to ensure an equilibrium between planned demands and planned supplies even in the short run. When Hicks came to abandon this equilibrium assumption he assumed instead that prices are determined exogenously. To distinguish the two methods Hicks adopted the flexprice/fixprice terminology. The former refers to the price flexibility found in competitive market structures while the latter refers to the 'sticky' prices which are more common in less competitive markets – these prices are not completely rigid but they do not necessarily change in response to a disequilibrium between demand and supply.

These two methods of price determination are obviously extremes and in his *History* book (1969) Hicks attempted to trace out the development of different types of market structures to indicate the conditions under which one or other tended to dominate. A crucial factor in this development has been the role of the *merchant*. Markets developed from barter to monetary forms of exchange largely because a merchant of some sort was prepared to act as a stockholder i.e. was prepared to buy goods in order to sell them later at a profit. In this role the merchant performed the function of price-*maker* and determined prices in relation to stocks – raising prices when stocks were (abnormally) low and vice versa. The margin between his buying and selling price was a reflection of the service he rendered to consumers by reducing their transaction costs. The size of this margin depended on the degree of competition. Thus the most competitive markets tended to be highly organised markets in which transaction costs were further reduced by the establishment of strict trading rules – like the stock exchange. In these markets margins could be so low that all transactors appeared to be price-*takers*. It was this type of highly organised market that formed the basis of Walras's model. However it was the (slightly) less competitive, unorganised markets (in which merchants were active) that Marshall used in his model.

Since the unorganised, flexprice markets were the dominant form historically, Marshall's method was closer to reality. However, these flexprice markets have been increasingly replaced this century by fixprice markets. This development has been caused largely by technological factors – basically economies of scale and product standardisation. These factors have tended to diminish the role of merchants and enhance the power of producers to fix price.

For Hicks the distinction between flexprice and fixprice markets is vitally important specifically because they have different implications for *stocks* and *flows* (1956b, 1979c). This can be more easily appreciated by analysing Keynes's model of the *General Theory*. According to Hicks, Keynes was aware of the change that had taken place in market structures since Marshall's time and therefore realised the importance of the fixprice method. Consequently Keynes characterised some markets as flexprice (e.g. the bond market) while others are taken to be fixprice markets (e.g. labour and goods). In addition, in the (flexprice) bond market, the *price* of bonds is determined almost entirely in terms of stock relations (liquidity preference) while in the (fixprice) labour and goods markets the *quantities* of these items are determined almost entirely in terms of flow analysis (the multiplier process). Thus in the fixprice markets a disequilibrium between demand and supply generates *quantity adjustments*. In this way the flexprice/fixprice distinction enables Hicks to illuminate one of the central features of the *General Theory* model, i.e. the multiplier process, which is shown to depend on quantity adjustments in fixprice markets.

More recently Hicks has used these insights into the fundamentals of Keynes's multiplier theory to indicate that theory's shortcomings. Specifically Keynes had concentrated his analysis of fixprice markets entirely on the flow relations and, whereas in the 1930s the vast stocks of idle resources made this concentration legitimate, it certainly cannot be so regarded in the postwar period. Therefore in his *Crisis in Keynesian Economics* Hicks attempts to make good this defect by highlighting the crucial role played by stocks in sustaining the multiplier process and thereby enabling increases in expenditure to be translated into increases in output. Basically an expenditure-induced expansion requires a relatively high level of stocks in fixprice markets because the initial expansionary impact reduces existing stocks and only eventually raises output. 'But there cannot be a fall in stocks unless there are stocks to fall. Thus it is impossible to tell the multiplier story properly in terms of the *flow* relations between income and saving to which Keynes (in the main) confined himself. The state of stocks . . . must be considered too' (1974). However, he further notes decisions regarding stocks depend crucially on producers' expectations.

By analysing the problems of stocks and of expectations in the multiplier process Hicks offers some illuminating insights into the present debate about the effectiveness of fiscal policy and the 'crowding-out' debate because ultimately this is what the multiplier theory is all about. (On this point see Coddington, 1979).

This discussion affords a useful introduction to our next topic – liquidity. As Hicks points out, this concept ought also to have been analysed in terms of stocks and flows but Keynes's analysis concentrated narrowly on the stock side of the question. Thus a broader and more meaningful theory of liquidity is feasible if proper account is taken of stock-flow interactions.

*Liquidity and sequential choice*

In the area of monetary theory (perhaps more than any other area) Hicks has again attempted to extend and refine Keynes's analysis. He notes that Keynes's concentration on money and bonds (in the *General Theory* at least) had left a lot to be done. His recent contributions have concentrated on Keynes's motives for holding money, on the 'true' meaning of liquidity and on the sort of minimum financial structure that must be posited once Keynes's narrow money-bonds model is abandoned. All three are interrelated, e.g. the attempt to make headway with the liquidity concept dictates a certain type of financial structure.

In the *Two Triads* (1967, Chaps. 1–3) Hicks ingeniously links together the transactions, precautionary and speculative motives with the three main functions of money – medium of exchange, store of value and measure of value. However, although his analysis was not entirely sound in this respect (see Harris, 1969) there is one part of the analysis to which he continues to hold, i.e. he insists that the transactions demand is not a voluntary demand to hold money – 'It is the money that is needed to circulate a certain quantity of goods at a particular level of prices'. The portfolio approach, which attempts to explain this demand in terms of voluntary choice theory, is therefore rejected by Hicks.

Moreover, the simple version of the portfolio theory is also rejected as a viable explanation of the other parts of Keynes's demand for money – the precautionary and speculative motives. Hicks rejects the portfolio approach because it is not sufficiently '*in time*' and therefore does not adequately come to grips with the concept of liquidity.

For Hicks liquidity is concerned with the spectrum of (more or less liquid) assets. Liquidity preference is not concerned solely with the demand for money but with the movement along this spectrum of assets. The portfolio approach (for which Hicks had laid the foundations back in 1935) deals with a *single choice* – between what is known and what is unknown but where the latter is reduced to a probability. However, in Hicks's analysis liquidity is a property of a *sequence of choices*. The distinction is not simply between the known and the unknown but between what is known *now* and those things that may become known in the *near future* (with the passage of *time*). '[Liquidity] is concerned with the passage from the unknown to the known – with the knowledge that if we wait we can have more knowledge' (1973, pp. 38–9).

This point can be elaborated in terms of two decision points – Hicks calls them 'Christmas' and 'Easter'. A decision must first be made (say) at 'Christmas' on the basis of the possible eventualities as seen at that date; but only one of these will actually occur. However, between 'Christmas' and 'Easter' some of these possible eventualities will be ruled out by subsequent events. Choice at 'Easter' then depends crucially on which particular eventualities survive. Therefore it 'becomes relevant to the "Christmas" choice whether it carries with it a *wide* or a *narrow* band of "Easter" alternatives – whether, that is to say, the choice admits of *flexibility*' (Hicks, 1973, p. 41). Hicks insists that this extra dimension of risk bearing *over time* is ignored in the standard portfolio approach.

The flexibility referred to in this context should be seen in a *market* context, i.e. the ease with which it is possible to buy or sell existing assets. When transactors become 'locked-in' to their current holding of assets – because selling them would incur a capital loss – their flexibility of action is correspondingly reduced. Therefore a liquid asset is one that can be sold at short notice without loss – if an asset is not liquid, sale at short notice will often involve a loss in comparison with the price that could be obtained by waiting. Many assets, such as real capital assets, are very illiquid because there are few markets on which to resell them; other assets, such as bonds, are also illiquid because, although they are easily marketable, their price is highly unstable and therefore a quick sale may involve a loss. Holding imperfectly liquid assets therefore narrows the band of opportunities available at 'Easter'. However, it is *outside* the financial sector that the full implications of liquidity are likely to be found since the assets of the industrial sector are much more illiquid than those held by financial firms. This has important implications for the sort of financial structure with which economic models should be concerned.

For Hicks, the general concept of liquidity is concerned with the balance sheet of the decision maker – its liabilities and assets. For financial firms both their liabilities and assets are financial but for industrial firms only their liabilities are financial – their assets are *real*, and since there are few markets on which such assets can be sold, the concept of liquidity for industrial firms is much more problematic. However, it is at the boundary between the financial sector and the industrial sector that liquidity considerations are vital. Thus if the industrial sector can expand its holdings of real assets (i.e. the capital stock) without seriously impairing its liquidity, then an expansion is more likely to take place. Liquidity in this sense is a vital ingredient of economic growth (Hicks, 1979a, Chap. VII).

*The impulse theory of growth and the traverse*

Hicks's theory of growth differs fundamentally from other contributions in this area. In the first place he notes, 'The theory as I understand it is in essentials a mathematical theory; but I have been anxious that in my statement of it I should keep myself writing *economics*' (*Capital and Growth*, 1965). He is also very critical of steady-state, equilibrium growth theory because 'it has encouraged economists to waste their time upon constructions that are often of great intellectual complexity but which are so much out of time, and out of history, as to be practically futile' (1976). However, he was not fully aware of this sterility when he wrote *Capital and Growth* and therefore he tried to develop an equilibrium growth model that would be capable of describing real-world changes. He now admits that the model was basically a failure because it could not deal with unexpected changes and it did not make adequate allowance for flexibility – it was too dependent on the technical characteristics of the capital stock.

However, in *Capital and Growth* Hicks did make a start on breaking out of the equilibrium straitjacket imposed by steady-state theories and he now sees the book's most important contribution as its introduction of the concept of the *Traverse* – the movement from one growth path to another when the steady state is disturbed by an innovation. This concept was further developed in *Capital and Time* (1973) where he showed that the prospects for a smooth convergence from one equilibrium growth path to another were exceedingly slim. Therefore the analysis of the short run, disequilibrium effects of the innovative process is vitally important – Hicks calls this the 'Early Phase'.

Half of the book '*Capital and Time*', is devoted to the Traverse and a neo-Austrian growth theory is adopted in an attempt to analyse the growth process *sequentially*. Here Hicks was attempting to say something about the impact of change upon an economy which is not initially in a steady state. However, one reviewer at least was not very impressed with Hicks's neo-Austrian theory. 'Professor Hicks is an illustrious addition to the ranks of those who have not got very far with non-steady-state capital theory . . . [even though] Hicks tries skilfully to plug [the gaps in his analysis] with the concept of "minor switches", alternative possible endings to a process already in midstream. That helps but not very much' (Solow, 1974).

Perhaps in response to criticisms of this sort Hicks has delved deeper into these disequilibrium growth situations and restated the process in terms of his concept of the *Impulse* (1977, Chaps. 1, 2 and 9). The main distinction that is here introduced is the old one between autonomous and induced invention (first introduced in 1932). However, he now sheds some new light on this distinction by illustrating it in a *dynamic* context.

The Impulse traces out a sequential process initiated by an *autonomous* invention and carried forward by *induced* inventions which are made possible by price changes (these price changes in turn are caused by the scarcities which are thrown up by the original invention). The process is one in which a major technical innovation widens the range of technical possibilities, raises profitability in many areas and induces further expansion. The scarcities encountered in the process of this expansion will then induce further changes in technical methods.

As Hicks puts it: 'this sequence may be rather fundamental. The mainspring of economic progress it suggests is invention; invention that works through the rate of profit. Each invention gives an Impulse . . . but the Impulse of any single invention is not inexhaustible. The exhaustion is marked by falling profit (and scarcities but) . . . substitution on the spectrum of techniques is just one way of overcoming the scarcities that arise out of the Impulse' (Hicks, 1977, pp. 15–16). He therefore calls for a study of past Impulses to help throw light on the growth process (with a major new technical innovation, the micro chip, already at hand, the importance of this aspect of Hicks's recent work should be readily apparent).

*Causality*

Hicks's latest work *Causality in Economics* (1979a) seems to have developed from his analysis of stock-flow relations in sequential processes (as illustrated in our previous discussion of the multiplier, liquidity and growth). As its title implies, the book is concerned with causal relationships and Hicks identifies three distinct types – static, contemporaneous and sequential. The first refers to long-run classical theories, e.g. to what extent are good transport facilities the cause of the higher relative wealth of certain areas? The second refers to Marshallian and Keynesian period analysis – relationships based upon facts gleaned from the past which are used to predict the future, e.g. the demand for $X$ is taken to be a function of price, incomes, etc. but where the former is taken to be the dependent variable (effect) and the latter the independent variable (cause). The third refers to the more popular sort of causality in which effect follows cause – the former is dated later than the latter. It is concerned with the time lags that inevitably surround decisions, e.g. to what extent did a prior rise in costs cause a rise in prices?

In this (very brief) summary we have used mostly economic examples to indicate the main ideas involved. Hicks, however, gives illuminating examples from many branches of the social sciences, history, and the natural sciences – it is a most interesting book. Its main concern (as it appears to this reader) is to distinguish between contemporaneous and sequential causality and to indicate the conditions under which one or other is a legitimate exercise. Again the main points can be brought out in relation to Keynes's model of the *General Theory*.

As pointed out above that model was a stock-flow model. The consumption function relates to flows, the Marginal Efficiency of Capital schedule relates to both stocks and flows and liquidity preference schedule relates to a stock. Hicks points out that it is exceedingly difficult to trace out causal relationships in a situation in which stock and flow relationships have to be fitted together. This is especially the case where contemporaneous causality is being attempted. The problem is that most of the model is stated in terms of flow equilibrium (i.e. $I = S$) but the stock relations cannot be reduced to the equilibrium method without making fairly drastic assumptions about expectations. He therefore insists that the causal relations must be deduced sequentially.

The important thing to note about sequential causality is that between cause and effect there is an intermediate stage in which economic decisions are made. The analysis of this intermediate stage is vitally important to understanding the process of change in economics. The time lag involved can be split into (at least) two parts – the *prior* lag between cause and decision and the *posterior* lag between decision and effect. The cause is the *signal* to react but the reaction is not normally compelled – the decision can be delayed and therefore so will be the effect. Only in special cases will cause and effect be immediate, e.g. when wages fall and borrowing power and savings and zero expenditure *must* be reduced. The time lag between cause and effect therefore will often depend on the availability of reserves (liquid assets, stocks of goods etc.). Again, it is the integration of stocks and flows that is crucial to the analysis. Indeed, liquidity in its most general sense is here seen as the major ingredient in sequential causality because liquidity is synonymous with freedom – freedom to *postpone* undesired action or to respond *immediately* to encouraging signals.

Finally, it is worth pointing out one common theme. The proper integration of stock-flow analysis within a historical setting, which Hicks feels is so important for resolving issues of causality also plays an important part in his analysis of the *multiplier* process, the *liquidity* spectrum and the *impulse*. Taken together they are indicative of the 'general theory' towards which the Elder Hicks is progressing. It is a theory that aims to offer solutions to real-world problems by tracing through causal sequences using properly specified economic relations. Much of his insights into these processes he admits he has obtained from the work of Keynes. However, 'in all this I have been in a wide sense, but only in a wide sense, Keynesian; not in the sense of any literal adherence to his work, but in the sense of trying to do what I think he would have tried to do, if confronted with different real problems from those with which he was confronted' (1979b).

CONCLUSION

Since 1963 Hicks has been concerned to convey to economists the process by which he came to make his greatest contributions to the subject. En route he is not averse to castigating some of his earlier efforts – quite a contrast to some eminent scholars who attempt to justify their contributions in the face of criticism almost to the point of religious fervour. To paraphrase Leijonhufvud (1979) Hicks seems intent on involving us in a personal commentary on his self-education in economics. It gives one a privileged sense of listening in on Hicks making up his mind on the crucial issues of value, capital, growth and money: the issues that have interested him through a long career. It is a unique approach and it has made the writing of this essay considerably easier.

It is to be regretted that his later works are not being given the attention they deserve. However, I think it is true to say that much of his earlier work was thirty or forty years too soon for most economists to fully appreciate its significance. I venture the guess that most of the work of the Elder Hicks will similarly turn out to be pregnant with relevant insights in about ten years time (assuming the learning curve of the profession is getting steeper!)

NOTES

1.  In correspondence with the author, Professor Hicks has been most helpful.
    Recently he distinguished between the elasticity of substitution in his *Theory
    of Wages* and the similar concept introduced by Joan Robinson in her
    *Economics of Imperfect Competition* (1933). Hicks writes: 'My elasticity of
    substitution was a measure of the cross-effect of the supply of one factor on
    the marginal productivity of the other (two factors and constant returns to
    scale). It is to be distinguished from Joan's elasticity of substitution (appearing
    six months later). In subsequent discussion it was shown that, in the two-
    factor constant returns to scale case, the two definitions are equivalent. The
    expression of Joan's definition as a property of an isoquant is due to Lerner
    (1934, p. 68)'. In Hicks (1970) he points out that Joan Robinson's version is
    best defined on the assumption that the *price* of the other factor is fixed while
    his own version is best defined on the assumption that the *quantity* of the
    other factor is fixed. In the two-factor case one is the reciprocal of the other
    but in the three-factor case the two diverge. This is important because one
    needs at least three factors in order to exhibit the character of
    substitution – complementarity relationships and this leads Hicks to suggest
    that Joan Robinson's should have been called the elasticity of substitution
    while his own could be better referred to as the elasticity of complementarity.
2.  In the two-good case moving along the indifference curve implies $dU = 0$
    where $U$ stands for total utility. Therefore taking the total differential of $U$
    gives:

    $$dU = 0 = (\partial U/\partial x)dX + (\partial U/\partial Y)dy = MU_x dX + MU_y dY$$

    since $\partial U/\partial X$ is the marginal utility of $X$ etc. Thus rearranging terms (and
    ignoring the negative sign) gives $dY/dX$ (slope of indifference curve)
    $= MU_x/MU_y$ ratio of MUs.
3.  The correspondence quoted in note 1 continues: 'It was from Lerner's
    isoquant that I proceeded to see that the same geometrical device could be
    used for an indifference curve. Hayek, incidentally, claims that he was the first
    to see this, and that he pointed it out to me. That may be so, but of course he
    did not see the consequences, which were drawn in Hicks and Allen (1934a).
    Though that latter paper was written up with my name attached to the
    "literary" version and his to the mathematical, what actually happened was
    that I worked out the two-goods case in both forms and that he extended it to
    the three goods (whence complementarity etc.)'.
4.  However, although it may be possible to justify the exclusion of certain minor
    topics in a study such as this a discussion of Hicks's restatement of welfare
    economics and his analysis of the trade cycle was reluctantly excluded from
    the final draft only because of space constraints. Briefly (1939b and 1941) he
    redefined Pareto's welfare optima in terms of compensation criteria and
    rigorously restated Marshall's concept of consumers' surplus so as to make it
    operational for purposes of economic policy. He was then able to demonstrate
    the social-welfare loss associated with monopoly. Recently Hicks has
    provided us with a synthesis of his views in this area (1974b and 1975). In his
    trade-cycle book (1950) Hicks constrained a basically explosive

multiplier–accelerator type model to oscillate between 'ceilings' and 'floors' thereby producing one of the first non-linear models of the trade cycle. Recently he has built on this work in an attempt to develop dynamic growth models; these are discussed elsewhere in this text.

5. Referring in the preface of the first edition of *Value and Capital* (1939) to Ursula's work on public finance, Hicks writes 'there is no part (of this book) which has not profited from the constant reminder which I have had from her work that the place of economic theory is to be the servant of applied economics'.

## REFERENCES

Baumol, W. J., 1952 'The Transactions Demand for Cash: An Inventory Theoretic Approach', *Quarterly Journal of Economics*.
Blaug, M., 1978 *Economic Theory in Retrospect* (Cambridge University Press).
Coddington, A., 1979 'Hicks's Contribution to Keynesian Economics', *Journal of Economic Literature*.
Friedman, M., 1956 'The Quantity Theory of Money: A Restatement' in *Studies in the Quantity Theory* (University of Chicago Press).
Hahn, F. H., 1975 'Money and General Equilibrium', *Indian Economic Journal*.
Harris, L., 1969 'Professor Hicks and the Foundations of Monetary Economics', *Economica*.
Hicks, J. R., 1928 'Wage Fixing in the Building Industry', *Economica*.
—— 1932 *Theory of Wages* (Macmillan).
—— 1934a 'A Reconsideration of the Theory of Value' (with R. G. D. Allen), *Economica*.
—— 1934b 'Leon Walras', *Econometrica*.
—— 1935 'A Suggestion for Simplifying the Theory of Money' (reprinted in *Critical Essays*, 1967), *Economica*.
—— 1936 'Mr Keynes's Theory of Employment', *Economic Journal*.
—— 1937 'Mr Keynes and the "Classics"' (reprinted in *Critical Essays*, 1967), *Econometrica*.
—— 1939a *Value and Capital* (Clarendon Press).
——1939b 'Foundations of Welfare Economics', *Economic Journal*.
——1941 'Rehabilitation of Consumer's Surplus', *Review of Economic Studies*.
—— 1942 *The Social Framework: An Introduction to Economics* (Clarendon Press).
—— 1946 *Value and Capital* 2nd edn. (Clarendon Press).
—— 1950 *A Contribution to the Theory of the Trade Cycle* (Clarendon Press).
—— 1956a *A Revision of Demand Theory* (Clarendon Press).
—— 1956b 'Methods of Dynamic Analysis' in *25 Essays in Honour of Erik Lindahl* (Stockholm).
—— 1959 *Essays in World Economics* (Oxford University Press).
—— 1960 'A Survey of Linear Theory', *Economic Journal*.
—— 1963 *Theory of Wages* 2nd edn. with reprints and commentary (Macmillan).
—— 1965 *Capital and Growth* (Oxford University Press).

—— 1967 *Critical Essays in Monetary Theory* (Oxford University Press).

—— 1969 *A Theory of Economic History* (Oxford University Press).

—— 1970 'The Elasticity of Substitution Again: Substitutes and Complements', *Oxford Economic Papers*.

—— 1973 *Capital and Time* (Oxford University Press).

—— 1974a *The Crisis in Keynesian Economics* (Basil Blackwell).

—— 1974b 'Preference and Welfare' in *Economic Theory and Planning: Essays in Honour of A. K. Dasgupta* (Oxford University Press).

—— 1975 'The Scope and Status of Welfare Economics', *Oxford Economic Papers*.

—— 1976 'Some Questions of Time in Economics' in *Evolution, Welfare and Time in Economics: Essays in Honour of Nicholas Georgescu-Roegen* (Lexicon Books).

—— 1977 *Economic Perspectives* (Oxford University Press).

—— 1979a *Causality in Economics* (Basil Blackwell).

—— 1979b 'The Formation of an Economist', *Banco Nationale Del Lavoro Quarterly Review*.

—— 1979c On Coddington's Interpretation: a Reply, *Journal of Economic Literature*.

Keynes, J. M., 1936 *The General Theory of Employment, Interest and Money* (Macmillan).

Leijonhufvud, A., 1979 'Review of Hicks's *Economic Perspectives*', *Journal of Economic Literature*.

Lerner, A., 1934 *Review of Economic Studies*.

Morishima, M. 1977 'The concept of Monopoly and the Measurement of Monopoly Power' in *Walras' Economics* (Cambridge University Press).

Robinson, J., 1933 *Economics of Imperfect Competition* (Macmillan).

Samuelson, P., 1947 *Foundations of Economic Analysis* (Harvard University Press).

Solow, R. M., 1974 'Review of Hicks's *Capital and Time*', *Economic Journal*.

Tobin, J., 1958 Liquidity Preference as Behaviour Towards Risk', *Review of Economic Studies*.

Weintraub, E. R., 1979 *Microfoundations* (Cambridge University Press).

Woolfe, J. N., 1968 *Value Capital and Growth: Papers in Honour of Sir John Hicks* (Edinburgh University Press).

# 8 Michal Kalecki: A Comprehensive Challenge to Orthodoxy

Josef Poschl and Gareth Locksley

Michal Kalecki was born in Poland in 1899. He died in 1970 after a distinguished and sometimes controversial career at Oxford, the United Nations (where he encountered McCarthyism), and in Poland (where he clashed with Stalinism).[1] Originally he studied engineering but the sad state of the Polish economy in his youth forced him to leave these studies unfinished. By a series of fortuitous accidents Kalecki joined the economics profession. He brought to it certain technical skills in mathematics and statistics, insights into the nature of firms, and above all a deep concern for his fellow man forged by his experience of the Great Depression. Further, perhaps because he had been a journalist, Kalecki had that rare ability to express new and exciting ideas clearly and succinctly,[2] in contrast to many of the great 'tree destroyers' of our time.

Kalecki's contribution to economics is wide-ranging, covering the dynamics of the advanced capitalist economies – the subject matter of this chapter – planned socialist or underdeveloped economies and war economies.[3] His work is characterised by a strong practical content, as one would expect of the man who was concerned with the UN's *World Economic Reports* and the Polish Planning Commission's Perspective Plan. Further, Kalecki's writings contain a pronounced sociopolitical element, for his main concern was to effect policy changes that would improve the conditions of the masses. In this very real way Kalecki was a political economist who devoted his attention to *real* problems by attempting to construct a complete system of theories integrating the micro and macro elements and applying this to, say, the crucial issue of income distribution as well as income determination.

Kalecki could be considered a *pre*-Keynesian, for in an article (1933) somewhat shorter than the chapter you are reading he outlined the major features of the *General Theory* some years before Keynes. However he is perhaps best considered as the leading inspiration for the *post*-Keynesians. For example, the influential *Cambridge Journal of Economics*, claiming 'strong emphasis on realism of analysis', cites Kalecki together with Marx and Keynes as its intellectual mentors. However Kalecki's work, given its nature and enormous relevance, possesses for us one really surprising feature – and that is the limited recognition which it has gained. Lawrence Klein comments: 'Kalecki was truly a phenomenon, known well to a select few but with a lasting impact on the economics of our age . . . some scholars generate "fan clubs", and Kalecki had his, although it was reserved, discrete, and not apparent to the outside world, including the bulk of professional economists'.[4]

This lack of appreciation cannot be explained solely by Kalecki's natural modesty and his unwillingness to market himself as have some economists. No, an important consideration must be the nature of ruling ideologies and their relation to challenges to them, an issue Kalecki recognised (1943b). The purpose of this essay is to outline the main elements of Kalecki's comprehensive challenge to orthodoxy; to indicate some of the instances where his ideas have been influential and to discuss why his ideas have failed to gain as wide an audience as they deserve.

Many of the widely accepted ideas of today concerning advanced capitalist economies were developed in the 1950s and 1960s when these economies were experiencing an unprecedented period of economic growth. However the experience of the 1970s has again focused attention on the crucial issue of the causes and conditions which generate a trend towards recovery and growth within a framework of cyclical fluctuations. Further, there is a growing dissatisfaction with 'inflationary gap' explanations of inflation based on general excess demand in relation to supply. Re-examination of macroeconomic theories of employment and income has resulted in some cases in a search for a set of microeconomic foundations and thereby to a rediscovery and acceptance of Kalecki's ideas. At the same time the post-Keynesians have been endeavouring to construct a complete, logically consistent complex of theories dealing with employment, prices, income distribution, accumulation and growth.[5] In its entirety Kalecki's work embraces these issues and any attempt to evaluate his contribution to contemporary economics must adopt this same approach. This is precisely what has *not* been done in the past.

Post-Keynesians have rejected the Hicksian *IS/LM* interpretation of Keynes's work. They consider that *IS/LM* overemphasizes some aspects whilst rudely neglecting others, thus giving a false impression of the essence of Keynes's ideas. They feel that it is impossible to repair this 'deformation' within mainstream economic thinking. Instead they have chosen to draw on Kalecki's concepts, for his work is influenced by the Marxian tradition rather than the Marshallian approach which contaminates Keynes's work.[6]

Post-Keynesians have consciously attempted to formulate a complete theoretical complex influenced by the heated discussions following the publication of Kuhn's *Structure of Scientific Revolutions* (Kuhn, 1962). The problem was that important criticisms of some aspects of orthodox economics (for example studies of monopolistic competition, or the work of Veblen and even that of Keynes) could not break its hold over the profession and policy making. Typically the criticisms would be translated into 'common terms', i.e. they were filtered and their emphases changed; then they were treated as an example of a special case, a slight aberration from the powerful general line. Certainly they were not discussed as an alternative to the orthodoxy; rather they were destined for incorporation in a modified form or to be forgotten. Disequilibrium economics can be considered to have passed through this process.

In this context post-Keynesians were well aware of the need to develop a total theoretical system, for all new contributions to economics are evaluated by comparison to the ruling theory. Such a process ensures the continuation of orthodoxy as all isolated criticisms will be translated or transformed and thereby made to appear a mere footnote. What then are the central elements of Kalecki's analysis of developed capitalism?

FIRMS AND MARK-UPS

Kalecki's crucial consideration is the microeconomic foundations of macroeconomic phenomena. Therefore he is concerned with the nature of a firm's production function and its pricing behaviour. So whereas the simplified '45° Keynesianism' can be criticised[7] for ignoring the level of prices and wages and their impact on aggregate demand, Kalecki is exempt from such attacks.

Kalecki emphasized that the general conditions prevailing in the production of raw materials were very different from those in manufacturing (1954). The conditions in the raw materials sector explain why their prices are demand-determined. For example, supply cannot respond to changes in demand in the short run. Further, given the number of competitors, individual producers occupy a relatively weak position and output is the only choice variable open to them for achieving some acceptable level of sales revenue in the long run. Kalecki views prices in the manufacturing sector as being determined by the enterprises themselves (1971b).

In Kalecki's theory of mark-up pricing, demand enters in an indirect manner through demand-determined prices for raw materials or wages. Because of the nature of inputs (they are reproducible), in the typical enterprise variations in output can be achieved at constant marginal cost up to full capacity. Thus average variable costs are also constant and these form the base for a mark-up factor in price determination. Enterprises, however, face constraints when choosing their mark-up. It must be enough to cover overheads and to generate some minimum profit (even where capital utilisation is low), whilst it should not be so high as to attract the attention of powerful competitors. Kalecki's firms inhabit an interdependent oligopoly where reactions can shift the relative profitabilities within the industry.

Kalecki's initial notion of mark-up (1938) drew on Abba Lerner's concept of 'degree of monopoly' (Lerner, 1934), which was the reciprocal of the price-elasticity of demand. However Kalecki found Lerner's formulation unsatisfactory as it relied on the traditional profit-maximising behaviour of a pure monopoly which was far from the reality of the manufacturing sector. Kalecki argued that firms do not follow some precise strategy aimed at profit maximisation. Instead, in oligopolistic structures, firms adopt some rule of thumb that takes into account the reaction of competitors. Within this framework he sees a hierarchy of profitability in an industry which only changes when there is some shift in relative power brought about by, say, technical progress. In this context, the size of the mark-up on average variable costs is an indicator of the relative power of a firm in a particular industry. Though mark-up is indicative of a firm's power it is not an explanation of this power. To provide an *explanation* Kalecki adopts a minimum 'mechanical' approach, simply listing the most important factors. These include: the degree of concentration; the level of effective collusion (including price leadership); the practicability of competition in the form of advertising instead of price wars; shifts in overhead costs in relation to variable costs; and the power of the trade unions. This list is strikingly relevant yet notably absent from the orthodoxy.

Though Kalecki concedes that the relation of overhead to variable costs has some influence on the size of the mark-up (during a boom as the ratio declines so will the mark-up, whilst in a slump the rising proportion of overheads in total costs places an upward pressure on the mark-up) his concept is not just a full-cost theory, for he includes competitors in the model (1954).

DETERMINANTS OF NATIONAL INCOME AND ITS DISTRIBUTION

Kalecki first formulated his macroeconomic framework (1933, 1935) to examine the debate between Rosa Luxemburg and Tugan-Baronovski (Kalecki 1972b) over the conditions necessary (the availability of lands to be conquered or sustained entrepreneurial demand) for permanent capitalist growth. He refined this framework to study the level, movement and distribution of national income.

If we assume constant input coefficients and market shares (between manufacturing sectors and firms) we can examine labour's share in national income. Clearly in the manufacturing sector labour's share is determined by the various mark-up levels and the relation between the price of raw materials and wages (i.e. the price of inputs). High levels of mark-up represent a large difference between price and marginal costs and thus a relatively low share for wages in national income. With a given mark-up labour's share will be low when raw materials costs are high in relation to labour costs.

This is Kalecki's starting point when analysing the multiplier. Here, income distribution is made an explicit determinant of the level of aggregate income. His analysis contains further unusual elements. He assumes different marginal propensities to save for different groups and develops the concept of the multiplier within Marx's reproduction schema (1954, 1968a). Here there are two classes of actors, workers and capitalists, operating in the context of the Gross National Income ≡ Gross National Expenditure/Output identity. This can be represented as in Table 8.1. In Department III (wage goods) part of the output is consumed by the workers who produce it. The remainder is sold to the workers in the other Departments. This sale equals the wage bill in Departments I and II and the profits in Department III. The value of production in Departments I and II is the sum of their wages and profits. We have seen that the wages in Departments I and II equal profits in Department III. Thus total profits equal the value of production in Departments I and II (see Appendix).

TABLE 8.1

| Gross profit $(P)$ | Gross investment $(I)$ | Department I |
|---|---|---|
| | + Capitalist consumption $(C_c)$ | Department II |
| + Wages and salaries $(W)$ | + Workers' consumption $(C_w)$ | Department III |
| = Gross national income $(Y)$ | ≡ Gross national expenditure $(Y)$ | |

Kalecki uses this scheme extensively to examine the consequences of different propensities to save, of wage rises and of different levels of autonomous expenditure (by private investors, the government or from abroad).

A cornerstone of Kalecki's reasoning is his demonstration that the aggregate income of entrepreneurs is proportional (and with the assumption that workers do not save, exactly equal) to their aggregate demand for investment and consumption goods in each period (e.g. 1971a). If we assume that workers spend all they earn then

$$P \equiv I + C_c \text{ (from Table 8.1)}$$

After an injection of investment (workers cannot, like capitalists, autonomously change their expenditure) national income expands to the point where profits (taken out in accordance with the mark-up) are equal to the sum of capitalists' consumption and investment. The relation between the expansion and the injection is of course the multiplier (see Appendix).

So capitalists' income expands to meet the level of production of capitalists' goods, assuming that there is no government or foreign trade: budget deficits and export surpluses create additional accumulation in the business world equal to their level.

Within this framework it can be seen that employees' aggregate income is a by-product of the individual decisions made by entrepreneurs. With the factors determining the distribution of income given, national income will be positively related to the level of entrepreneurial expenditure on investment and consumption and other elements of autonomous expenditure. Of course with autonomous expenditure given, labour's aggregate income will be positively related to its share in national income.

Concomitantly, income distribution determines the distribution of profits between economic sectors. High unit labour costs in the economy as a whole will effect high output in the firms producing wage goods and thereby high profits in this sector. So, far from squeezing profits, high labour costs merely redistribute profits. Clearly a general rise in wages would have a similar outcome. Below full capacity higher wages can be paid for by increased aggregate production (Kalecki, 1939, 1954, 1971a). Thus we can see that orthodox microeconomic rationality does not hold for macroeconomic relationships.

But what is the effect of a rise in real wages on investment decisions? In answering this question, Kalecki draws a distinction between short- and long-term rates of interest. He observes that there is a positive functional relationship between the velocity of circulation of money and the short term interest rate. They tend to vary in sympathy with the business cycle because the value of transactions fluctuates more than the supply of money from banks. The long-term interest rate is determined by the average of expected short-term rates over the time horizon, adjusted by past experience and the risk of depreciation of long-term assets. This average does not reflect cyclical fluctuations and if, for some reason, it falls, the impact of this is dampened by a counteracting and simultaneous decrease in the risk of depreciation (Kalecki, 1954).

Only the long-term rate is relevant for investment decisions. But due to its relative stability, it can be ignored as one of the major determinants of the volume of aggregate investment. The most decisive factors that influence investment expenditure over the next time period are: recent tendencies in profit levels; the existing stock of physical capital; the potential for financing investment internally; and technical progress which once incorporated improves a firm's relative position in an industry (Kalecki, 1968b). With the exception of technical progress, these factors tend to accentuate instability. Consequently Kalecki's theory of the business cycle, in which investment decisions are the dominant element, emphasizes *dynamics* rather than comparative statics.

Kalecki rejects the orthodox assumption of decreasing marginal productivity of labour (with less than full capacity utilization), for he believes it provides a misleading presentation of the relation between real wages and aggregate employment (1939, 1971a). We have seen that though an increase in real wages effects a reduction in profits in the investment and entrepreneurial goods sectors, this is compensated by additional profits in the wage goods sector. As aggregate profits are not squeezed in the short run (following a rise in real wages) there are no detrimental effects on future aggregate investment and entrepreneurial consumption. With a given level of entrepreneurial expenditures and capacity utilization, there is a positive relationship between real wage and output and employment. An increase in real wages raises output because labour has a high propensity to consume. With a relatively inelastic supply of labour (the majority working an institutionally given number of hours per week) the situation could be described by Figure 8.1.

In this closed economy with no government, the $L_D$ function represents aggregate demand for labour at various levels of real

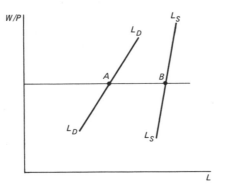

FIGURE 8.1

wages, assuming a constant level of investment expenditure and given propensities to save. The function has a positive slope because higher real wages imply higher employment (and profits) in the wage-goods sector with unchanged production in the other sectors. The prevailing level of real wages is arrived at as a result of the operation of the same factors determining the level of mark-up and the relation between wages and material costs as well as certain structural factors. The level of unemployment at this wage rate is represented by the distance $AB$ and an increase in the volume of investment would shift the $L_D$ function to the right and reduce unemployment. Note that reductions in real wages *do not* deplete the ranks of the unemployed and that union-induced wage rises are not the cause of unemployment; rather it is the weakening of their bargaining power (for example in slumps) that is a portent of unemployment (1971a).

Kalecki applies an analogous reasoning to the question of taxation (1937) to illustrate the contention that taxation will not reduce investment levels, an issue of particular relevance when government spending is being blamed for so many ills. Consider an increase in taxes to finance additional government expenditure with the level of budget deficit unchanged. If the taxes fall on employees' disposable incomes the resultant shift from private to public demand will leave the level of aggregate production unchanged. But if profits provide the taxes and they cannot be compensated by a rise in the mark-up, aggregate production could actually increase! Because investments are based on past decisions there will be no current reduction in investment and production. If there is no reduction now there will be none in the future. Further, if the government expenditure employs idle labour there will be an increase in demand for wage goods and an increase in their provision.

In an analysis of US statistics (1972a), Kalecki compared the structure of national income in 1937 with that of 1955. He concluded that the share of consumption in national income had decreased sharply, partly due to increased taxation of private consumption and partly because of the enhanced power of Big Business whose mark-up was relatively high. That national income doubled during the period whilst the share of consumption declined relatively was only possible because government had increased its relative share, financed by corporate taxes. With a falling share of consumption in national income, private investment on its own could not have produced such a favourable development of national income. Thus Kalecki is highlighting the *supportive* role of government in the process of capital accumulation.

Thus we find in Kalecki an integration of the micro and macro aspects of the economy. Building from the behaviour of oligopolists he formulates a relevant pricing policy where mark-up is a crucial factor. This he applies to the interdependent issues of the distribution and level of national income where autonomous expenditure by entrepreneurs is the crucial force behind the cyclical movements of an advanced capitalist economy. Using Marx's reproduction schema he applies his insights to the most pressing of our problems and arrives at policy formulations quite at variance with the orthodoxy. His analysis is simple, complete, yet rich in detail. Concerning the very pertinent question of growth, Kalecki regarded the neo-classical theories as an inadequate and unacceptable portrait of the development of a capitalist industrialised economy. Paradoxically he viewed such theories as suitable only as abstract reflections on the growth path of a planned economy! For Kalecki, whether growth emerges from short-run cyclical movements is dependent on the existence of 'development factors'. Most important here is the intensity of technical progress because it lowers production costs. Without this there would be insufficient investment opportunities for long-run economic growth for capitalism as a whole. In one of his last papers (1968b) Kalecki outlined a theory of capitalist growth in terms of moving equilibrium and incorporated both short-term fluctuations and technical progress whilst denying the validity of purely mechanistic theories.

Having summarised Kalecki's comprehensive challenge to orthodoxy, what then has been his impact on the bulk of economists? How have his insights been developed?

POST-KALECKI

Josef Steindl used Kalecki's approach in an analysis of certain (neglected) long run developments in advanced capitalist economies. In his book *Maturity and Stagnation in American Capitalism* (Steindl, 1952) and a later article (1979) Steindl explored the viability of capitalism's powers of recovery. His central question is: can a mature capitalist economy return to its growth path after it has experienced a severe shock, or will it stagnate?

Steindl follows Kalecki's methodology and categorisation of industries by structure (oligopolistic and competitive). These differences in structure result in different patterns of competitive behaviour and have different consequences for profit margins, internal accumulation and capacity utilisation. If a (primary) depression occurs in the volume of investment and economic activity there will be different reactions in the two sectors. The logic of oligopolistic competition will cause a secondary squeeze on investments which tends to prolong economic stagnation. For in response to the shock, the decrease in the margin of net profits over total costs will be smaller and the degree of capacity utilisation lower than in the competitive sector. Investment is here determined by recent internal accumulation, the degree of capacity utilisation and indebtedness, and the rate of profit, all of which are sensitive to the shock. So in order to maintain the 'gearing ratio' between capital and equity, investment expenditures are cut and the economy stagnates. Obviously the general trend towards increasingly oligopolistic structures throughout advanced capitalist economies is reducing their potential to recover from shocks.

Clearly this represents a particularly relevant piece of analysis given that stagnation characterised much of the 1970s and is likely to occupy a central position in the 1980s. Yet virtually no attention has been paid to Steindl's work! This can be partially explained by the inopportuneness of the analysis: it appeared in a period when stagnation was not in evidence (Steindl explains the absence of stagnation by reference to Kalecki's article on the economic situation in the US (1972b) in the preface to the second edition).[8] However at the same time there was considerable interest in industrial structures which form the basis of Steindl's analysis. The most plausible explanation of the disregard for this work is that it could not be incorporated into the prevailing theoretical structure.

Robinson and Eatwell adopt and develop Kalecki's macro-economic framework in their *Introduction to Modern Economics* (1973). They use a two-sector, two-good, two-class model which pays particular attention to the monetary aspects of the production and exchange of goods by dealing with money supply and the rate of interest. We can use this to examine the debate about money supply. The model assumes that the production of investment goods is related to demand originating in the consumption goods sector. Entrepreneurs issue bills against themselves to cover their needs for consumption goods (for themselves and their workers) occuring between the placement and delivery of orders. When orders are completed, bills equal in value to the orders are cancelled. So consumption goods serve as money, being used for the payment of wages and dividends. Thus the stock of money always adjusts to the volume of aggregate production.

What would happen if the markets for goods and money are in equilibrium while the supply of labour exceeds demand? Is there an adjustment process that will eradicate unemployment? The model assumes that the number of employees and the quantity of capital employed are determined by the level of aggregate demand and that the average product of labour and capital employed are constant. It is further assumed that the real wage equals the marginal (and average) product of labour, that prices are derived via a mark-up and that investment is a function of aggregate profits.

Now a decrease in the real wage will increase the profit per worker but will adversely affect the demand for consumption goods. So employment will fall and aggregate profits remain constant. Consequently there is no incentive to increase investment and move towards full employment. A similar outcome was demonstrated earlier in this chapter.

These results are totally at variance with those derived from the *IS/LM* model, which relies on an exogenously fixed supply of money, on investment being determined by the rate of interest, and on the concept of decreasing marginal product of labour.

We have seen that Kalecki restricted the use of supply and demand analysis of price formation to primary production. In the manufacturing sector he applied a mark-up interpretation of price formation with entirely different laws of motion. This has attracted considerable criticism because of the difficulty of precisely specifying the size of the mark-up and its consequences for inflation.[9] Robinson and Eatwell (1973) hold that there is a minimum level of mark-up necessary to cover overhead costs and 'normal' profits, taking into account expected capacity utilisation. This being the case, the minimum will vary across industries and will be positively related to capital–output ratios. Industries with high capital–output ratios typically possess barriers to entry which will facilitate 'extra' profits. Such listings of the factors determining the level of mark-up may appear unsatisfactory, but they can nevertheless be superior to more 'rigorous' economic analysis. Their strength is that they assign social and political factors a role in the actual determination of economic reality; for example, trade-union power is not exclusively economic.

However, Alfred Eichner has attempted a rigorous analysis of the size of the mark-up in *The Megacorp and Oligopoly: Micro Foundations of Macro Dynamics* (1976). His microeconomic foundations are explicitly derived from Kalecki. He posits, drawing on empirical evidence, that the size of the mark-up is conditioned by a firm's desire for internally generated funds to finance its investments. In this sense there is an *internal* demand for and supply of internal funds. Price adjustments – i.e. adjustments of mark-ups over constant marginal costs – can alter intertemporal cash flow by changing the return on investments thereby financed and because sales may decline following price rises. The demand for additional funds is related to the Marginal Efficiency of Investment (including returns to advertising and R & D) which is the return, measured in future cash flow, expected from incremental current investment. The supply of internal funds, i.e. the size of the mark-up, is limited by reactions to price rises. Clearly there is the possibility of a substitution effect and an entry factor besides meaningful government intervention. These two functions, supply and demand for additional funds, then interact to determine the size of the mark-up.

Eichner extends the concept of the mark-up, like Kalecki, to the question of income distribution, within the context of politically influenced wage determination. He maintains that 'the "cost-plus" pricing model, together with an institutionally or politically determined wage rate, provides the micro foundations for post-Keynesian macro-dynamic theory' (Eichner, 1973). He is particularly illuminating over the aggregate short-run adjustment process between savings and investment. Here, given that household savings play a minimum role in business accumulation, it is *business* savings and investment that diverge because actual sales differ from expected sales, especially when the economy is pushed off its secular growth path. Thus we have a different adjustment process from the usual Keynesian formulation. 'Any surplus [deficit] of savings relative to investment within the [oligopolistic] sector will, of course, have to be offset by a deficit (surplus) in some other sector, for in aggregate the Keynesian condition that $S = I$ still holds' (Eichner 1973). Thus an increase in investment does not initiate a pronounced multiplier process, for adjustment is achieved by a change in income distribution – a phenomenon noted by Kalecki in relation to foreign trade. This reasoning also lays the foundation for a wage–price spiral. To achieve planned cash flow prices will be raised and once we include a trade union strategy of maintaining some historic relationship between wages and profits, the possibility of a spiral becomes self-evident. Eichner (1976) extends the analysis to illustrate the ineffectiveness of governmental attempts to steer the economy thus complementing Steindl.

These are glaringly crucial issues. Interestingly Eichner comments in his preface, 'The appearance of this work has also been retarded by the hostility of other economists to the ideas which it contains' (1976).


IDEAS FOR AN EPILOGUE

Following the incorporation of the 'Keynesian Revolution' into the orthodoxy and teaching of economics, many aspects of Kalecki's work, like the multiplier, will seem very familiar, while others will appear very unusual. Taken in their entirety, Kalecki's ideas constitute a complex system whose solutions are very different from those of orthodox theory. Palpably, advanced capitalist economies are characterised by oligopolistic structures and a substantial body of evidence attests to the pervasiveness of mark-up pricing. Kalecki uses these realities to explain both the distribution of income between classes and the level of aggregate production. He also extends from these microfoundations to explanations of the dynamic movements in an economy. He proposes an alternative theory of growth that can also explain the persistent increase in the general level of prices. Within the Kaleckian framework the function of competition policy and its multifarious agencies is not just to protect the weak consumer who lacks countervailing power. Rather its concern is with the distribution of income both between the oligopolistic and competitive sectors of the economy and between the economic classes. In that competition policy affects income distribution it influences the growth of an economy. Why has competition policy in virtually all economies failed? Perhaps this can be answered by returning to one of our original tasks.

Why have Kalecki's ideas not reached a wider audience? True, there have always been pockets of interest, but this is far from a general consideration of a thoroughgoing alternative to the ineffectiveness of current policies.

Perhaps Kalecki himself provides the answer in his important article 'Political Aspects of Full Employment' (1943b). Here it is argued that even if we know how to maintain full employment it will not be a permanent state of affairs. He stresses the considerable opposition of business interests to full employment. Capital is conceived of as a coercive social force, rather than mere machines, interested in reproducing the capitalist system, the status quo. He foresaw a 'political business cycle'[10] developing as business interests alternatively gave and withdrew their support for full employment policies. Their interests prevail because they possess certain control mechanisms. Perhaps the most valuable is their domination of economic thinking – often termed 'soundness'. So the ideas that prevail are those of the ruling class.

Kalecki's ideas are a challenge to 'soundness', in both capitalist and socialist countries, and this may explain their limited exposure. It is the hope of the authors that this essay will stimulate its readers to a greater study of Kalecki and that they will use his work to challenge orthodox economic ideas.

APPENDIX: A SIMPLIFIED REPRESENTATION OF KALECKI'S MODEL

1. *Pricing*

Assume a one-sector economy with vertically integrated firms. Prices are arrived at by adding some mark-up ($m$) to prime unit costs, in this case wages ($w$). (Kalecki includes an additional factor that takes into account the prices of other firms in his multisector model.)

$$p = w + wm$$

Thus e.g. if $m = 0.25$ then $p = 1.25\,w$

## 2. *Income Distribution*

Mark-up determines the relative share of profits, $\Pi$, in aggregate income.

$$\Pi = m/(m+1) \tag{i}$$

Thus with $\qquad m = 0.25, \; \Pi = 0.25/(0.25 + 1) = 0.2$

Capitalists spend a proportion of profits ($q$) on consumption goods, i.e. $q$ is their (marginal and average) propensity to consume. Kalecki assumes that workers spend all they earn, whilst for capitalists $0 < q < 1$.

## 3. *National Income*

From Table 8.1 we have seen that

$$P = I + C_c \tag{ii}$$

Here $P$ = total profits = $\Pi Y$ and $C_c$ (capitalists' consumption) = $qP$ or $C_c = q\Pi Y$. Substituting in equation (ii) gives us

$$\Pi Y = I + q\Pi Y$$

Thus the equilibrium level of income is

$$Y_e = 1/(\Pi(1-q))I$$

The multiplier ($k$) is

$$k = 1/(\Pi(1-q)) \tag{iii}$$

That is, $k$ is determined by the relative share of profits in national income ($\Pi$) and capitalists' propensity to consume ($q$). Substituting equation (i) into (iii) we can see that the multiplier is also partly determined by the mark-up

$$k = (m+1)/(m(1-q))$$

Thus if $m = 0.25$ and $q = 0.50$

then $\qquad k = (0.25 + 1)/(0.25(1 - 0.50)) = 1.25/0.125 = 10$

For a given $m$, $k$ is thus positively related to $q$; for a given $q$, $k$ is inversely related to the mark-up, $m$. The level of national income is also related to the 'degree of monopoly' (through the mark-up) and thus we have the microfoundations for a macrodynamic theory.

## 4. *The System in Three Departments*

Department I makes investment goods
Department II makes capitalist consumption goods
Department III makes consumer (wage) goods

The value of output, $V$, in any Department equals the sum of profit ($P$) and wages ($W$)

$$V_i = P_i + W_i$$

The output of Department III is partly consumed by the workers who produce it, and the surplus is bought by the workers employed in the other departments.
   Thus

$$P_3 = W_1 + W_2 \tag{i}$$

The value of production in Departments I and II is

$$V_1 + V_2 = P_1 + P_2 + W_1 + W_2 \tag{ii}$$

Substituting (i) into (ii) we obtain

$$V_1 + V_2 = P_1 + P_2 + P_3$$

Thus total profits equal the value of production in Departments I and II, that is the value of investment goods and capitalist consumption goods.

NOTES

1. For a collection of essays dealing with Kalecki's work and life see the special issue of the *Oxford Bulletin of Economics* (Lipinski, 1977).

2. His most important essays are collected in several short volumes, 1939, 1943a, 1947, 1966, 1969, 1971b, 1972a, 1972b.
3. For a complete list of Kalecki's writings and an in-depth analysis of his work, see Feiwel (1975).
4. Lawrence Klein's foreword to Feiwel (1975).
5. See for example Robinson and Eatwell (1973) and Kregel (1972) for textbooks which attempt this task.
6. See Robinson (1964).
7. See, for example, Hotson, Habibagahi and Lermer (1976).
8. See Ostleitner (1980) for a discussion, within Kalecki and Steindl's framework, of economic policy at low growth rates.
9. See Kaldor (1976), Cowling and Waterson (1976), Pulling (1978) and Sherman (1977) for empirical studies of mark-up and its influence on inflation.
10. See Feiwel (1974) and Locksley (1980) for discussion of this concept.

REFERENCES

Cowling, K., and Waterson, M., 1976 'Price-Cost Margins and Market Structure' *Economica*.
Eichner, A. S., 1973 'A Theory of the Determination of Mark-up under Oligopoly', *Economic Journal*, Dec.
—— 1976 *The Megacorp and Oligopoly: Microfoundations of Macrodynamics* (Cambridge University Press).
Feiwel, G. R., 1974 'Reflections on Kalecki's Theory of Political Business Cycle', *Kyklos*.
—— 1975 *The Intellectual Capital of Michal Kalecki* (University of Tennessee Press).
Hotson, J. H., Habibagahi, H. and Lermer, G., 1976 *Stagflation and the Bastard Keynesians* (University of Waterloo Press).
Kaldor, N., 1976 'Inflation and Recession in the World Economy', *Economic Journal*, Dec.
Kalecki, M., 1933 *Essays on Business Cycle Theory*, (IBUGC; in Polish).
—— 1935 'Essai d'une Theorie du Mouvement Cyclique des Affaires', *Revue d'Economie Politique*, no. 2.
—— 1937 'A Theory of Commodity, Income and Capital Taxation', *Economic Journal*, Sep.
—— 1938 'The Determination of Distribution of the National Income', *Econometrica*, Apr.
—— 1939 *Essays in the Theory of Economic Fluctuations* (Allen and Unwin).
—— 1943a *Studies in Economic Dynamics* (Allen and Unwin).
—— 1943b 'Political Aspects of Full Employment', *Political Quarterly*, no. 4.
—— 1947 *Studies in War Economics* (Basil Blackwell).
—— 1954 *Theory of Economic Dynamics: An Essay on Cyclical and Long Run Changes in Capitalist Economy* (Allen and Unwin).
—— 1966 *Studies in the Theory of the Business Cycle 1933–1939* (Basil Blackwell).

—— 1968a 'The Marxian Equations of Reproduction and Modern Economics', *Social Science Information*, no. 6.

—— 1968b 'Trend and Business Cycle Reconsidered', *Economic Journal*, June.

—— 1969 *Introduction to the Theory of Growth in a Socialist Economy* (Basil Blackwell).

—— 1971a 'Class Struggle and the Distribution of National Income', *Kyklos*.

—— 1971b *Selected Essays on the Dynamics of the Capitalist Economy 1933– 1970* (Cambridge University Press).

—— 1972a *The Last Phase in the Transformation of Capitalism* (Monthly Review Press).

—— 1972b *Selected Essays on the Economic Growth of the Socialist and Mixed Economy* (Cambridge University Press).

Kregel, J. A., 1972 *The Reconstruction of Political Economy: An Introduction to Post-Keynesian Economics* (Macmillan).

Kuhn, T. H., 1962 *The Structure of Scientific Revolutions* (University of Chicago Press).

Lerner, A., 1934 'The Concept of Monopoly and the Measurement of Monopoly Power', *Review of Economic Studies*.

Lipinski, E., 1977 'Michal Kalecki', *Oxford Bulletin of Economics*.

Locksley, G., 1980 'Political Business Cycle: Alternative Interpretations' in Whiteley, P. (ed.) *Models of Political Economy* (Sage).

Ostleiner, H., 1980 'Wirtschaftspolitik bei Neidrigern Wachstum' in Fischer, H. (ed.) *Rote Markierungen '80* (Wein).

Pulling, K., 1978 'Cyclical Behaviour of Profit Margins', *Journal of Economic Issues*, June.

Robinson, J., 1964 'Kalecki and Keynes' in *Problems of Economic Dynamics and Planning in Honour of Michal Kalecki* (Warsaw).

Robinson, J. and Eatwell, J., 1973 *An Introduction to Modern Economics* (McGraw-Hill).

Sherman, H., 1977 'Monopoly Power and Stagflation', *Journal of Economic Issues*, June.

Steindl, J., 1952 *Maturity and Stagnation in American Capitalism* (Monthly Review Press).

—— 1979 'Stagnation Theory and Stagnation Policy', *Cambridge Journal of Economics*, Mar.

# 9 Wassily Leontief: Input–Output and Economic Planning[1]

## Martin Cave

Wassily Leontief is associated in the minds of most economists with one thing only – the development of the input–output system, the first empirical implementation of a general equilibrium model of the economy. This is a project to which he has devoted nearly all his professional life – nearly fifty years altogether – and its success can be measured in the widespread use made of input–output by governments and business. However, Leontief's contribution to economics is to be found not merely in his development of input–output but also in his conception of the subject as a practical, problem-solving discipline grounded in the collection and processing of actual data and the use of simplified but applicable analytical tools. The development of input–output is one positive expression of this distinctive view of economics which Leontief has consistently espoused throughout his lifetime; the same approach also finds expressions as we shall see, in his distaste for the dominant trends in contemporary economics.

Wassily Leontief was born in St. Peterburg in 1906, the son of a university professor. Academically he was something of a prodigy, being admitted to Leningrad University at the age of 15. His early studies were done against the background of the 1917 Bolshevik revolution, the civil war which occupied the next three years, and the period of slow economic recovery in Russia in the early 1920s. During this time Leontief was a socialist of independent views, which differed from those of the Bolsheviks, and he spent some of this period in prison. In 1925, after a serious illness, he left the USSR for Berlin.

In Berlin he worked with the economic historian Werner

Sombart and the statistician Ladislaus von Bortkiewicz,[2] until in 1928 he moved to the Institute of World Economics at Kiel. A chance conversation in a café with a party of Chinese visitors led to an offer of employment as adviser to the Minister of Railways in China. Leontief accepted and spent a year there planning the railway network. This required him to travel widely throughout the country collecting data, for which purpose he often had to devise ingenious methods. He was to return to China over forty years later and his earlier experience there gave him a useful yardstick for evaluating the success of the Communist régime.

In 1931, shortly after his return to Kiel, Leontief – who by this time had published several articles in German academic periodicals – received an invitation to join the National Bureau of Economic Research in New York. After a brief and not wholly satisfactory stay there, he moved in the same year to the Economics Department at Harvard. He accepted on condition that he receive financial support for a research project. The money was made available, although the project was not enthusiastically received by his future colleagues, and this marked the start of Leontief's life-long research on input–output models. His association with Harvard was nearly as long. Apart from a brief interruption for the war years[3] he remained there until 1975, and it was while at Harvard that Leontief received the Nobel prize for economics in 1973. In 1975, however, he moved to the Institute of Economic Research, a research institute created for him at New York University. Leontief's decision to move was prompted by dissatisfaction with what he regarded as Harvard's excessive concentration on orthodox theoretical economics, to the exclusion both of practical work and of radical approaches. When he left the department at Harvard, the University chose not to reappoint an economist working in the input–output field.

At the Institute for Economic Research Leontief continues to work on input–output models, devoting much of his time to a model of the world economy developed originally for the United Nations. He has also been deeply engaged in the recent debate over the desirability of some form of national economic planning in the United States.

Leontief's major publications are readily accessible. His first major study on input–output *The Structure of the American Economy 1919–29* was republished in an amended version covering the years 1919–39 in 1951 and reissued in 1976 (Leontief,

1951). A larger collective work on the same theme, edited by Leontief, was first published in 1953 (Leontief, 1953). Leontief published a set of later essays on input–output in 1966 (1966a), and his collected essays on economics were made available in two volumes in 1966 and 1977 (1966b, 1977a). His model of the world economy was also published in 1977 (1977b). These works have been extensively translated. In addition, Leontief has written widely on the development of economics, on economic policy, on the arts, and on his visits to Japan, China and Cuba. These last articles are particularly recommended as offering an insight into Leontief's thinking which may elude those who are acquainted only with his technical economic writings (1969, 1970 and 1973).

INPUT–OUTPUT ANALYSIS

Any account of Leontief as an economist must begin with his work on input–output. The input–output model is a way of representing the interdependence between the various sectors of the economy. Sector $A$ supplies inputs (raw materials, semi-finished goods etc.) to sectors $B, C$ and $D$ and itself receives inputs from sectors $X, Y$ and $Z$. $X, Y$ and $Z$ may themselves either ship inputs to $B, C$ and $D$, or receive inputs from them. The whole economy can thus be represented as a complex inter-relationship of sectors. An input–output table is a statistical representation of these inter-sectoral relationships. We illustrate this in figure 9.1 for a simple economy comprising three sectors.

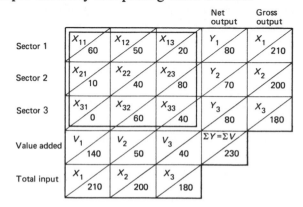

FIGURE 9.1

The three-by-three array or matrix within the double lines shows the shipments made between the sectors. The first element $(X_{11})$ expresses the output of sector 1 which is used as an input into sector 1 itself (seed planted to grow more corn, for example). $X_{12}$ indicates the quantity of output of sector 1 supplied for use within sector 2, and so on. $Y_1$ is the net output of sector 1, going to final demand (consumption, investment etc.). $X_{1,}$ is the gross output (net output plus intermediate inputs) of sector 1. $V_1$ is the value added within the first sector – the sum of wages and other factor incomes.

Interpreting the table in this way, we identify the destination of all output produced by sector 1 by reading along the first row. Reading down the first column we identify the value of inputs used in sector 1 – both intermediate inputs and primary factors. The first row and the first column must therefore have the same sum, as the revenue from the output of sector 1 is exhaustively divided among intermediate inputs and primary factors. The first of these relationships is the more important; the first row of the table can be written out in equation form as follows:

| Gross output | | Intermediate inputs | | Final demand |
|---|---|---|---|---|
| $X_1$ | $=$ | $X_{11} + X_{12} + X_{13}$ | $+$ | $Y_1$ |

The input–output table for an economy is by itself merely an accounting framework, a means of representing the inter-industry flows in the economy in a particular period. In the above account we have implicitly assumed that all flows are measured in monetary units, and this is the normal practice with input–output tables. We could alternatively have described the flows in physical units – so many tons of coal used as an input in the production of so many tons of steel. This is indeed the way in which Leontief himself prefers to think of the input–output system, and the foundation of the input–output model – rather than the accounting framework for inter-sectoral flows which we have described – is precisely the assumption that there is a direct, technologically-determined relationship between the output of one sector and the inputs from other sectors necessary to produce that output. Each ton of steel – it is assumed – requires so many tons of coal as an input in its production. (Or, holding prices constant, each dollar's worth of steel requires so many cents worth of coal to produce it).

Doubling the output of steel will require twice as much coal as an input. It is this special assumption about the nature of technological relationships in an economy which turns the accounting framework we have described above into a model suitable for analysis and projection of the economy.

Let us define $a_{ij}$ as the input of $i$ necessary to produce a unit of $j$. (Its value can be calculated by using the formula $a_{ij} = X_{ij}/X_j$). Then the equation above can be written:

$$X_1 = a_{11}X_1 + a_{12}X_2 + a_{13}X_3 + Y_1$$

The assumption of fixed input coefficients is equivalent to assuming that the $a_{ij}$s are constant and independent of the output levels. If we make this assumption we can then use the equation to calculate the gross output of sector 1 required to meet a specified level of final demand ($Y_1$) and also to supply sectors 2 and 3 with their required inputs. However inputs required for sectors 2 and 3 depend on those sectors' gross output levels ($X_2$ and $X_3$), and to the extent that they produce inputs for sector 1, their gross output levels depend themselves on the output level of sector 1, which we are trying to determine. In other words, the whole set of input–output equations must be solved simultaneously.

There are now straightforward techniques developed by Leontief for solving the simultaneous system of equations and computing the total gross output required in each sector to produce any given bill of final goods (see appendix). But whereas Leontief and his collaborators in the 1930s had to make the computations painfully and largely by hand, modern computer technology makes the solution simple.

The input–output model also allows the investigator quickly to calculate the consequences of a change in the structure of final demand. We can illustrate this by reference to an example which Leontief himself has considered on several occasions. Suppose the government reduces military spending as a result of a disarmament agreement. The immediate impact will fall on the armaments industry, but that sector's suppliers will also be affected indirectly, as will its suppliers' suppliers, and so on. The input–output model enables the investigator to calculate the total impact, direct and indirect, of such a change on the output of all the sectors of the economy. The consequences for employment can be calculated if output per man in each sector is known. A similar set of calculations will reveal the consequences of replacing military spending by alternative forms of government spending or by increased private final demand.

We consider other and more complex uses of the basic input–output model below. First, however, it is worthwhile considering the antecedents of the model and the way in which Leontief developed it. The notion of interdependence within the economy had been current for nearly two centuries. In 1758 Francois Quesnay, the Physiocratic economist, had published his *Tableau Economique*, a tabular representation of the relations between the output and expenditures of farmers, landowners and manufacturers (Quesnay, 1972; for a modern examination see Barna, 1975). The data however were fictitious. Marx's model of simple and expanded reproduction in a two-sector model also illustrated the interdependence of department I (producer goods) and department II (consumer goods) (Marx, 1956, Part III) and Walras formulated a mathematical model of interdependent markets or general equilibrium (Walras, 1954, Lesson 20).[4] These last two contributions were made in the second half of the nineteenth century.

Early Soviet work devoted to compiling a balance of the national economy for the year 1923/4 has also been cited as an influence on Leontief's thinking. The work in question was a set of tables indicating the breakdown of production and inter-sectoral flows within industry. The distribution of national income between alternative uses was, however, shown separately. Leontief's review of this work appeared in Germany in October 1925 and, in Russian translation, in the December 1925 issue of *Planned Economy*, the journal of the State Planning Commission of the USSR (1977a, pp. 3–9). The present-day reader finds it hard to see the seeds of the input–output model in the short review, and Leontief himself disclaims the influence of the Soviet balance, pointing out that he left the USSR at the age of nineteen. However the lucky chance of the review enabled later Soviet writers to claim Soviet origins for input–output, and this gave the technique a degree of respectability in the USSR which it would otherwise have lacked.[5]

Leontief himself attaches more significance to his time in Kiel, particularly to some work he did on demand and supply for particular products. Certainly by the time of his removal to Harvard he had a clear notion of what he wanted to do, and of the data required. However it was nearly ten years before his monograph on the American economy was published, and the first version he developed differed in important respects from the model described above, which appears in the later, expanded, edition of the monograph.

The first version was in many respects more sophisticated than the later one. The economic system it describes embraces the household sector not as a recipient of consumer goods produced to satisfy final demand, as described above, but as an integral part of the model. Households form an additional sector or industry; its inputs are consumer goods and its output is labour supplied to other sectors.[6] Investment and savings are similarly incorporated in the system. If a sector is making a net investment, its expenditure exceeds its revenues, while for a sector making net savings revenue exceeds expenditure. A separate saving coefficient is established for each sector, such that total expenditure is equal to total revenue divided by the coefficient. Sectors making a net investment will have a savings coefficient of less than one (expenditure exceeds revenue); sectors making net savings – the household sector, for example – will have a coefficient in excess of one.

The version described in the previous paragraph is a closed model, which integrates all economic activity within a single framework. Leontief's later version, first published in 1944, was an open model which treats final demand as exogenous. This version – in many ways less elegant than the first – has proved more satisfactory for practical work, though dynamic input–output models do treat investment demand as endogenous (see below).

As noted earlier, the crucial assumption which underlies any application of the input–output model in either version, open or closed, is the assumption of fixity of input coefficients or perfect complementarity of inputs. On this point Leontief has consistently argued from the need to make simplifying assumptions in order to implement the model empirically – a preoccupation which underlies all his work. His formulation combines elements of both substitution and complementarity, as the separate outputs produced by a single sector are assumed to be perfect substitutes: it is only between the outputs of any *two* separate sectors that no substitution is permitted. Moreover he points out that many apparent instances of substitution between inputs are due to changes in the inter-industry composition of output – changes which the input–output model captures without appeal to input substitutability. Ultimately though, as Leontief recognises, the realism of the assumption of fixed input coefficients is tested in practical applications of the model.

APPLICATIONS

A proper account even of Leontief's own refinements and applications of input–output would require more space than we have available. Leontief and his colleagues initially calculated 44-sector input–output tables of the American economy in 1919 and 1929. For analytical work the sectors were aggregated to ten, and even then the calculations, made with punch-card equipment, were laborious. The development of computer technology after the Second World War eliminated manual calculations. Much larger models were computed within hours or minutes, and practical applications multiplied.

Leontief had by this time developed ways of incorporating the foreign sector into his model. The prices side of the model had also been developed and could be used to show, for example, the effects on prices throughout the economy of changes in wage rates or rates of profit. A dynamic version of the input–output model incorporated the investment required to augment the capital stock and allow the economy to grow (see Appendix), and inter-regional models were introduced. In 1948 Leontief became the founding director of the Harvard Economic Research Project, which was devoted to furthering input–output analysis. Several governments embarked at this time on the compilation of input–output tables, including the American government, whose first table, for the year 1947, was published in 1949. Input–output techniques came to be widely used in the preparation of plans for developing countries. The model did not however find universal acceptance. In the USSR and Eastern Europe it was regarded with suspicion and hostility as an economic tool which ignored the creativity of the socialist economic system, and no input–output tables were prepared in the USSR until 1958. Ironically, ideological obstacles also hampered government work on input–output in the USA. During the Eisenhower presidency, input–output was viewed as the thin end of the wedge of economic planning, and government-supported work was stopped.

Leontief himself demonstrated the versatility of input–output techniques with his influential work in the 1950s on the factor content of American foreign trade. Standard trade theory implied that the United States – a capital-rich country – would export capital-intensive and import labour-intensive commodities. Leontief, using his input–output model, demonstrated the reverse, that American export industries were less capital-intensive than American import-competing industries. This result, which became known as the Leontief paradox, was a watershed in international economics which called forth a number of desparate attempts to salvage the traditional theory. Leontief himself was highly critical of some of these efforts, and his own explanation of the phenomenon, which was in terms of the higher productivity of American labour, found a later echo in terms of 'technological' theories of trade flows and theories explicitly incorporating human capital in the analysis.

Leontief's most recent and most ambitious input–output model is one covering the whole world economy prepared for the United Nations. Work on this model started in 1973, and the original focus was a projection of the impact of economic activity on the environment. The input–output model can be adapted in a conceptually simple way to incorporate this aspect. Each sector produces not only its normal output but also a number of pollutants, in quantities which are directly related to the scale of activity in the sector, (the assumption of proportionality or of fixed coefficients seems particularly appropriate here). The model is completed by incorporating a sector or sectors for the abatement of pollution, which has associated inputs and which destroys (produces negative quantities of) pollutants. Thus amended the model can immediately identify the total output of all sectors required to produce a specified bill of final goods while limiting pollution to a specified level.

However the scope of the United Nations study was extended to an investigation of the future of the world economy. The world was divided into 15 regions and an input–output model was developed for each region comprising 45 sectors, of which 22 are manufacturing; eight pollutants are also distinguished and five of the sectors are pollution-abatement activities. Within each region current and capital input coefficients were projected for the years 1980, 1990 and 2000; from these the total input requirements (and pollution outputs) can be calculated for any rate of growth and structure of national income. The regions were also linked by trade and capital flows expressed in money terms; the calculations thus required the forecasting of relative prices, again using the input–output model to project the changes in costs associated with changes in factor prices and technological change.

The model as set out above cannot define a trajectory for the economy. To do so additional assumptions are needed, particularly on rates of growth of population and of output in each region. The study proceeded by developing scenarios based on alternative combinations of growth rates for the regions. The results are scarcely encouraging for those concerned about the income gap between rich and poor countries. If growth rates of developed countries are simply extrapolated, and if the assumption is made that developing nations achieve the growth-rate targets adopted by the United Nations for the Second Development Decade, then the income gap between rich and poor countries would remain in the year 2000 what it had been in 1970 – about 12 to 1. Yet the United Nations targets for the 1970s proved to be hopelessly unrealistic, particularly for countries poor in natural resources, so the assumptions even of this scenario are – as Leontief acknowledges – unrealistic.

The second major scenario models the implementation of the New Economic World Order, based on a greater willingness of developed nations to open their markets to exports from developing countries and on more generous capital flows from the former to the latter. The effect of these policies would be to reduce the income gap to 7 to 1 by the year 2000. Leontief concludes that 'the principal limits to sustained economic growth and economic developments are political, social and institutional in character rather than physical' (Leontief, 1977b, pp. 10–11). He is however acutely aware of just how serious these obstacles are.

Leontief continues to work on the World model, although lack of financial support has prevented him from developing it as he would wish. In the past two years he has used it to investigate the impact of cuts in military spending, in a study financed by the United Nations. He has also developed the treatment of population variables in the model (Leontief, 1979), and other studies are in progress. Work on adaptations of the model is going on in other countries as well, including the USSR.

As this brief account indicates, input–output analysis has

become a powerful and widely-used tool for applied economic research. An input—output model forms the core of forecasting models of national economies, such as the Wharton School econometric model of the United States or the Cambridge growth project in the UK. Centrally-planned economies have now abandoned their early hostility and use input—output models extensively, particularly for longer-term planning. Business firms also make much use of the model. As Leontief wrote in 1976, 'for a fee one can now purchase a single row of a table showing the deliveries of a particular product, say coated laminated fabrics or farming machine tools, not only to different industries but within each industry to individual plants segregated by zip code areas' (1977a, p. 152).

Within the economics profession, however, input—output has been less influential. Certainly, linear models of the economy abound. Many authors émploy in their theoretical work so-called generalised Leontief techniques, or representations of the economy which allow each sector a choice from among a number of discrete techniques, each with different fixed input coefficients (see for example Dorfman *et al.*, 1958). Sraffa (1960) has investigated theoretical properties of linear systems. What these works lack, however, is the potential for implementation in the real world to solve practical problems. The increased generality of many such models is purchased at the cost of making them inapplicable in practical work.

It is his emphasis on empirical implementation which marks Leontief out amongst contemporary economists. In 1970 Leontief chose the occasion of his presidential address to the American Economic Association to deliver an unfavourable assessment of recent trends in economics. In particular he criticised economists for establishing a scale of professional values which gives high marks to theoretical (usually mathematical) contributions and low marks to those engaged in the painstaking work of developing the data base from which well-founded practical conclusions can be drawn.[7] As a result, the means with which economists try to solve their problems are 'palpably inadequate', and economists display a 'continued preoccupation with imaginary, hypothetical rather than observable reality'. This scale of values is passed down from generation to generation by bias in the recruitment of academic personnel. Leontief calls instead for serious efforts to collect more accurate and more recent data and for a willingness to cross frontiers and collaborate with other disciplines, such as engineering and sociology. He believes, moreover, that much of what economists are trying to do is done much better by operations researchers or management scientists.

Views similar to Leontief's were expressed at the same time by several leading economists working in different areas of the subject. Nearly ten years later, however, in 1979, Leontief had seen little improvement in the situation. Academic journals are still replete with articles using complex mathematics to prove trivial results on unrealistic assumptions. Leontief now believes that it would serve little purpose for him to express himself again on the subject and that the major contribution he can make towards furthering his own conception of economics is the continuing example of his own work.

Before we consider in detail Leontief's views on more explicitly political questions, and particularly his controversial espousal of national economic planning in the United States, it may be worth outlining his other contributions to economics. Two topics here deserve particular attention – Leontief's work on aggregation and his perceptive and often critical remarks on Keynesianism.[8]

AGGREGATION

We have already made reference to the problem of aggregation in discussing the input–output model. In the model, the innumerable separate activities which make up the economy are aggregated into a number of sectors, the flow of products between which is then analysed. In other words, some kind of consolidation into sectors is required. A number of authors have contributed to the literature on this topic (see Green, 1964, Chap. 9). Leontief's own contribution to aggregation theory, which dates back to some early work on index numbers in the 1930s, was more fundamental. He was concerned with the following sort of problem. A functional relationship exists between a number of variables. In what circumstances are we justified in replacing that functional relationship with another in a small number of variables, where one or more of the new variables is found by aggregating or consolidating several of the original variables into a single number? The problem arises frequently in economics. We might wish to aggregate a number of commodities in a utility function into a single commodity group or to aggregate the inputs of separate kinds of capital services into a single capital aggregate in a production function.

His two 1947 papers on aggregation set out what became known as the Leontief condition for aggregation (Leontief, 1966b, Chap. 13). It states essentially that aggregation of two variables in the original function is permissible if and only if the marginal rate of substitution between the two variables depends only on those two variables, and is unaffected by changes in variables outside the group. For example, two food products can be aggregated into a single variable 'food' in a utility function, if and only if the marginal rate of substitution between them in consumption is unaffected by the quantities consumed of, say, housing or shirts. The inputs of two kinds of capital services can be aggregated into a single variable, 'capital', in a production function, if and only if the ratio of their marginal products is independent of the input of labour (Bliss, 1975, Chap. 7).

The implications of this result are substantial. On one hand it has stimulated demand theorists such as Gorman and Strotz to investigate preference structures which yield consumer demand functions in terms of commodity groups rather than individual commodities. On the other hand the Leontief condition, by imposing restrictive conditions for consistent aggregation, has cast serious doubt on the 'neo-classical parables' which seek to explain the distribution of income on the basis of production functions in which capital appears as a single aggregate. It has always been clear to Leontief that the Cambridge criticisms of simple neo-classical capital and distribution theory are well-founded.

KEYNESIANISM

Leontief has not always agreed with Cambridge views, however, and he has been particularly suspicious of the aggregative framework of Keynesian economics. Leontief took part in the debate in the 1930s which greeted the publication of the *General Theory*. His best-known objection to Keynes was expressed in an article entitled 'Implicit Theorising – a Methodological Criticism of the Neo-Cambridge School'. Leontief makes the same criticism of the Cambridge School of the 1930s, and of Keynes in particular, which Schumpeter made of Ricardo in a famous passage in his *History of Economic Analysis*:

> his [Ricardo's] interest was in the clearcut result of direct, practical significance. In order to get this he cut that general system (of universal interdependence of all the elements in the economic system) to pieces, bundled up as large parts of it as possible, and put them into cold storage – so that as many things as possible should be frozen and 'given'. He then piled one simplifying assumption upon another until, having really settled everything by these assumptions, he was left with only a few aggregative variables between which, given these assumptions, he set up simple one-way relations so that, in the end, the derived results emerged almost as tautologies (quoted in Bliss 1975, p. 119).

Leontief argues that Cambridge economists make extensive use of what he calls implicit definitions of economic terms. 'Given any number of compatible fundamental postulates expressed in terms of *ABC*, we can make, without infringing upon rules of logic, any other statement concerning the same elements provided that we introduce into it at least one new term, *X*'. This is so because we can implicitly define *X* to make our statement compatible with the initial proposition. The theorist who argues in this way can accuse any critic of an inability to understand the correct meaning of the terms in which the theorem is defined. 'Scientific discussion degenerates into a comedy of errors and mistaken identities' (Leontief, 1966b, pp. 63, 64–5).

In Leontief's view, Keynes' economic writings give numerous examples of this methodologically unsound procedure. In particular he condemns Keynes' implicit definition of aggregate supply and demand curves in terms which make them independent of one another, so that a shift in one is not accompanied by a shift in the other. Leontief's concern seems to be with the lack of an explicitly specified micro-foundation for the theory.

Leontief's criticism of Keynes was not limited to methodological issues. He also had theoretical doubts about the nature of the Keynesian underemployment equilibrium and at a practical level he doubted the efficacy of simple Keynesian remedies in a complex and interdependent economy. In a post-war theoretical paper Leontief first casts doubt on Keynes' assumption of a supply curve for labour expressed in terms of money wages, preferring the orthodox assumption, based on traditional maximising behaviour, that the supply of labour is a function of real wage rates. He goes on to question the Keynesian liquidity preference as a mechanism preventing the emergence of full employment through monetary expansion. He points out that liquidity preference must be zero in long-run equilibrium, because in the long run investors adjust their view of the normal interest rate downwards. The existence of involuntary unemployment must therefore be justified in terms of a dynamic argument incorporating the assumption of disequilibrium or temporary equilibrium (Leontief, 1966b, Chap. 8). These criticisms, voiced by Leontief in the 1940s, were subsequently developed independently by later writers, such as Clower, who explicitly reinterpreted Keynes' work as an attempt to model disequilibrium phenomena.

PLANNING

Leontief's analysis of the inadequacy of the Keynesian policy prescription leads us to an examination of his views on economic planning. Essentially Leontief has recognised that government fiscal intervention can be used to protect the economy from catastrophic recessions, but he regards it as inadequate to deal with inflation:

> according to prevalent academic doctrine a proper combination of fiscal and monetary policies should be capable of securing steady economic growth with reasonably full utilisation of productive capacities, high levels of employment and stable prices. After many years of trial in many countries and under a great variety of circumstances, practical experience with the application of this approach has proved disappointing. Neither the Keynesian nor the so-called monetarist prescription seems to work (Leontief, 1978, p. 73).

Leontief explains this by the inadequacy of three or four simple macro-economic-policy instruments to cope with the complexity of economic management in an advanced economy. As always he is concerned less with large macro-aggregates than with the shifting inter-relationships between the sectors of the economy.

Since the 1960s – and with increasing urgency in the harsher economic climate of the 1970s – Leontief has argued instead for the introduction of a system of national economic planning in the United States. The argument is made in terms of the failure of the market system to generate *by itself* an efficient allocation of resources. The market operates as a giant computer, grinding out solutions to the equations of the general equilibrium system by a process of trial and error. However, the errors in the passage to equilibrium (unemployment, unused capacity, etc.) are costly and can be eliminated by supplementing, not replacing, the market mechanism by a plan or projection for the development of the economy as a whole. The plan would thus be a consistent inter-sectoral projection of the economy which supplements in quantitative terms the price information provided by the market. A system of rolling plans would operate, with annual recomputation of the five-year projection in the light of new data.

Not surprisingly the technique Leontief recommends for making the projection is the input–output model. Leontief pointed out in an early essay on planning in the *Harvard Business Review* that corporations make independent estimates of the size of their future markets, but these estimates are inevitably wrong because firms lack the necessary data. He described it as a frustrating and costly guessing game (Leontief, 1966a, p. 6). On the other hand, a plan compiled centrally using input–output techniques would trace the direct and indirect effects of one sector on another and produce a consistent forecast. The actual construction of the plan would be in the hands of a non-political agency loosely connected with the executive branch of the United States Federal Government with regional offices in each state. The planning board would be supplied with data by government statistical services, whose operations would have to be seriously overhauled to provide the planners with the necessary data.

Leontief further proposes that planning be integrated with the democratic political process through the construction of articulated and consistent alternative scenarios for the development of the economy. The ideas of politicians would be translated into alternative plans which would be publicly discussed and voted on by the electorate or adopted by legislative wrangling and political log-rolling. Implementation of the plan would be achieved by the market, assisted where necessary by government regulatory action. Inasmuch as the plan adopted would be internally consistent it would form the basis of firms' expectations, and be self-fulfilling. This mechanism would be supplemented by selective government intervention and regulation. The government's own adherence to its part of the plan would itself have a profound impact on the private sector. Leontief believes that if industry is put in a tunnel with a light at the end of it (i.e. the opportunity of profit) it will move in the desired direction.

There is some overlap between Leontief's proposals and the system of indicative planning operating in some Western countries, such as France or Norway. Indeed, part of Leontief's argument about the self-fulfilling nature of a consistent intersectoral plan is strongly reminiscent of the view of indicative planning as a form of 'generalised market research' expounded by Pierre Massé, the French planning commissioner of the early sixties. (Leontief's proposal differs from French practice, however, by the incorporation of more democratic choice between alternative plans.) The French experience has not been entirely happy, however, and the problems of getting private enterprise – or even the government itself – to abide by the plan have been acute. Leontief's views on this point seem too sanguine.

Leontief has played an important role in the debate in the United States on economic planning. With Leonard Woodcock of the auto workers' union he was co-chairman of the Initiative Committee for National Planning. In the Congress, legislation was proposed by Senators Humphrey and Javits which would have created an Economic Planning Board and a Council on Economic Planning. Leontief himself had reservations about the form of the legislation, which in his view concentrated too much on the elimination of unemployment and too little on planning the structural shifts which will inevitably take place as a result of technological advance. The principal impact of the planning system would thus be on a structural rather than demand-deficient or Keynesian unemployment. However much of the momentum behind the movement for national economic planning in the US has now been dissipated, although the economic problems that planning is intended to mitigate have become even more severe. Leontief now believes that the economy will have to go through further crises before the need for planning is recognised.

Leontief's views on other social and economic systems than capitalism have to be inferred from his occasional writings or from asides in papers devoted to other topics. He regards Marx as an important precursor of much modern economic analysis, particularly of the business cycle. His assessment of the traditional system of central planning, as practised in the USSR for example, is unfavourable; the planning methods used are rudimentary, the institutional structure is rigid and the system lacks an incentive to replace the profit motive. Leontief takes a more favourable view of a reformed socialist economy such as Hungary, which does harness the profit motive within the framework of socialist ownership. He has also given a favourable evaluation of economic developments in the less-advanced socialist economies of Cuba and China. In the case of the latter he was able to compare the economy at the time of his visit in 1973 with the widespread misery and abject poverty prevailing at the time of his earlier visit in the 1920s. He approved in particular of the Chinese concentration on agricultural development (Leontief, 1973). His remarks on Cuba were more ambivalent. Whilst obviously sympathetic to the regime, he regarded its economic difficulties in the early 1970s as an inevitable consequence of its excessive reliance on moral as opposed to material incentives (Leontief, 1971).

These final paragraphs have taken us some distance from Leontief's technical contributions to economics. However, one thread which runs through all Leontief's work is a conviction that economics is a practical subject. He does not underrate theory – indeed his own contributions to theory are considerable – but argues that economics is ultimately justified by its ability to explain and then perhaps change the world. His own political views have led him to favour particular kinds of economic and social change, but the methods he has developed need not be directed towards those ends.[9] His primary concern has been with developing usable models of the economy which can be implemented with real data. It is this preoccupation which throughout his professional life has separated him from most contemporary economists. He has always acted on the principle expressed in the passage from Quesnay which he chose to introduce his first book: 'dans la recherche pour la verité par le calcul, toute la certitude est dans l'évidence des données'.

APPENDIX: THE SIMPLE MATHEMATICS OF INPUT–OUTPUT

1. Input–output is based on the use of certain simple operations in matrix algebra. The basic equations of the static input–output model, set out in matrix form are:

$$X = AX + Y \qquad (1)$$

where   $X$ is an $n$-dimensional column vector of gross outputs of the $n$ sectors
$Y$ is an $n$-dimensional column vector of net outputs, or shipments to final demand, of the $n$ sectors
$A$ is an $n \times n$ matrix of input coefficients $a_{ij}$.

We can solve equation (1) for $X$, to yield

$$X = (I - A)^{-1} Y \qquad (2)$$

The matrix $(I - A)^{-1}$ can now be interpreted as the matrix of total, direct and indirect, input coefficients. It can be computed directly by inversion, or by the expansion

$$(I - A)^{-1} = (I + A + A^2 + A^3 \ldots) \qquad (3)$$

i.e.        $$X = (I + A + A^2 + A^3 \ldots) Y.$$

The expression shows how the total output of an economy is made of final output ($Y$), plus direct inputs into that final output ($AY$), plus inputs into those inputs etc. For the economy to be capable of producing net output, the matrix $(I - A)$ must satisfy the so-called Hawkins–Simon condition that its principal minors are positive. This will ensure that the sequence in the expansion converges.
2. The dynamic model is formulated using the matrix $B$ of capital coefficients. Element $b_{ij}$ of matrix $B$ expresses the amount of capital produced by sector $i$ which must be accumulated to produce one extra unit of output in sector $j$. The basic equation

(assuming full capacity utilisation) becomes

$$X = AX + B\Delta X + C \tag{4}$$

where $\Delta X$ is an $n$-dimensional column vector of increases in
output in the $n$ sectors
$C$ is an $n$-dimensional column vector of net outputs of the
$n$ sectors, excluding investment demand.

The system (4) determines the development of gross output in the
economy for any sequence of values of $C$.

One of Leontief's most recent innovations is the dynamic
inverse (Leontief, 1977a, Chap. 5). This is a dynamic equivalent of
the static inverse matrix $(I - A)^{-1}$. Unlike the static inverse which
is a single matrix, the dynamic inverse is a dated sequence of
matrices showing the total inputs (direct and indirect) which must
be produced prior to the delivery of a unit of final output in a given
year. The dynamic inverse thus captures the time phasing of
output required to produce a unit of final output in any year.
Leontief computed the dynamic inverse for a 52-sector model of
the US economy based on 1947 and 1958 data. Other applications
of this highly promising technique are however still fairly rare.

3. A simple price model. We assume that labour is the only
primary factor. The price of the output of sector $i$ is given by

$$p_i = a_{1i}p_1 + a_{2i}p_2 \ldots + a_{ii}p_i + a_{ni}p_n + a_{oi}\omega$$

where $a_{oi}$ is the input of labour per unit of output $i$
$\omega$ is the wage rate.

In matrix form:

$$p = A'p + a_o\omega$$

where $p$ is the column vector of prices
$A'$ is the transpose of matrix $A$ (found by converting the
rows of $A$ into columns)
$a_o$ is the column vector of labour-input coefficients.

Solving for $p$,

$$p = (I - A')^{-1} a_o\omega.$$

i.e. prices are proportional to the total (direct and indirect) input of labour. More complicated relationships naturally apply when the number of primary inputs exceeds one. These relationships are explored theoretically in Sraffa (1960). Leontief's own framework enables him to compute directly the effect on prices of a 10 per cent change in wages or profits, either in all sectors or in one sector only (Leontief, 1951, pp. 188–202).

NOTES FOR FURTHER READING

Leontief (1951) is the classic treatment which introduces the input–output model and contains many applications. A simple mathematical statement is given in Leontief (1966a), Chap. 7. For a simplified account of Leontief's latest model, see in particular his Nobel Lecture (Leontief, 1977a, Chap. 10). Leontief's views on economic planning are set out in Leontief (1966a, Chap. 1; 1966b, Chap. 20 and 1977a Chap. 11). The second of these three volumes also contains all his major contributions to economic analysis, including his criticisms of Keynes (Chaps 5, 7–9) and his article on aggregation (Chap. 13).

NOTES

1. I am grateful to several people at Brunel University and elsewhere for comments on an earlier version of the chapter. Professor Leontief was kind enough to see me in New York in September 1979 and I greatly benefited from our conversation.
2. In view of Leontief's later pre-occupations, it is interesting to note that one of Sombart's best-known works, published in 1906, is entitled *Why is There no Socialism in the United States?* (Sombart, 1976). As well as his contributions to statistics, von Bortkiewicz also published in 1907 an early solution to the so-called 'transformation problem' in Marxian economics.
3. One of Leontief's colleagues during his war service for the US government was George Dantzig, who shared his interest in linear economic models and shortly after the war became the first Western writer to publish a solution method for what became known as linear programming. For an acknowledgement of Leontief's influence see Dantzig, 1963, pp. 17–18.
4. Dorfman in his evaluation of Leontief's work (Dorfman, 1973, pp. 436–7) gives emphasis to Walras' influence. However Leontief himself cites Marx and Quesnay as more important influences on his own work.
5. See, for example, Nemchinov (1964, pp. 2–13). In this Soviet work published in 1959 Leontief is described as a 'well-known American bourgeois economist

who took a degree at the University of Leningrad in the mid-1920s and was later the author of a method based on principles similar to those of the first Soviet balance sheet for the national economy' (1964 p. 12, fn. 2).

6. Readers may note the parallel with the von Neumann model of growth, produced at the same time, which embodies the same assumptions (Neumann, 1945).

7. His criticisms extended to much econometric work, which he characterised as 'an attempt to compensate for the glaring weakness of the data base by the widest possible use of more and more sophisticated statistical techniques' (Leontief, 1977a, p. 27).

8. For a technical account of Leontief's other writings on economics, see Dorfman, 1977, especially pp. 432–4.

9. He sees no reason, for example, why even the planning system he proposes for the United States would make much difference politically, remarking, without much enthusiasm, that 'the wealthy with the support of their retainers can be expected to continue to rule the roost' (Leontief, 1977a, p. 158).

REFERENCES

Barna, T., 1975 'Quesnay's *tableau* in modern guise', *Economic Journal*, vol. 85, pp. 485–96.

Bliss, C., 1975 *Capital Theory and the Distribution of Income* (North-Holland).

Dantzig, G., 1963 *Linear Programming and Extensions* (Princeton University Press).

Dorfman, R., 1977 'Wassily Leontief's contributions to economics', *Swedish Journal of Economics*, vol. 79, pp. 430–49.

Dorfman, R., Samuelson, P. and Solow, R., 1958 *Linear Programming and Economic Analysis* (McGraw-Hill).

Green, H. A. J., 1964 *Aggregation in Economic Analysis* (Princeton University Press).

Leontief, W., 1951 *The Structure of the American Economy* (Oxford University Press). (Reprinted by International Arts and Sciences Press, 1976).

—— 1953 *Studies in the Structure of the American Economy* (Oxford University Press). (Reprinted by International Arts and Sciences Press, 1976).

—— 1966a *Input–Output Economics* (Oxford University Press).

—— 1966b *Essays in Economics: Theories and Theorising*, vol. 1 (Oxford University Press). (Reprinted by Basil Blackwell 1977).

—— 1969 'Notes on a Visit to Cuba', *New York Review of Books*, 21 August, pp. 15–20.

—— 1970 'Mysterious Japan – a Diary', *New York Review of Books*, 4 June, pp. 23–9.

—— 1971 'The Trouble with Cuban Socialism', *New York Review of Books*.

—— 1973 'Socialism in China', *Atlantic Monthly*, March, pp. 74–81.

—— 1977a *Essays in Economics*, vol. 2 (Basil Blackwell).

—— 1977b *The Future of the World Economy* (Oxford University Press).

—— 1978 Issues of the Coming Years', *Economic Impact*, vol. 8, no. 4, pp. 70–6.

—— 1979 'Population Growth and Economic Development: Illustrative Projections', *Population and Development Review*, March, pp. 1–27.

Marx, K., 1956 *Capital*, vol. 2 (Lawrence and Wishart).

Nemchinov, V. S., 1964 *The Use of Mathematics in Economics*, (Oliver and Boyd).

Neumann, J. von, 1945 'A model of general economic equilibrium', *Review of Economic Studies*, vol. 13, pp. 1–9.

Quesnay, F., 1972 *Tableau Economique*, edited by Kuczyuski, M. and Meek, R. (Macmillan).

Sombart, W., 1976 *Why is There no Socialism in the United States?* (Macmillan).

Sraffa, p., 1960 *The Production of Commodities by Means of Commodities* (Cambridge University Press).

Walras, L., 1954 *Elements of Pure Economics* (translated by W. Jaffé) (George Allen and Unwin).

# 10 Lionel Robbins: Methodology, Policy and Modern Theory

Maurice Peston

Lionel Robbins was born in 1898. He served in the First World War and, perhaps as a result of that experience, developed, like so many others of his generation, a desire to change society. He enrolled as a student at LSE, specialising in political ideas and having Harold Laski as his tutor. He learned his economics from Edwin Cannan and Hugh Dalton. He then worked as Beveridge's research assistant for a year, spent some time as a fellow and lecturer at New College, Oxford, and then returned in 1929 to take the chair of economics at LSE. He held that chair until 1961 when his formal retirement began. It is necessary to underline the word 'formal' because even in the academic year 1979/80 he continues to lecture.

Lionel Robbins is an economist of many paradoxes. His great work on methodology, for example, has usually been interpreted as *a priorist* and anti-empirical, yet he has always been concerned with the problems of the real world. On philosophy and policy he has associated himself with the school of thought which is strongly anti-socialist and anti-interventionist, but has not hesitated to be closely involved with governments in almost every possible way. He has made some extremely important contributions to mainstream economic theory, but does not discuss most of these in his autobiography. Finally, an extraordinarily large number of the major figures in the profession were on his staff or were his pupils, but he has founded no school of thought and published no 'principles of economics'. In this last connection it must be noted that while he was no econometrist or mathematician, he was the head of the department which fostered the career of Bill Phillips with all the consequences that has had for LSE as a world centre for econometric theory.

In this essay I shall limit myself to four issues; (a) the nature of economic science, (b) the classical view of economic policy, (c) the supply of effort problem, and (d) the control of inflation. Before doing that, however, there is one additional general remark to be made. Lionel Robbins's writings have been extremely fruitful as statements of problems or problem areas. Whether he has been right or wrong (and he has never been tardy in admitting error) he has concentrated on key issues, and arguments with him have invariably been fruitful. His attack on interpersonal comparisons of utility led to all sorts of new developments in welfare economics. His alleged *a priorism* stimulated the programme of obtaining qualitative predictions based on qualitative restrictions on the underlying functions. His querying of the rationality of a socialist state clarified that topic and again gave rise to innumerable advances in welfare economics.

METHODOLOGY

*An Essay on the Nature and Significance of Economic Science* (Robbins, 1932) is one of the great works of twentieth-century economics. This is clearly so if it is viewed solely as a statement of a problem area or class of problems, but the book also has greatness because of its attempt at solutions. The latter may now be regarded as a magnificent failure, but from the vantage point of the 1980s it looks less of a disaster than does the naive empiricism of the previous three decades.

What is the nature of the Robbins contribution? In the first place he asks the direct question, on what foundation do the basic propositions of economics (and especially value theory) lie? Secondly, he sees that these propositions do have and are meant to have empirical relevance. Thirdly, he rejects historical inductionism, or support via the notion of 'history shows'. Fourthly he recognises the limitation of controlled experimentation in economics. Fifthly, he argues that the correctness of microeconomics does not depend on the validity of particular psychological doctrines. (In this connection it is interesting to note his rejection of behaviourism partly on the grounds that the subjective theory of value cannot be properly understood without a psychical element.) Sixthly, he adopts the position that economics is value free in the sense that it does not depend on individual valuations being regarded as ethically appropriate. Seventhly, in various parts of the book he emphasises the importance of abstraction, of the particular assumptions made. (A good example of this is the use of the assumption of perfect foresight, although for other purposes, such as the theory of profit, uncertainty must be the dominant theme.)

Given this position he then argues that the propositions of economics are deductions from various postulates, 'and the chief of these postulates are all assumptions involving in some way simple and indisputable facts of experience relating to the way in which the scarcity of goods which is the subject-matter of our science actually shows itself in the world of reality'.[1] In addition to these ultimate truths there are 'the assumptions of a more limited nature based upon the general features of particular situations or types of situations which the theory is used to explain'.[2] It must be recognised that Robbins mentions both sorts of assumption. Equally, there can be no doubt that he is correct in stating that economics consists of theoretical assumptions and generalisations, particular propositions, and a wide range of inferences. The difficulty is the one he faces, namely whether all these are true, and what it is of an empirical nature that economists have established. In this connection it seems to the present writer that the usual objection to Robbins, his assertion of simple and indisputable facts, represents a mistaken emphasis. Many if not all of his facts may be indisputable but this does not mean that a great deal of significance can be derived from them.

His view on methodology did develop. An extremely interesting statement appeared in 1959.[3] This was noteworthy partly for what Robbins did say and partly for what he did not. On the latter there is no mention of simple facts, intuitively known for certain. On the former there is a definite acceptance of the hypothetico-deductive method as enunciated by Popper. Robbins says succinctly, 'We devise theories to explain the world and we test them by asking whether they perform this function in specific instances . . . as economic theory becomes more advanced and complicated, the need for testing becomes more and more imperative'.[4]

Later on Professor Robbins went further still and argued that his methodological position had been too essentialist. He claims that he tried to get the problem of testing by reference to reality sorted out in the second edition, but agrees that he was really not successful. His justification, and it is a fair one, was his 'reaction . . . against the ridiculous claims of the institutionalists and the cruder econometricians and an attempt to persuade Beveridge and his like that their simplistic belief "in letting facts speak for themselves" was all wrong'.[5] His move to the Popperian position and his willingness to accept sophisticated econometrics, while apparently reasonable, may have been a trifle premature. For while the logic of the hypothetico-deductive method may seem compelling, its practical usefulness is less so. Lionel Robbins's initial doubts about the ability of economists to establish empirical laws have surely been borne out by the experience of econometric estimation and testing in the past decade. Almost every empirical generalisation, above the level of the trivial, has a tendency to collapse, and almost all that remains is economics as an analytical method which can be applied tentatively and with much judgement to an extremely uncertain world.

Let us, however, revert to the question of whether there are 'simple and indisputable facts of (economic) experience'. What Lionel Robbins had in mind, for example, was scarcity, by which I do not believe he meant so much that economics was the science of scarcity, but rather that the rejection of the existence of scarcity would be to deny the most obvious facet of experience. He is not saying that he could not conceive of a world without scarcity, but that it was not this one. Moreover, he was not denying the existence of unemployment; nor is the existence of scarcity incompatible with unemployed labour with a low, even zero, opportunity cost.

He is arguing that all decision makers in society are constrained, and for most the constraints are effective in that their wants exceed their resources and they are not satiated. Note that he is aware of the existence of ascetics and altruists, but still insists that scarcity applies to them. It is simply that their tastes are different.

More generally, even if wants are not limitless, they need merely exceed the free bounty of nature for scarcity to exist. Even in those circumstances there remains the not totally uninteresting question of the allocation of the hours of the day and the days of a lifetime.

It seems to me, therefore, that Robbins is not mistaken in insisting on the indisputable fact of scarcity, both in saying that it is indisputable and in insisting on its empirical character. I think also that one can cite other facts of similar standing, the most noteworthy of which is the existence of uncertainty. I do not mean by this the Popper proposition concerning the self-contradictory nature of a statement purporting to predict the whole of the future, but the much simpler point that even the most elementary characteristics of the next day cannot be known for certain.

What must be discussed is whether these facts are as important as Robbins thinks. It may well be that he is in error not so much in suggesting that they exist, but in exaggerating what can be derived from them alone. There are two sides to this. One is that we need a great deal more than these facts to get anywhere in economics at all; the other is that we can make progress in economics without paying explicit attention to them. (I ignore the well-known criticism of Robbins that some indisputable intuitions turn out to be highly disputable. The most obvious of these is that some economists are perfectly convinced that they have well defined wants expressible in a utility function while others are equally convinced of the opposite. It is also worth adding that the doubtful nature of some 'Robbins facts' is also characteristic of 'Friedman facts', i.e. those observations that determine the correctness of a theory as shown by its predictions. Here too what is more usual is the contentious character of testing rather than the agreement of 'objective observers'.)

Even the most simple examples clarify the matter. Robbins did not and would not doubt the validity of the theory of the firm; but that theory in the form in which it appeared and was discussed in the thirties tended to ignore uncertainty. And in this respect (if not in any other) it has made scant progress since then. Equally, the existence of scarcity does not tell us that 'the price of pork fluctuates with variations in supply and demand'. It does not even tell us that there will be a price of pork. Of course, it is possible to say that *ex definitione* if pork is scarce, a unit increase in the quantity available must imply a decrease in the availability of something else, and that decrease is the price of pork. But that is a purely theoretical consideration adding nothing to the notion of scarcity. If Robbins is saying anything at all, it must be about the price of pork as commonly understood or something similar; and this need not be determined by supply and demand. Despite its scarcity pork may be distributed to people by dividing the total quantity produced by the number of people, everybody receiving an equal share which they regard as fair and satisfactory. It is possible, therefore, for Robbins's sentence to be false, and 'the price of pork is fixed by government decree' to be the true one.

For the price of pork to depend on demand and supply a great deal more must be the case than the existence of scarcity, and much of that extra, experiential though it may be, is neither simple nor indisputable. We require the existence of a market (which is not necessarily a market place, but something more abstract) involving suppliers and demanders. Something must be said about how the price is fixed and how it comes to change and whether it is absolute price or relative price. It is difficult to avoid questions about the fulfilment of supply plans and demand plans, and one is led inexorably to that elusive concept, equilibrium. In other words, even to begin to assess what is apparently the most elementary 'law' of economics, one becomes involved with theory going beyond the fact with which one started.

And, of course, one is already in deep methodological water, for 'market', 'supply', and 'demand' are the names of concepts in economics and 'price' may be. Certainly, they are not Robbins's facts, but were, of course, invented by philosophers or political economists. They may have empirical counterparts, but these are to be sought and agreed upon, and may remain doubtful. Indeed, were this not so there arises the ultimate paradox of doubting the value of economic theory which Robbins initially set out to defend. If the theory cannot be wrong what significance lies in it being right? If supply, demand and all that were not *additions* to thought why is all the fuss made about discovering them?

The answer is that at the very least the theory draws our attention to and helps us to interpret experience. It guides us to look at the supplies of pork coming forward at the existing price and to the quantities that people are endeavouring to buy. It claims:

(i) that if the former is reduced compared with an earlier occasion or the latter increased, the price will rise,
(ii) that if the price is rising, the former must have been reduced or the latter increased.

Experience (not particularly simple) may confirm all this to the point of it being indisputable, but it is theory that is being, and needs to be, tested. The rise in price may not be open to doubt and the reduction in supply may certainly have happened, but that they go together is a contingency, and one which substantiates the theory. For their existence to be a necessity is of no help to the theory, but rather renders it nugatory.

Let us, however, now proceed and accept for the sake of argument that demand and supply are forces that indisputably act on price, doing this precisely in the way that Robbins claims. In particular let us accept that proposition (i) has been substantiated on many occasions and is undoubted. What does this remind us of in natural science? Surely it is such low level propositions as 'the sun always rises' or 'the seasons always follow each other'. They are undisputed facts of experience and are not incompatible with physical theory. But they play little, if any, part in such theory and go unnoticed. Thus, even if no other difficulties arose with Robbins's view, does it not cause us to set our sights extremely low, limiting us to little more than commonsense? Robbins's facts in themselves do not get us very far and devotion to them may prevent our progressing further.

There is yet one final card to be played. If one enquires as to which part of economics is most closely geared to the simple and indisputable, notably to supply, demand, price, and scarcity, the answer is surely general equilibrium theory. Yet this is the most abstract area of economic discourse, the one the conclusions of which are most distant from ordinary experience and which, while seemingly irrefutable, and in Robbins's terms entirely soundly based, is more or less irrelevant to the real world.

ROBBINS AND THE CLASSICAL ECONOMISTS

Lionel Robbins has made many contributions to the study of the history of economic thought. Current interest in this branch of scholarship owes as much to him as to Viner and Schumpeter, and it is impossible in a brief essay to discuss all his contributions. It is important, however, to pay some attention to one particular contribution, his study of the classical approach to economic policy. His book on the subject (Robbins, 1952) is both hermeneutic and exegetical, the former also taking him close to an apologia. He himself places considerable emphasis on clarifying what the classical economists actually had to say, but he also recognises the importance of the context in which they said it.

There are a great many questions that emerge from Robbins's book that are worth noting. He himself refers to the rather commonsensical and robust arguments used by the classical economists to account for the adjustment processes of the system of economic freedom. Economic policy for the most part, therefore, is about supplementing that process but for the most part allowing it to continue. Robbins says, 'their claim, in essence, was not so much that the system of markets was always tending to some refined equilibrium adjustment, but rather that it provided a rough pointer and a rough discipline whereby the tumultuous forces of self-interest were guided and held in check'.[6] Now, there is a genuine intellectual difficulty here in considering the economic functions of the state. These cannot be considered independently of whether the economy has a tendency within a reasonable time scale to move towards a position of equilibrium and preferably one of full employment. Although the classical economists did recognise the existence of economic fluctuations, and obviously were aware of inflation and balance of payments difficulties, the economic functions of the state did not appear to include a stabilization role. Their rough and ready theory in both its normative and positive modes must have taken it for granted that the system was self-equilibrating. Their economic function of the state was predicated on this so that Keynes's famous remark is relevant

> If we suppose the volume of output to be given, i.e., to be determined by forces outside the classical scheme of thought, then there is no objection to be raised against the classical analysis of the manner in which private self-interest will determine what in particular is produced, in what proportions the factors of production will be combined to produce it, and how the value of the final product will be distributed between them.[7]

But even here Robbins reminds us that matters are not at all clear cut. How can we account, for example, for McCulloch's advocacy of state assistance for the unemployed, if the classical economists were supposed to assume perpetual full employment?[8]

The second of Robbins's contributions follows from the first and it is to remind us that the classical economists were not extremists in the sense of taking all their assumptions to their logical conclusions. McCulloch and Senior could be pretty exacting and harsh on occasion, but the latter did say 'It is the duty of a government to do whatever is conducive to the welfare of the governed', and the former stated 'to appeal to [the principle of laissez-faire] on all occasions savours more of the policy of a parrot than of a statesman or a philosopher'.[9]

Finally, some remarks must be made on their attitude to socialism. Setting J. S. Mill on one side for the moment, they were strongly anti-socialist. Robbins was able to show that they saw a much bigger role for the government than that usually associated with the state but it stopped well short of social democracy, let alone pure socialism. One reason for this was the slippery slope argument – once the state really started to intervene there was no knowing where it would stop. We are given a remarkable quotation by Senior from de Tocqueville

> If, on the other hand the State, in order to escape from this train of consequences, does not itself find work, but takes care that it shall always be supplied by individual capitalists, it must take care that at no place and at no time there be a stagnation. It must take on itself the management of both capitalists and labourers. It must see that the one class is not injured by over trading, or the other by competition. It must regulate profits and wages – sometimes retard, sometimes accelerate, production or consumption. In short, in the jargon of the school, it must organise industry. This is Socialism.[10]

Apart from the felicity of language this could be written by a member of the radical right today. But it is also interesting to note that it could be used to justify some backtracking on other grounds for state intervention. It is not easy to see how logically Senior and other classical economists could justify the amount of intervention that they did if they feared the slippery slope to Socialism. What seemed to happen, therefore, is that common sense replaced logic.

As for Mill, he was a passionate, emotional man who agonised on these issues. Robbins's chapter on his views is a brilliant one. There is no point in summarising it. It should be read and then used as Robbins intends as an incentive to become acquainted with the original literature.

Robbins's essay (1930) on the supply of effort problem is a remarkable example of a standard method to reach a conclusion which should have been obvious in the first place. What is strange is how such great economists as Pigou and Knight should have got the analysis wrong in the first place. Incidentally it should be recalled that their mistake was not the vulgar one of arguing that a tax cut will cause a man to work more but the reverse, namely that he will certainly work less when the net wage rises.

The analysis can be set out as follows:

Income equals the wage-rate times hours worked i.e.

$$Y = W \cdot L$$

It follows that the percentage change in income equals the percentage change in the wage rate plus the percentage change in hours worked

$$y = w + 1$$

where lower-case letters mean 'percentage change in'. The elasticity of demand for income in terms of effort is $y/l$

i.e. $$y/l = (w/l) + 1$$

If this is greater than unity, $w$ and $l$ have the same sign, i.e. as the wage rate increases so does effort. This is the Robbins formulation (see Figure 10.2) which he himself stated was well known and accepted. He then points out that the price of income in terms of effort is the inverse of the wage. The higher the wage the less effort that has to be put in to acquire a unit of income.

Price on the vertical axis in Figure 10.1 is the effort price of income i.e. $1/W$. Robbins then argues that in the 'normal' case the demand for income will vary inversely with price, i.e. the demand curve is downward sloping.

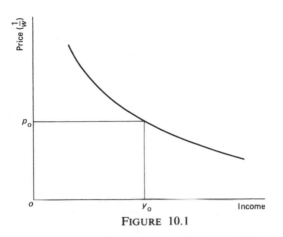

FIGURE 10.1

If price is $p_o$, income demanded will be $y_o$. What then is $p_o Y_o$? This is equal to $y_o / W_o$ i.e. the number of hours worked. It is, of course, obvious that as $p$ falls $pq$ (in this case $y/w$) rises if the elasticity of demand is greater than unity, which is the Robbins proposition.

Nowadays this conclusion is arrived at by any first year student using indifference curves. This is illustrated in figure 10.2.

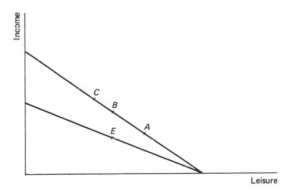

FIGURE 10.2 *The initial equilibrium is at E. A rise in the wage is essentially a fall in the price of income. Assuming income is a normal good, this is still compatible with the new equilibrium being at A. B. or C. i.e. with less work, the same amount of work, or more work.*

Which demonstration is superior? This is not really an answerable question but it must be noted that the strength of Robbins's approach is first its emphasis on the price of income and secondly on elasticity. The first of these need not be neglected in the indifference curve treatment while the second is not amenable to indifference curve analysis at all. In addition, a benefit of the Robbins exposition is its commonsense nature, namely its emphasis on income being a normal good the demand for which varies inversely with the cost of acquiring it. If his had remained the usual exposition, the tendency to believe that effort must vary directly with the wage rate might not have persisted or remained as influential as it has. The Robbins approach indicates that there is no presumption that tax cuts (expected to endure) will increase the supply of effort. Empirical studies of some subtlety and detail are required, therefore, to ascertain the effects of such cuts and it would be surprising if they indicated a simple and uniform response. It is a great pity that in the fifty years since the article first appeared so few empirical investigations have been undertaken, and the nonsense that Robbins exposed so elegantly remains in the minds of such a wide variety of influential people.

MACROECONOMICS

Turning to his views on macroeconomics, these have shown an interesting evolution. Robbins' book *The Great Depression* (1934) is, he says, 'Something which I would willingly see forgotten'.[11] In his *Autobiography of an Economist* (1971) (a fascinating book which is beautifully written and should be read by all students) he states that he was mistaken in opposing the views of Keynes and his followers that increased public expenditure would ease the path away from the bottom of the slump. He also asks himself how he got to his erroneous position in the first place. His answer is one which some economists today might well ponder.

> The trouble was intellectual. I had become the slave of theoretical construction which, if not intrinsically invalid as regards logical consistency, were inappropriate to the total situation which had then developed and which therefore misled my judgement. I realized that these constructions led to conclusions which were highly unpalatable as regards practical action. But I was convinced that they were valid and that therefore it was my duty to base recommendations as regards policy upon them.[12]

To this quotation must be added Keynes's famous footnote, 'It is the distinction of Professor Robbins that he almost alone, continues to maintain a consistent scheme of thought, his practical conclusions belonging to the same system as his theory'.[13] It is an interesting philosophical question whether, if theory leads to conclusions which make no sense in practice, the correct response is to be 'so much the worse for theory' or 'so much the worse for practice'.

More seriously there are available two important statements by Lionel Robbins on policy at the macroeconomic level. The first was in his Marshall Lectures, *The Economic Problem in Peace and War* (1947). The significance of these lectures is mostly seen in his reiteration of the case for the decentralised free-market economy despite the apparently opposite experienced in the war. The lectures still contribute the best short (although not, of course, necessarily valid) modern statement of that position.

But at the macroeconomic level he argues that Keynes and Robertson were right in believing that the decentralised system would need to be supplemented by government actions if aggregate demand is to be maintained at an appropriate level. He says that the government must take an annual look at the relationship between likely aggregate expenditure and desired aggregate expenditure and adjust policy to bring the two into line. The objective he sets for the government is avoiding both inflation and deflation, but he is careful not to put this in terms of a policy of crudely planning for full employment. His argument here is extraordinarily prescient. First, he is worried about the statistical definition of full employment. Secondly, he believes that circumstances will arise in which unemployment will not be the result of deficient demand. His example is a remarkable one.

The changes . . . in the international conditions of supply and demand to which nearly every community is likely to be exposed, whatever its internal organisation, will not necessarily exhaust themselves without occasionally causing structural unemployment; and we are surely raising false hopes if we claim that measures acting on over-all expenditure will prevent this kind of unemployment or cure it when it occurs.[14]

His third objection concerns wages policy. He says that at high levels of activity wages will rise leading either to unemployment or inflation. 'This theoretical dilemma carries with it a corresponding dilemma for policy: in such circumstances are you to allow unemployment to develop, or are you to take steps which, if repeated, will involve a continued depreciation of the value of savings?'[15] In connection with this dilemma, he was not prepared at the time to advocate a thorough-going wages policy but wanted to wait and see what would happen in the next few years.

Subsequently his view developed but, before noting that, it is worth while considering his position on monetary matters, especially in relationship to what is called monetarism. This is best seen in his essay commenting on the Radcliffe Report (Robbins 1963). In that, while not denying the significance of a broad view of liquidity, he asserts that money in its narrower, more conventional sense is important in accounting for inflation and deflation. While money is not everything,

> in making this the pretext for relegating the supply of money to a subordinate, and even passive position, the Committee, like the Banking School and many others before them, seem to me to be in danger of an error of analytical perspective no less one-sided in pure theory and even more damaging in practice than that of those – if they exist – who ignore the short period vicissitudes of velocity and trade credit.[16]

Given that, he went on to say that the supply of money was an instrument susceptible of control, and that monetary policy was feasible and useful especially in helping to deal with inflation. He added, however, 'in the strongly inflationary conditions of the post-war period, I am clear that sole reliance on monetary policy would have been both unwise and undesirable'.[17]

It is for that kind of reason that Lionel Robbins cannot be called a 'monetarist' in the technical sense. This can be seen more clearly by examining a more recently published collection of his Speeches to the House of Lords (Robbins, 1979). In these he argues for the necessity of an incomes policy within the public sector and does not rule out an incomes policy more generally as a temporary expedient. But he argues that the main policy weapons must be fiscal and monetary policy. He also reverts to his earlier comments on the inflation–unemployment dilemma, by stating that the government should finance aggregate demand to guarantee high employment with low inflation, but not to provide the money for nominal incomes sought beyond that level.

This eclecticism based on good sense was most apparent in his speech on the counter-inflation measures of November 1972. He emphasised both demand-pull and cost-push elements in causing inflation, but drew special attention to the role of the money supply. But as a transitory device he did accept the need for the tough measures introduced by the then government to act directly on prices and incomes. The reason for this was that merely to cut back on effective demand by reducing the rate of growth of the money supply would involve too high a cost in employment and output. To quote him,

> the serious recommendation of the extreme monetarists, the sort of overtone which emerges when Mr. Enoch Powell makes one of those monolithic pronouncements on the principles of economic liberation (will) . . . usually make me want to stand on a chair and sing 'The Red Flag'. Alas! I do not think that things are as easy as the Powellite pronouncements would suggest. I do not deny . . . that inflation might be stopped by violent measures of this sort; but much else would be stopped as well.[18]

To summarise, Lionel Robbins's views on macroeconomics and policy moved, during the 1940s, close to those of Keynes. In particular, he has taken a broad view of possible instruments and a rather robust view of objectives. He has not been the sort of extremist who has thought that only one instrument was necessary and one objective desirable. On inflation, in particular, he has stressed the importance of money without going on to say that limitation of the money supply is all that is necessary. In a curious way, therefore, the views he took in the post-war period were those that Keynes himself might have put forward had he lived.

NOTES

1. Robbins (1932) p. 74.
2. Ibid. p. 100.
3. Robbins (1959), also reproduced in E. Henderson and L. Spaventa, (eds), *Guest Lectures in Economics*, Milan, 1962.
4. Ibid p. 43.
5. Robbins (1971) p. 149.

6. Robbins (1952) p. 16.
7. Keynes (1936) pp. 378–9.
8. Robbins (1952) pp. 44–5.
9. Quoted in Robbins (1952) p. 45 and p. 43 respectively.
10. Ibid p. 139.
11. Robbins (1971) p. 154. Despite this the book went into several impressions, and was assessed by *The Times* as 'one of the few books written on the economic crisis in recent years that can be described as a real intellectual achievement'.
12. Ibid p. 153.
13. Keynes (1936) p. 20.
14. Robbins (1947) p. 70.
15. Ibid p. 71.
16. Robbins (1963) p. 210.
17. Ibid p. 213.
18. In this connection David Laidler is right to remind us that Robbins was an economist who always believed that money was important, but wrong to refer to his views as 'monetarist'. Laidler (1976) p. 485.

REFERENCES

Keynes, J. M., 1936 *The General Theory of Employment, Interest and Money* (Macmillan).
Laidler, D., 1976 'Inflation in Britain: a Monetarist Perspective', *American Economic Review*.
Robbins L., 1930 'On the Elasticity of Demand for Income in Terms of Effort', *Economica*.
—— 1932 *An Essay on the Nature and Significance of Economic Science* (Macmillan).
—— 1934 *The Great Depression*, (Macmillan).
—— 1947 *The Economic Problem in Peace and War* (Macmillan).
—— 1952 *The Theory of Economic Policy in English Classical Political Economy* (Macmillan).
—— 1959 'The Present Position of Economics', *Rivista di Politica Economica*.
—— 1963 'Monetary Theory and the Radcliffe Report' reprinted in *Politics and Economics; Papers in Political Economy* (Macmillan).
—— 1971 *Autobiography of an Economist* (Macmillan).
—— 1979 *Against Inflation* (Macmillan).

# 11 The Economics of Joan Robinson

Thanos Skouras

Even before the outbreak of the Second World War, Joan Robinson had already made such contributions to economic theory that guaranteed her a place in the history of economic thought. Her book on imperfect competition and her work, in close association with Keynes, on the theory of employment and output, were at the forefront of economic thinking in these 'years of high theory' (Shackle, 1967). Her work since then has covered most aspects of economic theory culminating in her books on the analysis of growth and in her attack on the neoclassical theory of capital and interest in the 1950s and 1960s. It is impossible, in a brief paper, properly to survey Joan Robinson's work. This is not only because of its volume (her essays are collected in 1951, 1964, 1965, 1973) and variety but also because of its contrast to the dominant and familiar modes of thought in economics. As John Eatwell (1977) observes, despite the fact that

> Joan Robinson is acknowledged to be one of today's foremost economic theorists with an impressive list of path-breaking contributions to her name . . . many economists, even those who regard themselves as 'theorists', approach her writings with apprehension and confess to bewilderment. Her books and articles are often outstanding examples of English prose, and the ideas are novel and exciting, but they do not fit within the framework used by most economists to define their subject.

What I propose to do here is to concentrate on a few central aspects of Joan Robinson's work attempting to present them in as simple a manner as possible. If, as a result of this, Joan Robinson's writings are made accessible to a somewhat wider audience, this chapter will have served its purpose.

My presentation will be under the two broad headings of the Theory of Value and the Theory of Accumulation. This division of economic theory is suggested by Joan Robinson herself in the preface of her probably most important book (1956). Nevertheless, some of her central ideas are of such wide import, affecting nearly the whole of economic theory, that they cannot neatly be fitted even within these broad categories and this is occasionally reflected in my discussion.

THEORY OF VALUE

Joan Robinson's first book was an attempt to forge new tools in order to deal with deficiencies in the then prevailing theory of prices, which was essentially Marshall's formalisation by Pigou. This theory has been out of fashion with later general equilibrium theorists, but in the absence of convincing applications and any substantial contact between general equilibrium theory and the real world, it is still found in elementary textbooks and constitutes the bulk of what students learn in microeconomics courses. It is therefore instructive to examine briefly what Joan Robinson deemed to be wrong with that theory.

Under competitive conditions, each firm produces such an output that marginal cost equals price. An implication of this is that firms can never be found to operate below optimum capacity as denoted by the lowest point on their average variable cost curve. Thus, the experience of the slump when most plants were working part-time and manifestly below capacity cannot be squared with this theory.

Let us illustrate this argument by means of a simple diagram (Figure 11.1). We look at three plants and we draw their average variable cost curves since average variable cost is what they must cover to continue in operation in the short-run.

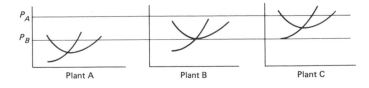

FIGURE 11.1

If price is $p_A$, then all three plants are producing well above their optimum capacity making short-period profit equal to the difference between marginal and average variable cost. If price is $p_B$, then plant C will not cover its operating costs and it will shut down. But plants A and B will still operate at or above optimum capacity. It is evident that no matter how low the price, the plants that do not shut down will always operate at or above optimum capacity. The standard competitive theory then clearly implies that, even in the short-run, under-capacity working is impossible.

But irrelevance and incongruity with observed facts was not the only problem with the competitive model. The logic of the Marshall–Pigou theory had already been criticised by Sraffa (1926). Sraffa had argued that the notions of diminishing returns and long-run supply curves that are universally upward-sloping, which were essential to that theory, could not be logically sustained. Having demonstrated that this theory is ridden with internal contradictions, he suggested, on the grounds of realism, that a new theory should recognise that a firm's size is limited not by increasing costs but rather by 'the difficulty of selling the larger quantity of goods without reducing the price'.

Joan Robinson took up this 'pregnant suggestion' (as she called it) and, in her *Economics of Imperfect Competition* (1933), she considered firms confronted by downward-sloping demand curves. For this purpose she developed the concept of the 'marginal revenue curve' which, it is not difficult to show, allows the possibility of under-capacity operation with positive short-run profits.

But though imperfect competition was more realistic than perfect competition, it was still not much more than 'a box of tools for the analytical economist'. It was essentially a refinement of the Marshall–Pigou theory that hardly stepped outside the confines of that tradition. Joan Robinson's contribution consciously steered clear of 'the fundamental problems on whose solution depends the validity of the whole supply-and-demand-curve analysis'. Thus, despite the fact that her book together with Chamberlin's *Monopolistic Competition* (1933) opened up a whole new branch of traditional price theory that has been since well established in textbooks, Joan Robinson's increasing awareness of the fundamental problems underlying the whole supply-and-demand-curve analysis and her preoccupation with Keynesian theory and the problems of the slump caused her to outgrow her book nearly as soon as she had finished it.

What then are the fundamental problems of demand-and-supply-curve analysis? For Joan Robinson the first and foremost problem is undoubtedly that of time. Demand-and-supply-curve analysis is an analogy from physical mechanics. 'For mechanical movements in space, there is no distinction between approaching equilibrium from an arbitrary initial position and a perturbation due to displacement from an equilibrium that has long been established. In economic life, in which decisions are guided by expectations about the future, these two types of movement are totally different' (Robinson, 1974). As expectations about the future are based on past experience, history plays a paramount role in determining the reactions of economic agents. This whole area is a conceptually difficult one and we can do no more here than attempt to sketch the basic problem.

The point is that in order to decide on the quantities that will be demanded or supplied at a particular price, buyers and sellers need to have a notion of normal price or at least an expectation of a normal price-range that will be established before long. Plans to buy and sell are based on such expectations which are therefore logically prior to the plans. Such expectations are themselves based on historical experience and this is one of the ways that history affects future outcomes. The other ways that history affects future events is by determining the technical conditions of production and capacities on the supply side and the consumption habits on the demand side. (The influence of existing capacities has been explained by Marshall who clearly recognised the irreversibility of the long-run supply curve). But let us return to the more fundamental former point. We can see what it entails by considering a non-equilibrium price $p_A$. $D_A$ is the quantity demanded and $S_A$ the quantity that the suppliers would be willing to sell at this price *if this were the equilibrium price* (Figure 11.2).

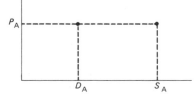

FIGURE 11.2

In the event, only $D_A$ can be sold and traditional analysis would argue that as a result of $D_A < S_A$, price will tend to fall. But if historical experience leads buyers and sellers to expect that this is an abnormally low price and that it will most likely be higher in the near future, then the price will not fall. Buyers will be willing to buy more and sellers will be willing to sell less so that the apparent initial excess of $S$ over $D$ may even be reversed. In any case, even if it is not reversed, suppliers may well be willing to hold on to their merchandise and increase their stocks on the expectation of larger gains when the price rises.

The quantity that buyers would be willing to buy and sellers willing to sell at a particular price will be different depending on whether, (1) this price is seen as the equilibrium price, (2) this price is lower than the expected normal price, or (3) the price is higher than the expected normal price. It is evident that in cases (2) and (3) the drawing of demand and supply schedules presupposes a knowledge of the equilibrium price and cannot serve for its determination. Traditional demand and supply analysis, even when enriched by reaction functions giving rise to fluctuations, is built on case (1): buyers and sellers are assumed to react as if any price that is considered might be the equilibrium price. It is in this way that their memory of the past and their expectations about the future are eliminated and it becomes possible to construct curves the intersection of which determines the equilibrium price.

The only circumstances in which it is plausible that buyers and sellers would react to a price as if it were equilibrium price, is when the market (or strictly speaking the economy) has not changed for some time and the particular price has been long-ruling. But of course for all prices other than the long-established one it still makes no sense to draw demand and supply functions without taking into account the expectations that have been formed about the normal price. It is evident that demand and supply functions that *do* take normal price expectations into account are not meant to determine the equilibrium price but to analyse disequilibrium situations. The traditional demand and supply analysis that is supposed to determine equilibrium price is even, in the circumstances of an unchanging market, quite inappropriate. Though it is true that only in these circumstances the traditional analysis will give an answer consistent with the ruling price, it is misleading to pretend that this ruling price has been determined by the intersection of the demand and supply curves. It is only when we assume that the price is given, and unchanging for some time past, that the demand and supply analysis can 'find' it. And apart from the point of intersection, the rest of the curves are still without any meaning and can serve for nothing. In short, it is only when the normal price has been long-established that the illusion of its determination by demand and supply schedules can be sustained.

Traditional theory can thus at best only deal with comparisons of different, unchanging imaginary states rather than analyse the effects of change. A system is in equilibrium only if expectations are such as to warrant it and this is likely only if it has been in equilibrium for some time. It is therefore possible to compare equilibrium positions that are similar in all but one respect, though such exercises in comparative statics cannot support any conclusions as regards the effects of change in any respect. The former does not at all involve time while in the latter time, that is historical experience and expectations about the future, cannot be ignored.

Joan Robinson's insistence on the irrelevance of theory that does not take time seriously has two critical implications. First, it constitutes a general critique of common methodological practice in economics and secondly, it is a specific critique of the nature of neoclassical theory. As regards the first, the implication is that all conclusions from comparative statics are suspect. The method of comparative statics is useful only as a preliminary exercise in the process of constructing and understanding the properties of a model. After this preliminary stage, the model must be capable of incorporating relevant historical and institutional detail if it is to serve for an analysis of historical change. And it is exactly this crucial step that neoclassical theory, in all its forms, consistently fails to make. Demand and supply analysis, both in its Marshallian partial and Walrasian general-equilibrium varieties, is constructed in a way that rules out history. Neoclassical theory could *only* be suitable for comparative statics; uncertainty about the future and the influence of institutional and historical factors require a drastic amendment of the fundamental assumptions of neoclassical theory in a manner that causes the neoclassical edifice to collapse (for a development of this theme, see Robinson, 1971).

It should be clear that the difficulties that the whole of neoclassical analysis has in dealing with time are, for Joan Robinson, much more grave than those associated with 'reswitching'[1] and 'the measurement of capital'. The latter do not challenge the inability of neoclassical theory to handle time but demonstrate that, even within its chosen field of comparative statics, the results of neoclassical theory are inconclusive and, contrary to popular opinion and textbook pronouncements, do not lend themselves to any interesting or useful generalisations.

Let us here digress briefly to consider the 'capital debate' of the 1960s in which Joan Robinson was one of the main protagonists. The start of the debate can be dated to Joan Robinson's critique of the neoclassical aggregate production function (1953–4). This was a particularly convenient construction as it clearly and simply established a number of distributional relationships in accord with basic general equilibrium neoclassical theory. In particular, it established that higher capital–labour ratios, which are expected to result in the process of accumulation, are associated with a lower rate of profit or, equivalently, that a higher wage is associated with a more capital-intensive technique. This went hand-in-hand with the notion that the rate of interest is equal to the marginal product of capital which here could be directly derived from the aggregate production function (being its first derivative with respect to capital).

The upshot of the capital debate, which lasted well into the 1960s, was a rejection of both these neoclassical views. As regards the second notion, it was shown that it was invalid to determine the rate of interest from the marginal product of capital in the production function, since the value of capital presupposes a knowledge of the interest rate. It follows that the aggregate production function had to be abandoned as a basis on which such a proposition can be made and neoclassical theorists had to retreat to general-equilibrium analysis for a defence of marginal productivity.

As regards the first view, the neoclassicals had to finally admit (Samuelson, 1966) that 'reswitching' of techniques is perfectly possible and that there is no monotonic relationship between the rate of interest and capital intensity of technique. It is therefore *not* the case that more capital-intensive techniques are generally associated with lower interest rates and neoclassical growth theory has thus lost what was perhaps its simplest and most appealing result. The consequence of this is that, even within comparative statics, neoclassical theory has little of interest to say and proves to be generally indefinite and inconclusive.

But of course Joan Robinson goes further than this. She has

always insisted that these results are simply exercises in comparative statics and that the ultimate difficulty of neoclassical theory is that it cannot transcend the limits of comparative statics. It is for this reason that she has stated 'the problem of the "measurement of capital" is a minor element in the criticism of the neo-classical doctrines' (Robinson, 1974). It is also for the same reason that she never paid too much attention to 'reswitching' though she had been aware of this possibility since her *Accumulation of Capital* (Robinson, 1956) (in which she had dubbed it the 'Ruth Cohen curiosum'). Equally, she has insisted on referring to the 'pseudo-production function' to emphasise the artificiality of a construction that involves 'a comparison of timeless equilibrium positions' rather than a tool for the analysis of 'effects to be expected from a change taking place at a particular moment'.

It should be noticed that an analysis of change that takes time and history seriously does not imply for Joan Robinson that calendar time should be introduced into one's modelling. Economic models are 'tools of analysis' or 'engines of thought' and they are not meant to faithfully replicate reality. What is important is that they are *not* in conflict with historical events and can possibly provide rough guidance to an economic historian rather than that they portray in detail actual historical events. Given this view of economic theory, the fact that calendar time is empirically observable does not mean that it is necessarily the best notion to use in the modelling of change. On the contrary, the notion of 'calendar time' is of such a low order of abstraction that it does not fit in with the other theoretical concepts that have been developed by and have, in turn, themselves formed the quite highly abstract mode of economic analysis.

Leaving aside the criticism of the neoclassical theory of price, does Joan Robinson espouse an alternative theory of value? There is little doubt that she looks with favour at the classical theory of value as interpreted by Sraffa (1960). This theory explains prices on the basis of exogenous variables that are quite different from those of the neoclassical approach. The data of classical theory are: the level and composition of output; the conditions of reproduction of commodities; the real wage rate (or the profit rate). In contrast, the neoclassical theory is built on the following data: the utility functions of individuals; the existing technology; the initial factor endowments; the distribution of factor endowments (See Eatwell, 1979).

On the basis of these two alternative sets of data, relative prices emerge in neoclassical theory as the equilibrium of the opposed forces of demand and supply and in classical theory as the long period position that will be established from the competitive tendency to a uniform rate of profits.

But despite Joan Robinson's sympathy for the classical theory, she does not see this as a properly historical theory that overcomes her fundamental criticism of the method of comparative statics. Classical theory, for Joan Robinson, also abstracts from the influence of expectations about the future and the frequent irreversibility of the outcomes of past decisions that dominate any process of change, with the consequence that it too is limited to dealing only with comparisons of stationary states. Her regard for the classical school thus seems to be founded, on the one hand, on their common criticism of and opposition to the dominant neoclassical school and, on the other, on the more positive reason that in the classical school, and especially in Marx, economic theory is not divorced from historical analysis.

Value theory has been traditionally concerned with the determination of long-run prices. But there can also be concern for the formation of prices in certain short-period situations. Of course, there is an infinity of short-runs depending on the degree of adjustment postulated, so that there can be no general theory of short-run prices, but certain short-run conditions seem to be of some relevance for the understanding of real world events. Thus Joan Robinson has been concerned with the analysis of price formation under the short-run conditions of plant, money wages and expectations all being fixed. Following Kalecki, she distinguishes between two types of markets: those in which prices tend to fluctuate depending on the state of demand and supply; and those in which prices bear a relatively stable relationship to the cost of production. The former are common for many types of primary commodities while the latter are as a rule manufactures. In industry, firms tend to set the prices of their products by adding a profit margin, reflecting their market power and the degree of competition they face, on their costs. This is a basically common-sense approach and it has been often found useful in empirical work.

In concluding this section, it should be clear that there is no theory of value that fully satisfies Joan Robinson's own criteria of a good theory. Despite her adherence to Kalecki's short-run price theory and her approval of the Classical long-run theory of prices, she notes that 'all important and interesting questions lie in the gap between the two' (Robinson, 1978, p. xx).

THEORY OF ACCUMULATION

Joan Robinson's books and articles on the theory of accumulation constitute the bulk of her work in the 1950s and early 1960s. Her objective was to incorporate Keynes' principle of effective demand into long-run growth theory. The generalisation of Keynes' theory to the long-run was first attempted by Harrod (1948) but Joan Robinson's book (1956) was not only more rounded and richer in suggestions but also contained a version of principle of effective demand that originated with Kalecki rather than Keynes.

Though Joan Robinson has always acknowledged her debt to Kalecki and has recognised Kalecki's independent discovery of the principle of effective demand and his priority of publication, her identification with Keynes and even her own claim of being a Keynesian has confused readers reared on the dominant, 'Keynesian' interpretation of Keynes's theory.[2]

For this reason, it will be useful to look in some detail at the short-run theory she employs in her work. But before we do this, let us very briefly examine the sense in which Joan Robinson is truly a disciple of Keynes.

There is no doubt that Keynes and the collective work of the Cambridge circus in the 1930s was a major influence on her thought. But despite the fact that she wrote an introductory book (Robinson, 1937) to explain and popularise Keynes' ideas, she soon took a distance from Keynes' specific analytical formulations. As Keynes himself was habitually quick to revise or even to completely abandon his own analytical formulations, this did not mean for her that she stopped being a follower of Keynes. At a deeper level the lessons of the years of her association with Keynes have never been forgotten and have been always present in her work.

What are these lessons ? They concern methodological orientation in economic theorising. First of all, economic theory must be about actual, observed phenomena and it must be of relevance to problems in the real world. This may sound obvious but if taken seriously it disqualifies a large part of economic theory. The second, and most characteristic lesson that Joan Robinson draws from Keynes, is the importance, on the one hand, of uncertainty and expectations about the future and, on the other hand, of the frequent irreversibility of past decisions. Indeed, it is this, as we have seen, that makes history an indispensable dimension of economic theorising and which constitutes the main Keynesian attribute in economic modelling. Her opposition to neoclassical theory is, like that of Keynes, a direct consequence of this. Equally, the importance attached to the short-run and to the principle of effective demand is another major consequence of this lesson. The third lesson is the need for inclusion in economic theorising of relevant institutional detail. This has been again pursued by Joan Robinson, like the previous one, to its logical conclusion. She has emphasised the importance of institutional characteristics such as property relations in the operation of an economic system and she has gone further than Keynes by systematically including in her theorising the specification of the social relations of production. The central role that both this and history have in her approach to economic theory constitutes the bridge on which she brings together Keynes and Marx. Though, in her case, first taught by Keynes, these are lessons that have been confirmed and carried further by her study of Marx.[3]

Let us now close this digression and return to Kalecki's version of the principle of effective demand that Joan Robinson employs in her work on accumulation. We will present this by means of a simple diagram that was first used in a somewhat different context in Joan Robinson (1953) but was used again in a recent assessment of Kalecki's work (Robinson, 1977).

But first let us set out the assumptions we make concerning, on the one hand, the technical conditions of production and, on the other, the social relations of production. As regards the former, we assume that productive capacity is given and does not change significantly in the period under discussion. There are two types of output: consumption goods and investment goods. These are produced by given techniques that combine labour with productive capacity in fixed proportions.

The social relations of production are typically capitalist and are characterised by the presence of three types of agents. *Firms* organise production in the pursuit of profit. *Rentiers* are the legal owners of the firms but have no direct control over the production process, all effective decisions being taken by hired managers. The rentiers' income consists of the dividends paid by the firms, the magnitude of which is determined by management. *Workers* sell their labour time to the firms for a wage.

Wages are to a large extent spent on consumption goods while a smaller proportion of profits is spent. The reason for this is not only that rentiers tend to have larger incomes and therefore can afford to save a larger proportion of them but also, and more importantly, a considerable amount of profits is retained by the firms. Firms retain profits for a variety of reasons and it is an empirical fact that in many advanced capitalist economies these constitute the bulk of savings. The firms' retention ratio is treated as an exogenous variable but total profits and the share of profits in income are endogenous variables.

The money wage rate is another exogenous variable determined by bargaining between workers and firms. Demand conditions in the labour market, the inflationary trend in the price of consumption goods as well as the degree of organisation of the workers and the behaviour of their trade unions are all factors that may influence the determination of the bargaining outcome and ought to be considered in a theory of the money wage rate.

The price level emerges from the pricing decisions of individual firms. Firms mark up average variable costs according to the competition they face. Factors such as the degree of concentration, barriers to entry and product differentiation may enter into the determination of the size of the mark-ups. Markups, therefore, reflect the 'degree of monopoly'. In our aggregate model, the 'degree of monopoly' and the average mark-ups in the two sectors are taken as exogenous variables.

Average variable costs are constant and equal to marginal costs until capacity is reached, at which point they increase sharply. Average cost, on the other hand, falls with output up to full capacity because of the existence of overhead costs. Given that the mark-up is based on average variable or marginal cost, a higher degree of plant utilisation and employment implies a higher profit per unit of output for the individual firm and a larger share of profit in national income for the economy as a whole.

In our aggregate model (Figure 11.3), since we consider a closed economy, all costs are labour costs. Imported raw materials or intermediate products that are part of the cost of domestic production need not be considered as long as we abstract from foreign trade.

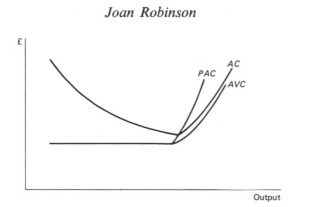

FIGURE 11.3

Given the labour cost per unit of output, which is itself dependent on the exogenous money wage rate and the technique in use, the average mark-up in each sector determines the prices of the consumption and investment goods. Given the price in the consumption goods sector and the money wage rate, the real wage emerges.

The final variable to be considered is the value of investment. Joan Robinson does not feel that there is any point in specifying an investment function since, as is evidenced by empirical observation and econometric studies, investment tends to be erratic and it cannot be reliably and systematically related to any quantifiable variable. The determinants of the propensity to accumulate need to be sought in the 'historical, political and psychological characteristics of an economy' (1962b p. 37) which shape firms' expectations of future profit, willingness to take risks and drive for growth. For this reason, investment is treated as an exogenous variable dominated by the 'animal spirits' of the business community.

Having described the assumptions that Joan Robinson makes regarding the variables which are included in her version of Kalecki's model,[4] let us now take a look at a diagram that demonstrates clearly the basic theoretical mechanism of her model (Figure 11.4).

On the $y$-axis we measure money values and on the $x$-axis both employment and consumption goods' output. It is possible to use the $x$-axis for both by choosing the labour unit so as to equal the labour time required for the production of one unit of consumption goods. Since the technique in use is given and unchanging,

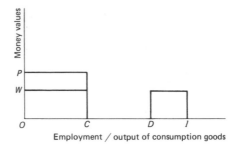

FIGURE 11.4

this presents no problem in the absence of overhead labour. In the case that there is overhead labour, the technique is specified in terms of variable rather than total labour and the labour unit is defined to equal the *variable* labour time required for the production of one unit of consumption goods. The use of a single technique in the production of consumption goods rules out the possibility of plants operating with varying efficiency. If we want to allow for this possibility, then we need to assume that the shares of different plants in total output are constant in the short-run. With this assumption, we can again define a single technique as the weighted average of the techniques in use and we can therefore again specify the labour unit so as to be able to measure *both* employment and consumption goods output on the same axis.

$OC$ is employment and output in the consumption sector, $DI$ is employment in the investment sector. We will take employment and output in the consumption sector as given provisionally. On the other hand, $DI$ is determined by the exogenously given value of investment and the mark-up in the investment-goods sector. The output of the investment-goods sector can be determined from the employment magnitude, $DI$, and the technique in use in that sector. $CD$ denotes the amount of employment that could be provided if idle productivity capacity was all put into use.

Given the money wage, the wage cost per unit of output is $OW$, the wages bill in the consumption sector is $OW \cdot OC$ and in the investment sector $OW \cdot DI$. The total demand for consumption goods is equal to the spending out of all wages and profits. Let us temporarily assume that there is no saving out of wages and no spending out of profits. Then the total demand for consumption goods is equal to the wages-bill in the consumption sector $OW \cdot OC$ *plus* the wages-bill in the investment sector $OW \cdot DI$. Placing this total demand over the output of consumption goods, $OC$, we form the rectangle $OP \cdot OC$ in which the sub-area $WP \cdot OC$ is equal to the wages bill on the investment sector, $OW \cdot OI$. $OP$ is then the price per unit of consumption-goods output that will clear the market and $PW$ is the gross profit per unit of output. $PW \cdot OC$ is the volume of gross profits made in the production of consumer goods if the price is such as to equate the total demand to the supply of consumer goods. It is evident then that gross profits in the consumption-goods sector are equal to the wage bill in the investment-goods sector. This is a most important result and will hold as long as, on the one hand, there is no saving out of wages and no spending out of profits and, on the other, the price of consumer goods is not set below the market clearing level.

It is also possible to determine the volume of total gross profits in both sectors though this is not shown in the diagram. Gross profits in the investment-goods sector are equal to the difference between the market value of investment goods and the wage-bill in that sector. Since the latter equals gross profits in the consumption-goods sector, it follows that total gross profits in both sectors equals the value of investment.

Net profits can also be determined if depreciation values are known. The latter depend on the production life of the different types of plant, the accounting conventions in use and the price of investment goods. The first two require additional exogenous information while the last one is dependent on the 'degree of monopoly' in the investment-goods sector and the associated mark-up which is an exogenous variable that we have already made use of in determining the level of employment in the investment-goods sector.

So far we have been assuming no saving out of wages and no spending out of profits. If we remove the less realistic part of this simplifying assumption and recognise that profits are at least partly spent on consumption goods, then it is clear that total demand for these goods is correspondingly increased and so is gross profit. Our results so far can be summarised by Kalecki's famous saying: 'Workers spend what they get, and capitalists get what they spend'. On the reasonable assumption that workers' savings are insignificant, capitalists' spending, whether on consumption goods in their capacity as rentier households or on investment goods in their capacity as business managers, comes back to them as profits and determines the volume and even the existence of profits.

If, in the interests of exactitude, we withdraw the assumption that all wages are spent since there are always some savings however insignificant, the qualitative change in our results is quite obvious. Saving out of wages reduces total demand for consumer goods and therefore it correspondingly reduces gross profit. Nevertheless, the diagram is not easy to use when this assumption is dropped and an algebraic analysis becomes preferable (for such an example, see Skouras, 1979).

A final endogenous variable shown in the diagram is the real wage which is equal to $OW/OP$. It should be noted that the level of the real wage, as well as the relative shares of wages and profits, and even the level of employment and outputs all crucially depend on the firms' pricing policy. Mark-ups are set according to the market circumstances facing each firm. If these are treated as exogenous, then the level of employment and output become endogenous variables. We have already treated the investment-goods sector in this way; let us now examine in more detail what an exogenous mark-up in the consumption-goods sector implies for employment and output in this sector.

The importance that pricing policy and the degree of monopoly have, not only on the real wage, but also on the determination of employment and output as well as on relative shares is illustrated in Figure 11.5. We will consider two possible mark-ups, the one implying price $OP$ and the other price $OP'$. When the mark-up is relatively high resulting in price $OP$, then the given demand arising from the investment-goods sector allows for the sale of $OC$ goods. If firms produce more than this, they will not be able to sell all their output at the profit margins implied by price $OP$.

A lower mark-up allows a higher level of sales without affecting the volume of gross profits. Since gross profits in the consumption goods sector are equal to the given wage-bill in the investment goods sector (we use here the simplifying assumption of all wages spent, all profits saved), the mark-up can only affect sales and the levels of employment and output. The given volume of gross profits as determined by the investment-goods' wage-bill is in this instance $OC-PW$ but it could equally well be, depending on the

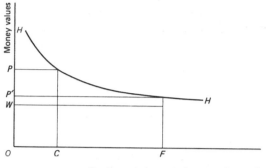

Employment / output of consumption goods

FIGURE 11.5

mark-up, any rectangular area under the rectangular hyper-bola $HH$. For instance, the relatively lower mark-up result-ing in price $OP'$ makes possible a volume of sales sufficient to warrant full employment of the available productive capacity and generates the same volume of gross profits ($OF \cdot P'W$ being equal to $OC \cdot PW$).

The model above integrates the theory of the firm, and in particular firms' pricing and output decisions, within the theory of effective demand. It shows clearly the way in which macro variables are affected by micro decisions and in this way it builds a bridge between macro-economic and micro-economic theory. It is instructive in this respect to consider the effects of a change in investment that the standard textbook treatment subsumes under the concept and analysis of the 'multiplier'. It can be immediately seen, by means of the present model, that an increase in investment will give rise to increased profits but the effect on employment and output will depend on the reaction of the corporate sector to the increase in demand. The standard multiplier is based on the assumption that firms, when faced with an increase in demand, expand production without altering their prices; another possible response, under quite plausible assump-tions regarding firm behaviour, is that both output and prices will go up. The value of the multiplier thus is also clearly shown to depend on microeconomic behaviour and, in particular, on firms reactions to changes in the state of demand.

This model is used by Joan Robinson to generate a variety of growth paths given, on the one hand, the desire of firms to grow (resulting from their 'animal spirits') and, on the other hand, the feasible rate of growth under the ruling conditions of the growth of population and technical knowledge. The analytical typology that she thereby produces is extremely rich and goes under such colourful names as: golden age, limping golden age, leaden age, restrained golden age, galloping platinum age, creeping platinum age, bastard golden age, bastard platinum age. The growth path that neoclassical growth theory is concerned with, that is full-employment steady growth, is only the special case of 'a golden age', dubbed so 'to indicate its mythical nature'. In contrast to this, Joan Robinson's typology emphasises the checks to growth, the inevitable imbalances, and the inherent instability of the system, and analyses their consequences. This analysis, which cannot be briefly summarised and will not be pursued here, abounds in interesting insights and contains all the important results of neoclassical growth theory transposed to a Keynesian or Kaleckian theoretical setting that is firmly based on the principle of effective demand. As a consequence, not only does it put such results in their proper perspective but it also makes a stab at an out-of-equilibrium, more realistic (Joan Robinson would call it 'historical') analysis that never loses sight of the Keynesian principle that capitalist enterprise 'cannot be relied on, unassisted, either to achieve stability in the short run or to maintain an adequate rate of growth in the long run' (Robinson, 1962b, p. 87).

CONCLUDING COMMENT

The foregoing account of Joan Robinson's work concentrated only on certain central aspects of her approach to economic theory. But her contributions to both economic as well as social theory (Robinson, 1970) are numerous and wide-ranging. In Samuelson's words (Samuelson, 1975), 'economics owes much to Joan Robinson for her many contributions across the whole spectrum of the subject: imperfect competition, Keynesian macroeconomics, international trade, Marxian-analysis contributions and critiques, growth theory, economic philosophy, and much more'.

Joan Robinson has two unique distinctions in the economics profession. She is the only great economist that has ever lived who is not a man. She is also the only great living economist who has not been awarded the Nobel prize. These two are the great scandals of the economics profession.

## NOTES

1. (Editor's note) The reswitching phenomenon needs a note of explanation. According to Joan Robinson and Piero Sraffa, a central feature of neoclassical explanations of income distribution (which explain income distribution by reference to marginal productivity of factors of production) is the view that there is some way in which one production technique can be described as more 'capital intensive' or 'roundabout' than another. A corollary of this is that at high ratios of capital rentals to wage rates one technique – the 'labour-intensive' technique – will be cheaper than the other, and therefore selected in preference to it. As wage rates rise relative to the return on capital, however, the advantage of this technique is eroded and eventually there is a 'switch' of techniques: the capital-intensive technique becomes the least-cost method of production. It is essential in order for the neoclassical system to be determinate that there should be only one wage-rental ratio at which such a switch occurs. However Sraffa (1960) has shown that when alternative techniques are examined in terms of dated streams of labour – on the lines of classical political economy – the possibility emerges of a 'reswitch'. This is a case where a technique with a particular pattern of labour inputs is chosen at a low wage-rental ratio, rejected at intermediate ratios, and is chosen again when wages have risen very high in relation to capital rentals.
2. For an influential distinction between 'Keynesian' and Keynes's theory, see Leijonhufvud (1968).
3. See Robinson (1942) for an assessment of Marx from a Keynesian perspective.
4. See Kalecki (1968) and his collection of essays (1971), which contains the most important elements of his model.

## REFERENCES

Chamberlin, E. 1933 *The Theory of Monopolistic Competition* (Harvard University Press).

Eatwell J. 1977 'Joan Robinson: Portrait', *Challenge*, vol. 20, no. 1.

—— 1979 *Theories of Value, Output and Employment*, (Thames Papers in Political Economy).

Harrod, R. F., 1948 *Towards a Dynamic Economics* (Macmillan).

Kalecki, M., 1968 'The Marxian Equations of Reproduction and Modern Economics', *Social Science Information*, vol. 7.

—— 1971 *Essays on the Dynamics of the Capitalist Economy* (Cambridge University Press).

Leijonhufvud, A., 1968 *On Keynesian Economics and the Economics of Keynes* (Oxford University Press).

Robinson, J., 1933 *The Economics of Imperfect Competition* (Macmillan).

—— 1937 *Introduction to the Theory of Employment* (Macmillan) (2nd edition 1969).

—— 1942 *An Essay on Marxian Economics* (Macmillan) (2nd edn 1966).

—— 1951 *Collected Economic Papers – Volume One* (Basil Blackwell).

—— 1953 *The Rate of Interest and Other Essays* (Macmillan) (2nd edn 1979 under the new title *The Generalisation of the General Theory and other Essays*).

—— 1956 *The Accumulation of Capital* (Macmillan) (3rd edn 1969).

—— 1960 *Exercises in Economic Analysis* (Macmillan).

—— 1962a *Economic Philosophy* (C. A. Watts).

—— 1962b *Essays in the Theory of Economic Growth* (Macmillan).

—— 1964 *Collected Economic Papers – Volume Two* (Basil Blackwell).

—— 1965 *Collected Economic Papers – Volume Three* (Basil Blackwell).

—— 1966a *Economics – An Awkward Corner* (Allen & Unwin).

—— 1966b *The New Mercantilism: an Inaugural Lecture* (Cambridge University Press).

—— 1970 *Freedom and Necessity: an Introduction to the Study of Society* (Allen & Unwin).

—— 1971 *Economic Heresies: Some Old-fashioned Questions In Economic Theory* (Macmillan).

—— 1973 *Collected Economic Papers – Volume Four* (Basil Blackwell).

—— 1974 *History versus Equilibrium* (Thames Papers in Political Economy).

—— 1976 *Economic Management in China* (Anglo-Chinese Educational Institute).

—— 1977 'Michal Kalecki on the Economics of Capitalism', *Oxford Bulletin of Economics and Statistics*, vol. 39, No. 1.

—— 1978 *Contributions to Modern Economics* (Basil Blackwell).

—— 1979 *Aspects of Development and Underdevelopment* (Cambridge University Press).

Robinson, J. and Eatwell, J., 1973 *An Introduction to Modern Economics* (McGraw-Hill).

Samuelson, P. A., 1966 'A Summing-up', *Quarterly Journal of Economics*.

—— 1975 'Steady-State and Transient Relations: A Reply on Reswitching', *Quarterly Journal of Economics*, Feb.

Shackle, G. L. S., 1967 *The Years of High Theory: Invention and Tradition in Economic Thought 1926–1939* (Cambridge University Press).

Skouras, T., 1979 'A Post-Keynesian Alternative to Keynesian Macromodels', *Journal of Economic Studies*, vol. 6, no. 2, Nov.

Sraffa, P., 1926 'The Laws of Returns Under Competitive Conditions', *Economic Journal*.

—— 1960 *Production of Commodities by Means of Commodities* (Cambridge University Press).

# 12 Paul Samuelson and the Scientific Awakening of Economics[1]

Adrian Kendry

He who goes out each morning to invent the wheel furthers his vanity more than his locomotion.

> *Paul Anthony Samuelson,*
> *Foundations of Economic Analysis*
> (Japanese edn, 1967) Foreword.

## PAUL THE POLYMATH

The death of Keynes in 1946 marked the end of the era of British supremacy in economic thought, an era stretching back to Adam Smith. The inheritance passed to the United States of America and the mantle descended upon Paul Samuelson. Thus, the passing of one great Cambridge economist was accompanied by the emergence of another, for Cambridge, Massachusetts has been the intellectual home of Samuelson since the mid-thirties. As part of a community noted for its intellectual leanings Cambridge contains, in particular, two distinguished institutions of research and scientific training – Harvard University and the Massachusetts Institute of Technology. In 1935, at the age of twenty, Samuelson made his way to Harvard where, for five years, he was taught economics that was truly iconoclastic. The long established modes of economic analysis, focusing upon a perfectly competitive, supply-determined world of full employment, gave way to the heresies of monopolistic/imperfect competition and the Keynesian Revolution. Samuelson assimilated these heterodox ideas fully, but the originality and importance of his

219

work stems from the manner in which he harnessed the other shockwave to hit economics – the mathematical revolution. In 1940 Samuelson moved to MIT and it is highly appropriate that, since then, he has been associated with this institution, renowned for its contributions to the natural sciences, for Samuelson has done more than any other economist to elevate economic analysis to a scientific plane. In the eyes of many of his colleagues, Samuelson is regarded as the doyen of American economists. Moreover, he commands the respect of generations of students and the public in general. Articles in 'Newsweek' and 'The New York Times' have identified him in a manner rivalled only by Milton Friedman among contemporary economists. The comprehensive and comprehensible textbook *Economics*, first published in 1948, has recently run to an eleventh edition.[2] Among fellow economists, Samuelson's stature is founded upon the quantity and quality of scientific papers published since 1937; up until 1979, the total stood at just over three hundred. In view of this prolific and diverse output (which does not include the seminal work *Foundations of Economic Analysis* (1947), nor the contributions to Dorfman, Samuelson and Solow (1958)), it is not surprising that Samuelson has received numerous accolades during his career, from both within and outside the economics profession. The crowning moment of his career came in 1970 when he became the second (and first American) Nobel Memorial Prize winner in Economics, an award made for the development of dynamic and static methods in economic theory and his contributions to the heightening of analytical awareness. What is quite remarkable about Samuelson is his refusal to sit back on his laurels; in the decade that followed, not only was his scholarly output maintained, but several new and important areas of enquiry were embarked upon. Putting aside, for the moment, any debate about content, Samuelson's writing is invariably impressive because of the literacy, wit, urbanity and mathematical sophistication that are displayed.

> Possibly I would have done well in any field of applied science or as a writer, but certainly the blend of economics of analytical hardness and humane relevance was tailor-made for me or I for it (1972).

Samuelson's boundless energy and enthusiasm for economics stems from a deep and passionate commitment to the understanding of economic behaviour in the mixed economies of the West. Samuelson's love affair with economic science has been a lasting one; the purpose of this essay is to reveal the origins and evaluate the progeny of this extraordinary symbiosis.

## SLEEPING BEAUTY AND THE DOUBLE KISS

Economics was a sleeping princess waiting for the invigorating kiss of Maynard Keynes . . . but . . . economics was also waiting for the invigorating kiss of mathematical methods (Samuelson, 1972).

The attack by Keynes in the 1930s upon the orthodox neo-classical theory of employment brought about a revolution in economic thinking and policy. If, for many economists, the message of state intervention and the control of aggregate demand was a difficult one to accept, it had, at least, the merit of being presented in a literary, although highly complex form and, as such, could readily be discussed and disputed within academic journals and the serious press. The mathematical revolution in economics during the thirties and forties offered no such consolation and brought despair to those who, having struggled to absorb Keynesian principles, were confronted with the transformation of new and old theories into mathematical form. Samuelson's role in this revolution was crucial, for although mathematical arguments had been employed by economists, such as Cournot, Walras, Pareto, Edgeworth and Fisher, in the nineteenth and early twentieth centuries, the use of mathematics in economics had been essentially piecemeal and ad hoc. Drawing upon an education that included formal training in advanced mathematics and the physical sciences, Samuelson set out to reveal the common mathematical structure which underpinned disparate areas of economics such as consumer behaviour, international trade and Keynesian theory. The debate between Keynes and the neoclassical orthodoxy concerning the deficiencies of macroeconomic theory tended to obscure the fact that economic theory as a whole was accompanied by analytical methods that were fuzzy and unsystematic. In attempting to rectify this, Samuelson has taken the stance of economist *qua* scientist; the scientific awakening experienced by economics, as a result, has been far-reaching and profound.

It is often said that PhD dissertations come and go, but that some live on for ever. The latter is certainly the case with Samuelson's prize-winning dissertation, completed in 1941 at Harvard, and published as *Foundations of Economic Analysis* in 1947. Samuelson's own affection for this piece of work has not diminished through the years, not surprisingly, since it remains a classic statement of the mathematical foundations of economic theory. It is worth noting here that Samuelson has cautioned against the view that accomplished mathematics necessarily implies accomplished economics. However, the presentation of an economic argument in laboured prose, instead of simple mathematical concepts, involves 'mental gymnastics of a peculiarly depraved type' (1947).

The objective of *Foundations* was to cleanse economic analysis of errors perpetuated through economic theorems which are imprecisely formulated and operationally meaningless.[3] This is the crux of Samuelson's scientific work and since controversy has surrounded the notion of operationally significant (i.e. empirically verifiable) theorems, it will be useful to examine this issue in some detail a little later on. Undeniably, the mathematical revolution swept all before it. Instruction at undergraduate and graduate level in the USA and UK has increasingly emphasised a knowledge of differential and integral calculus and linear algebra as a prerequisite for the understanding of micro-economic and macro-economic theory. Although a substantial time lag can exist, this trend reflects the increasing use of mathematics in articles in professional economic journals, particularly American ones.[4] The intellectual osmosis that has brought this about is clear: the current generation of professors and lecturers were schooled by mathematical revolutionaries such as Samuelson and, accordingly, conduct their own teaching and research in the *lingua franca* of mathematics. Hence, each new cohort entering the economics profession exhibits more and more sophisticated technical skills in mathematics (and statistics), thereby increasing the average level of competence and likelihood of mathematical methods being employed. The desirability of this state of affairs can be called into question on a number of grounds:

(i) Mathematical symbolism may disguise inadequate economics. Samuelson holds no brief for mathematical skills that are not accompanied by sound economic reasoning.

(ii) Those economists who, for reasons of age, fear or lack of opportunity, have not acquired mathematical fluency, have been confronted with serious problems of technical obsolescence. Insofar as this has resulted in such economists seeking sanctuary in the less technically demanding regions of the discipline, the breakdown of communication between the mathematically and non-mathematically inclined has intensified.

(iii) The extent to which mathematics imposes rigour rather than relevance, has been a much-debated question in the 1970s (Leontief, 1970; Gordon 1976). It is argued that the rigour of sophisticated mathematical formulation is inappropriate to a discipline such as economics, where the datum is incomplete and experimental methods are unreliable. This contrasts with the natural sciences where the 'hardness' of data and consistency of experimental method, permit the sophisticated use of mathematics.

Samuelson is well aware of criticisms of this kind and his work constitutes a spirited defence of the role of mathematics in economics. Mathematical formulation, argues Samuelson, can clarify the essential structure and properties of a model or argument. Keynes, with his suspicion of mathematical economics, avoided the mathematical presentation of complex ideas in the *General Theory of Employment, Interest and Money* (1936). In contrast, Samuelson reasons that subsequent mathematical interpretation probably assisted Keynes as much as anybody in understanding the significance of this book. Unlike the work of many mathematical economists, Samuelson's writings combine mathematical analysis with geometric and verbal clarity in such a way as to keep open (in all but his most recondite papers) the channels of communication to readers with little mathematical ability. Concerning the question of rigour and relevance, Samuelson has argued that the rigour of mathematical argument is appropriate insofar as it facilitates the development of propositions or theorems in economic theory that are meaningful in the sense of being empirically refutable. Unlike Physics and Chemistry, where the logic of scientific procedure is well established, economics has need of careful methodological discussion. As far as Samuelson is concerned, it is vital that the classification of procedures accompanying the construction of operationally meaningful propositions in economics, should be as clear and unambiguous as possible. Insofar as mathematics, as language, can sharply define such propositions, it is fully justified. Samuelson understands that the refutation of these propositions involves considerable philosophical problems as well as, perhaps, only being possible under certain ideal experimental conditions. He, himself, has not entered into the world of econometrics in order to specify suitable tests that might establish the relevance of the rigorous propositions he has advanced; by responding to intellectual comparative advantage, Samuelson is prepared to practise what he preaches! Although this has, undoubtedly, disappointed those who, with regard to his stature as an economist, have enjoined him to enter the statistical fray, Samuelson's failure to satisfy such aspirations cannot diminish the importance of his contributions to the development of a logical and consistent scientific method in economics.

COD-LIVER OIL AND METHODOLOGY

The old-fashioned virtues of administering cod-liver oil to children, as a means of correcting vitamin deficiencies, have been generally forgotten in the affluent West. The medicine might have been unpleasant, but it was good for you! The gradual neglect of methodological and philosophical considerations within economics has, similarly, deprived many students of distasteful but essential knowledge. The deficiencies are, often, readily apparent. What had disturbed Samuelson, in this respect, is the damage caused by the uncritical (or unknowing) acceptance of the plausible methodology of Friedman and the Chicago School.[5] Friedman's well-known view (1953) is that economic science advances through positive economics – the formulation of hypotheses that are to be judged according to the precision and scope of their conformity with the evidence of the predictions that the theory provides. Insofar as this mirrors the search of Karl Popper

(Magee, 1973) for a method of distinguishing science from non-science and echoes his recommendations that theories should be formulated unambiguously in order that they should be susceptible to refutation, Friedman's view is unexceptional.[6] However, Friedman continues by arguing that it is of no consequence nor relevance whether the assumptions behind a theory are unrealistic and that, in general, the greater the fruitfulness of a theory then, necessarily, the more unrealistic the assumptions.

Samuelson's response to this has been quite unequivocal; to regard a theory as all the better for its shortcomings is a 'monstrous perversion of science'. In describing the position adopted by Friedman above as the 'F-twist', Samuelson drew attention to the empirical invalidity of theorems deduced from counter-factual hypotheses. Perhaps the most important example of such a counter-factual hypothesis would be the perfectly competitive *laissez faire* model of economics that Friedman has consistently supported over the years. But, in criticising Friedman, is Samuelson inadvertently criticising himself? It has been suggested by Machlup (1964) that the 'F-twist' might also be described as the 'S-twist' since the operationally meaningful theorems that Samuelson derives are, of a necessity, empirically invalid since they draw upon unrealistic assumptions. The role of such theorems might then be said to illuminate the divergence between the predictions of a hypothesis and observed reality, by reference to the departure of the assumptions from real world conditions. For example, does Samuelson's famous theorem (1948, 1949) that the perfect mobility of commodities under free trade will equalise the rewards to factors of production in a two-region (USA and Europe), two-commodity, two-factor model (with no factor movement but partial specialisation according to the law of comparative advantage) fall into the 'F-twist'? Samuelson's response was that although neither the assumptions nor conclusions were empirically valid (when measured against the complexity of the real world), the accurate prediction of the theorem reflected the realism of the model, *viz*: the movement of goods by trade would improve European living standards by nearly as much as large-scale emigration. If there is a suspicion of hand-waving here, it is undeniable that the logic Samuelson has brought to bear on the discussion of economic methodology has yielded some extremely interesting concepts.

MAXIMISING AND THE LE CHATELIER PRINCIPLE

Samuelson's perception of the affinity between physical and economic science has led him to assign crucial importance to the following statements, in deriving meaningful theorems:

(i) Individual economic units behave, in bringing about equilibrium solutions, *as if* they are maximising agents. The equilibrium paradigm has dominated economic thought since the eighteenth century, most notably in the familiar mechanical form, as articulated by the 'Marginalist' School of Economics in the late nineteenth century. The view that this paradigm represents a teleological, ahistorical device which fails to recognise the irreversibility of economic processes, is one that continues to be propagated (Veblen, 1919) (Georgescu-Roegen, 1978). The strength of such criticism has partially been dissipated by Samuelson's revelation of the symmetry of behaviour between natural and economic science.

(ii) As economic models become increasingly complex, with time, as a variable, being explicitly introduced, often it will not be possible to treat such models as though some optimisation procedure is inherently at work. Nevertheless, the careful specification of the dynamic properties of an economic model enables the economist to analyse the stability of equilibrium.

What this amounts to is that operationally meaningful theorems require comparative static propositions (e.g. if a tax is imposed upon a producer, the price of the commodity will move in a specified direction) in order that their empirical validity/invalidity can be judged (eschewing the complications of the 'F-twist'). Such propositions can be tested by deriving the conditions for stability of an economic model, so that if the model was disturbed by some exogenous shock, adjustment towards a new equilibrium would or would not take place according to the numerical values of the slopes of the relevant functions.

The interest shown by Samuelson in the Maximum Principle is amply demonstrated in his papers on economics. He has shown that, just as

often the physicist gets a better, a more economical, description of nature if he is able to formulate the observed laws by a maximum principle, the economist is able to get a better, a more economical, description of economic behaviour from the same device (1971a).

This is not to imply that Isaac Newton's proverbially falling apple deliberately chose a trajectory of descent that minimised the integrand of the square of its instantaneous speed less some linear function of its position, for every moment of descent from the time of release to the time of inertia. But to describe the trajectory *as though* this was a minimising problem that was being solved, provides a useful heuristic method for the formulation of predictable regularities in nature. More importantly, it gives rise to refutable hypotheses on observable facts. Samuelson's most celebrated application of this idea occurs with his theory of 'Revealed Preference' (1938). Samuelson's concern was the emancipation of demand theory from the psychological restrictions of introspection and maximisation imposed on the consumer by the theory of utility. To deduce, from indifference curve theory, that what the consumer purchases is what he prefers and, with the assumption of maximising, what he purchases maximises his psychic satisfaction, rapidly leads to a tautology and does not give rise to refutable hypotheses. In formulating the 'Revealed Preference' approach, Samuelson developed a theory that was subject to empirical refutation, through postulating consistency of consumer choice.

Suppose a consumer buys a bundle $Q^A$ of two commodities 1 and 2, $Q_1^A$ and $Q_2^A$ representing the amount purchased of 1 and 2 when the prices of the two commodities are $P_1^A$ and $P_2^A$. Total expenditure is $P^A Q^A$ ($\equiv P_1^A Q_1^A + P_2^A Q_2^A$). If another 'bundle' of commodities 1 and 2, $Q_B$, could have been purchased by the consumer at the prices at which $Q_A$ was chosen but was not, it follows that $P^A Q^B \leqq P^A Q^A$, i.e. $Q^A$ is at least as expensive as $Q^B$ but, in being chosen, is 'revealed' to be preferred. Samuelson's 'weak' axiom of revealed preference asserted that consistency required that once $Q^A$ was 'revealed' as being preferred, $Q^B$ could never turn the tables and be 'revealed' as the preferred bundle.

The only conceivable way in which $Q^B$ *could* be revealed as being preferred, is if $P^B Q^A \leqq P^B Q^B$. (Some other price situation when the consumer buys $Q^B$ although $Q^A$ could be afforded.) For this case to be denied by the weak axiom, logically it must be the case that $P^B Q^A > P^B Q^B$. This is illustrated in Figure 12.1.

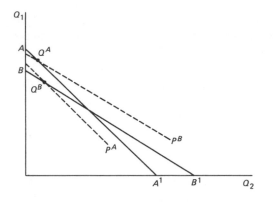

FIGURE 12.1    *The weak axiom of revealed preference*

A serious objection to the operational meaningfulness of this theory has been raised by Bharadwaj (1968). First, given that the observed choices would be separated over time, can it be valid to interpret two 'revealed choices', at two different points in time, as arising from price changes only, *ceteris paribus*? Secondly, the breakdown of consistency of choice would be attributed to changing tastes; economists have been reluctant, traditionally, to discuss the formation of tastes (Kendry, 1979) and even more reluctant to formulate testable hypotheses regarding taste formation (McCain, 1979).

Nevertheless, the 'revealed preference' theorem can be thought of in the context of implicit maximising (although, equally, consumer choice could be attributed to psychological impulses). A fascinating further application of this idea to economics comes from the Le Chatelier–Samuelson principle of thermodynamics. The principle has two parts: first, a change in the external conditions of a system will cause the equilibrium of that system to adjust as though it were minimising the impact of the change. Secondly, every additional constraint imposed upon the system will reduce the magnitude of change.

To illustrate the first part, suppose that an observer, focusing upon an imperfectly competitive firm, wished to determine the effect of a price change in one of the firm's inputs ($P_i$) upon the amount demanded of that input ($V_i$) *ceteris paribus*. Then, given that the Total Revenue function satisfies certain mathematical properties, to treat the firm as a profit-maximiser will give rise to the result that $\Delta P_i \Delta V_i < 0$, i.e. an increase in the price if the *i*th input, holding all other input prices constant, will lead to a reduction in the quantity demanded of the *i*th input by the firm. The point that Samuelson makes here is not that the typical firm maximises profits, but that the maximising paradigm enables the economist to formulate a proposition in comparative statics that can be defined as operationally meaningful. In the example given, the negative relationship between the price and the quantity demanded of the input implies, and is implied by, the firm's reacting as though it were minimising the loss of profit.

The second part of the proposition is of considerable importance to economics. If, for simplicity, there are only two inputs, land and labour, both being required in production, the Le Chatelier–Samuelson principle (Figure 12.2) asserts that the reduction in the quantity demanded of labour, resulting from an increase in the price of labour, will, when the *price* of land is held constant, be greater than the reduction when the *quantity* of land is held constant.

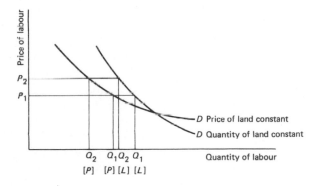

FIGURE 12.2    *The Le Chatelier–Samuelson principle and the responsiveness of demand to varying constraints*

The fixed supply of land case provides a physical constraint upon the firm that reduces the elasticity of demand for labour. In general, the principle says that the fewer the constraints, the more elastic is demand. It is interesting to note that this principle is not just confined to maximising procedures of the classical calculus type, but is equally relevant to linear programming optimisation (Samuelson, 1958). Samuelson has shown that the famous dietary problem of minimising the cost of nutrient intake subject to minimum daily requirements of various nutrients, also illustrates the Le Chatelier–Samuelson principle. For example, increasing the calorie requirement will, *ceteris paribus*, increase the implied cost (i.e. shadow price) of calories. Furthermore, adding another food to the required menu will reduce the rate at which the shadow price increases.

### DYNAMICS AND THE CORRESPONDENCE PRINCIPLE

The previous discussion concerning the usefulness of the Le Chatelier–Samuelson principle in deriving comparative static theorems, was predicated upon a knowledge of the dynamic properties of the model of the imperfectly competitive firm and the assumption that the firm operated under conditions of stability. Samuelson has named the fundamental relationship between static and dynamic analysis, the 'Correspondence Principle'. In giving this name, Samuelson has drawn, yet again, upon his scientific intellectual capital. As enunciated by the Danish physicist, Niels Bohr, in the 1920s the correspondence principle requires that new theories should also explain all of the phenomena for which a preceding theory was valid. Samuelson's adaptation stipulated that the 'new' theory of dynamics, brought about by examining the behaviour of a model in disequilibrium situations, would adjust over time in such a manner as to restore the equilibrium properties of the 'old' static theory. For this hypothesis of stability to be valid, the slopes of the various functions within the model must conform to certain magnitudes, magnitudes which are subject to empirical corroboration.

> By investigating the (sufficient) conditions for stability in theoretical models, it is therefore often possible to obtain the information necessary to determine the sign of the effects of a parameter shift in a comparative statics experiment (Samuelson, 1947).

The correspondence principle, therefore, emphasises the importance of the dynamic properties of, for example, a market model with Walrasian price adjustment. If such a market is in disequilibrium (see Figure 12.3b), the market clears through the assumption that excess demand/supply leads to a price increase/fall. It can be demonstrated (Figure 12.3a) that the sufficient condition for the market to have stable equilibrium is that the absolute value of the slope of the demand function should be less than the absolute value of the slope of the supply function. (Note that this allows for the supply function to be negatively sloped.) In such a case, the comparative static exercise of seeing what happens to price as demand increases, yields a 'normal' positive relationship.

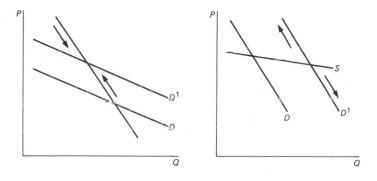

FIGURE 12.3a  *Stability of Wal-rasian adjustment*     FIGURE 12.3b  *Instability of Wal-rasian adjustment*

Does this example of the correspondence principle tie in with the Maximum principle? The answer is yes, in the sense that 'lying behind' the demand curve is the assumption that the consumer behaves as if intent upon maximising his satisfaction.

Samuelson's original contributions to the field of dynamics and maximising have gone far beyond this simple case. One of his most ambitious undertakings has been the attempt to apply the type of optimal control techniques employed in lunar rocket missions (the determination of an optimal trajectory over time, given initial payload, thrust and terminal descent) to the derivation of intertemporal paths of production that satisfy the usual microeconomic efficiency conditions and the intemporal paths of consumption that are optimal in the sense of yielding maximum rates of consumption per head over time. In negotiating the mathematical hazards of intertemporal optimal growth, Samuelson made some interesting conjectures about turnpikes (1958). All Americans know that should Paul Samuelson plan a West Coast lecture tour, beginning in Los Angeles, the short drive from Cambridge to the Massachusetts Turnpike is the only part of the journey, other than the concluding short distance off the highway into Los Angeles that has to be made away from the optimal, uninterrupted path, that comprises a succession of turnpikes and interstate highways. Could the same kind of procedure be applicable to the problem of formulating optimal growth policies in an economy?[7] Samuelson's answer was, in principle, yes;

> to develop a country most efficiently, under certain circumstances it should proceed rather quickly toward the configuration of maximum balanced growth, catch a ride so to speak on this fast turnpike and then at the end of the twenty year plan move off to its final goal . . . as the horizon becomes large, you spend an indefinitely large fraction of your time within a small distance of the turnpike (Samuelson, 1971a).

It would be foolish to pretend that this avenue of Samuelson's work gives rise to operationally meaningful theorems with any degree of ease; the specification problems are daunting, to say the least. Nevertheless, some attempt has been made at examining Soviet economic development in the context of turnpikes. Finally, in this section, it must be pointed out that the determination of stability conditions need not be associated with maximising behaviour. Samuelson's famous demonstration of the interaction between the multiplier and the accelerator (1939) and the conditions under which the time-path of national income would exhibit convergent or divergent fluctuations, is a case in point.

THE FUNDAMENTALS OF PAUL SAMUELSON

'A great man is a great nuisance' runs an old Chinese proverb and, in the sense that it is difficult to adequately portray all of his ideas and contributions to economics in an essay of this length, this is true of Samuelson. It is clear that he has been a fence-builder, trying to impose discipline on the science of economics. Rather like the use of barbed wire in preventing the encroachment of cattle farmers upon sheep farmers (and vice versa) and quietening the range wars in the old American West, Samuelson's 'operationally significant' economics has imposed internal discipline and acted as a restraint (with certain conspicuous exceptions!) upon those who would invade the domain of sociological and political enquiry. If Leon Walras, by virtue of his general equilibrium system, deserved the accolade of the 'Isaac Newton' of economics, Samuelson, by virtue of his contributions to the unity of dynamic and static methods within economics, has a claim upon the epithet of Einstein. The following themes emanate from his work and enable us to define, more sharply, the man and his ideas.

(i) Samuelson's knowledge of the genealogy of economics is both immense and profound. As he has commented, this reflects the fact that his bloodlines would do credit to the daughters of the American revolution. Having distinguished mentors (e.g. Schumpeter, Knight, Viner, Leontief and Hansen) clearly bestows an advantage on a student, but when he produces distinguished pupils of his own (e.g. Solow, Mundell and Bhagwati), the stimulus obviously has not been one-sided. Furthermore, Samuelson is a consummate scholar who has, no more, no less, devoted himself daily over the years, to the study of this 'hard' discipline. The encyclopaedic knowledge that Samuelson possesses could be wielded as a weapon of intimidation; instead, Samuelson has used this knowledge constructively, as the next point makes clear.

(ii) Samuelson's disdain for spurious originality has meant that some of his work is characteristic of a brilliant expositor, rather than original thinker, yet a proper concept of originality is crucial to an epistemological understanding of any science, including economics. 'There is nothing new under the sun' runs the old adage and, in revealing the contributions of, *inter alia*, Wicksell and Lindahl to the theory of public expenditure and collective goods, Samuelson seemingly qualifies his own work (1954, 1958). However, as is often the case, his contribution sheds light on the opaqueness of the accumulated wisdom of interpretations and assessments. In other cases, the penetrating role of mathematics is evident (for example, the mathematical derivation of multiplier, accelerator, stability conditions that had been alluded to verbally, by Alvin Hansen, the architect of American 'Keynesianism'). Intellectual integrity of the kind that Samuelson displays provides a salutary lesson for those who dispute the value of history in the teaching of economics. Intellectual candour is also a welcome quality and, on a number of occasions, Samuelson has generously admitted the error of his ways. Thus, for example, in the, by now, infamous debate between the two 'Cambridge Schools', concerning the measurement, valuation and theory of capital, Levhari and Samuelson, (1966) confessed that a proposition that denied the reswitching, at low rates of interest, of a technique that had also been the most profitable at high rates of interest, in an indecomposable economy, was completely wrong. Insofar as this resulted in an obsessive study of, and exaggerated claim for, the importance of the pathological case of reswitching, Samuelson might be said to have had the last laugh. However, only the completely biased would deny the value of Samuelson's expository paper on reswitching, published contemporaneously with the admission of error. Other recent cheerful confessions would include the recognition of the validity of Ohlin's *partial* factor-price-equalisation theorem of international trade (Samuelson, 1971b), an interesting example, in the context of the optimum growth rate for population, of Samuelson, for once, failing to specify sufficiently carefully the appropriate conditions for an unambiguous maximum.

(iii) Samuelson's description of economics as the science of the bourgeoisie does not represent an apologia for capitalism. As he has stated on many occasions, his overriding commitment is to the understanding of the behaviour of the 'mixed' capitalist economies. For Samuelson, this means understanding the manner in which individuals respond to prices, markets and the impact of government intervention (although much of Samuelson's work is cast in the methodologically individualist framework, he is not unaware of the economic power exerted by the family and other groups). Samuelson's textbook *Economics* epitomises this approach and is, perhaps, with 10-million copies sold in many languages, the most influential piece of literature, for extolling the *net* benefits of the capitalist system, ever to be published.[8] When Samuelson reflects that he would undertake whatever preparation was necessary to understand the workings of the capitalist economy, the fact that, by and large, this does not include the study of Marxian economics is because, for the most part, Samuelson identifies the operation of Soviet-type economies as containing little of economic interest, owing to the virtual absence of the bourgeois phenomena of markets and prices. Naturally, Samuelson's academic stance, as represented in *Economics*, invites the criticism that it conceals more than it reveals about the state of contemporary capitalism. The two-volume 'Anti-Samuelson' (Linder and Sensat, 1977) is a Marxist critique based on demonstrating the internal contradiction of the bourgeois theoretical approach contained in Samuelson's text. Samuelson, of course, would deny the existence of any logical contradictions in his work and point out that to criticise his economics for being bourgeois is to criticise it for being economics! It is another matter to criticise contemporary economics for being too narrow a searchlight on the unexplained recesses of the human condition and, in this respect, Samuelson is quite amenable to the incorporation of political, sociological and psychological enquiry into his assessment of wider social problems. However, this satisfies neither those who see economics of this kind as fragmented, teleological and non-evolutionary, failing to provide the foundations for a unified social science, nor those who see such economics as being incapable of explaining the historical development of capitalism, that arises from the inevitable contradictions between the re-lations and forces of production.

(iv) Whereas Samuelson's pre-eminent concern, in his early years as a writer, was with developing a holistic approach to scientific method in the disparate fields of economics, during the seventies, his attention was directed towards demonstrat-ing the unity of thought between Classical economists (which, in certain instances, included Marx) and revealing the isomorphic structure of Classical and Modern economics. Samuelson's view, as encapsulated in the aphorism 'within every classical economist there is to be discerned a modern economist trying to be born' might be regarded as danger-ously provocative, notwithstanding his disclaimer that the codification of classical economists will necessarily be over-simplistic and liable to distort in such a way as to both improve and libel the original works. Indisputably,

Samuelson's treatment of Marx, subjecting the three volumes of *Capital* to microscopic analytical scrutiny, is
provocative; Samuelson's contention, forcibly expressed in a
series of papers, is that Marx has an important place in the
development of ideas and, in terms of his non-analytical
contributions, to the tradition of radical thought within the
social sciences. However, Samuelson concludes that Marx is
found wanting, analytically, since the crucial innovatory
concept of equal rates of surplus value among industries,
introduced in volumes one and two, is found to be irrelevant
to the understanding of the laws of motion of the economic
system (1974). Not surprisingly, some commentators regard
this critique as an emasculation of Marx's contributions to a
historical explanation of capitalist development: 'he deals
with a Karl Marx who would have readily conceded to
having been "only a minor Post-Ricardian", were he to be
reborn with a faith that his economics could be so effectively
de-institutionalised and drained-off of history and politics'
(Bharadwaj 1968).

SUMMING UP SAMUELSON

In the treacherous maelstrom of economic beliefs, Samuelson
has, over the years, stood firmly upon the rock of scientific
impartiality. Challenged by economists of the Radical Right and
Left, Samuelson has adhered to the principle that controversial
facts can be stated without being admired or deplored. Formerly
identified as a brash and bright 'Young Turk', Samuelson is now
seen, by some, as a pillar of the establishment, seeking to avoid
judgement on controversial questions of economic policy.
However, in refusing to be labelled in terms other than a scientist,
Samuelson draws a clear distinction between those aspects of
economics that are susceptible to contentious, subjective, normative debate and the areas of the discipline that are grounded in
scientific objectivity. (A classic example of this distinction
occurring with the ethical foundations of the individualistic social
welfare function (Samuelson, 1947, 1977).) In consistently revealing a preference for deductive over 'seductive' economics,
Samuelson must be judged, for posterity, according to his own
logic.

## NOTES

1. I would like to acknowledge the assistance, cheerfully rendered, by C. A. Harvey, T. Flegg and P. Taylor in the writing of this chapter. As usual, they are to be entirely exonerated from the errors remaining.

2. Interestingly, it may be noted that, in the 1970s, Samuelson devoted some attention to analysing the optimum growth rate for population (1975). In an article by Deardorff (1976), it was pointed out that the extremum condition derived by Samuelson could conceivably be a *minimum*, i.e. the optimum growth rate would be the one that minimised the *per capita* lifetime utility of consumption. Judging by the contributions made by Samuelson's six children to the latest edition of *Economics*, one might argue that Samuelson's *personal* optimum growth rate of population is also a minimum condition – the smallest number to ensure the perpetuity of the book into an infinite time horizon!

3. 'By a *meaningful theorem*, I mean simply a hypothesis about empirical data which could conceivably be refuted, if only under ideal conditions. . . . Thus, with existing data, it may be impossible to check upon the hypothesis that the demand for salt is of elasticity − 1.0. But it is meaningful because under ideal circumstances an experiment could be devised whereby one could hope to refute the hypothesis' (Samuelson, 1947).

4. For evidence of this phenomenon, see Bennett and Johnson (1979).

5. For a recent reappraisal of the Friedman methodological stance, see Coddington (1979) and Auerbach (1979).

6. Unexceptional, that is, within the context of logical positivism. However, neither does it concern itself with the question as to whether the growth of knowledge occurs through gradual accumulation or discontinuous upheavals, nor with the question as to whether actual scientific practice, in the pursuit of such knowledge, corresponds to the positivist methodology. For a brilliant exposition of the relevance of these themes to the development of economic thought, see Blaug (1975).

7. Samuelson's inspiration for this turnpike theorem (which employs the advanced mathematical methods of variational calculus) came from Von Neumann's model (1945) of an expanding economy. In this model, maximum growth was necessarily achieved at every production time period.

8. For an amusing and informative account of the result of translating *Economics* (Fifth Edition) into Russian, see Gerschenkron (1978). The difficulties of translation and the problems of censorship are well documented, revealing anecdotes such as the following. Samuelson's second chapter, on national income, is headed by the well-known quotation from Lewis Carroll,

> The time has come the Walrus said
> To speak of many things . . .

No doubt bemused by this couplet, Soviet translators decided that 'Walrus' was a misprint for 'Walras', another vulgar bourgeois economist!

REFERENCES

Auerbach, P., 1979 'Scientific Hypotheses and their Domain of Applicability: Comment on Coddington', *British Review of Economic Issues*, Nov.

Bennett, J. T., and Johnson, M. H., 1979 'Mathematics and Quantification in Economic Literature: Paradigm or Paradox?, *Journal of Economic Education*, Fall.

Bharadwaj, K., 1968 'The Collected Scientific Papers of Paul A. Samuelson, *Indian Economic Journal*, pps. 501–26.

Blaug, M., 1975 'Kuhn versus Lakatos, or Paradigms versus Research Programmes in the History of Economics', *History of Political Economy*, Winter.

Coddington, A., 1979 'Friedman's Contribution to Methodological Controversy' *British Review of Economic Issues*, May.

Dorfman, R., Samuelson, P. and Solow, R., 1958 *Linear Programming and Economic Analysis* (McGraw-Hill).

Deardorff, S., 1976 The Growth Rate for Population: Comment', *International Economic Review*, June.

Friedman, M., 1953 'The Methodology of Positive Economics' in *Essays in Positive Economics* (University of Chicago Press).

Gerschenkron, A., 1978 'Samuelson in Soviet Russia: a Report', *Journal of Economic Literature*, June.

Georgescu-Roegen, N., 1978 'Mechanistic Dogma and Economics', *British Review of Economic Issues*, May.

Gordon, A., 1976 'Rigour and Relevance in a Changing Institutional Setting', *American Economic Review*, Mar.

Kendry, A., 1979 'Chess, Art and Economics', Unpublished paper presented to Midwest Economic Association, Chicago.

Keynes, J. M., 1936 *The General Theory of Employment, Interest and Money* (Macmillan)

Leontief, W., 1970 'Theoretical Assumptions and Non-observed Facts', *American Economic Review*, May.

Levhari, D. and Samuelson, P., 1966 'The Non-switching Theorem is False', *Quarterly Journal of Economics*, Nov.

Linder, M. and Sensat, J., 1977 *The Anti-Samuelson* (Urizen Books).

Machlup, F., 1964 'Theory and Realism: a Reply', *American Economic Review*, Sep.

Magee, B., 1973 *Popper* Fontana Modern Masters.

McCain, R., 1979 'Reflections on the Cultivation of Taste', *Journal of Cultural Economics*, June.

Neumann J., von 1945 'A Model of General Economic Equilibrium', *Review of Economic Studies*, vol. 13.

Samuelson, P. A., 1938 'A Note on the Pure Theory of Consumer's Behaviour', *Economica*, Feb.

—— 1939 Interactions Between the Multiplier Analysis and the Principle of Acceleration, *Review of Economics and Statistics*, May.

—— 1947 *The Foundations of Economic Analysis* (Harvard University Press).

—— 1948 'International Trade and Equalisation of Factor Prices', *Economic Journal*, June.

—— 1949 'International Factor-price Equalisation Once Again', *Economic Journal*, June.

—— 1954 'The Pure Theory of Public Expenditure', *Review of Economics and Statistics*, Nov.

—— 1958 'Aspects of Public Expenditure Theories', *Review of Economics and Statistics*, Nov.

—— 1966 'A Summing Up' *Quarterly Journal of Economics*, Nov.

—— 1971a 'Maximum Principles in Analytical Economics' in *Les Prix Nobel en 1970* (The Nobel Foundation).

—— 1971b 'Ohlin was right', *Swedish Journal of Economics*, Dec.

—— 1972 'Economics in a Golden Age: a Personal Memoir' in Holton, G. (ed.), *The Twentieth Century Sciences: Studies in the Biography of Ideas* (Norton and Co. Inc.)

—— 1974 'Insight and detour in the theory of Exploiration: a reply to Baumol, *Journal of Economic Literature*, Mar.

—— 1975 'The Optimum Growth Rate of Population', *International Economic Review*, Oct.

—— 1977 'Reaffirming the existence of "reasonable" Bergson–Samuelson Social Welfare Functions', *Economica*, Feb.

—— 1980 *Economics*, Eleventh Edition (McGraw-Hill).

Veblen, T., 1919 'Why is economics not an evolutionary science? in *The Place of Science in Modern Civilisation* (Huebsch).

## FURTHER READING

Stiglitz J. (ed.), 1966 *The Collected Scientific Papers of Paul A. Samuelson* Volumes 1 and 2 (MIT Press).

Merton R. (ed.), 1972 *The Collected Scientific Papers of Paul A. Samuelson* Volume 3, (MIT Press).

Nagatani H. and Crowley K. (ed.), 1977 *The Collected Scientific Papers of Paul A. Samuelson* Volume 4, (MIT Press).

# 13 Piero Sraffa's Contribution to Political Economy

## Alessandro Roncaglia

*Translated by Lesley North*

In 1960, when Piero Sraffa's main work *Production of Commodities by Means of Commodities* appeared, one reviewer commented that the book might perhaps have had something new to say at the end of the twenties when Sraffa drew up the outline of his approach, but by the time of its publication it had been superseded by contemporary economic analysis.[1] Since then the debate over Capital Theory has proved this opinion profoundly inaccurate. Sraffa's analysis has been used to criticise some of the central elements of dominant economic thought. In addition a more constructive function has also been attributed to the analysis – that of the scientific rehabilitation of the classical (Ricardian) and Marxian framework.

A lively and ever-widening debate began with differing evaluations of the meaning and importance of Sraffa's contribution.[2] On other occasions I have attempted to give my own interpretation; here I shall adopt a different method – tracing developments during the period of Sraffa's theoretical research.

EARLY INFLUENCES

Piero Sraffa was born in Turin on 5 August 1898; his father, Angelo, was a well-known professor of Commercial Law. Moving around with his father, Piero Sraffa studied at Parma and Milan, where he went to the *ginnasio superiore*. One of his teachers was Domenico Re, a socialist, who had a decisive influence on his political development. Later the family moved to Turin, where the young Sraffa attended the *liceo* and came into contact with young socialists. After this he registered at the University, in the Faculty of Jurisprudence, but was conscripted and took the exams without attending classes.

In 1919 Sraffa met Antonio Gramsci through the agency of the literary figure Umberto Cosmo, who had taught Sraffa in the first year at the *liceo* and was Gramsci's professor at the Faculty of Letters. Despite a seven-year age difference between the two, they soon became friends. In this way – without ever joining the Socialist Party nor, after its foundation at Livorno in 1921, the Communist Party – Sraffa followed his friend's political activity very closely. He contributed to *L'Ordine Nuovo* (founded and directed by Gramsci), producing translations from German and English and some short articles on economics.

In the summer of 1921, during a brief stay in London, Sraffa held press credentials for *L'Ordine Nuovo*. In London he came into contact with a group of English Marxists who would later edit the influential periodical *Labour Monthly*. On a short visit to Cambridge he also met Keynes, already an important person in the field of economics.

Sraffa gave Gramsci the greatest possible assistance after the latter's arrest in 1926. He organised direct help through Gramsci's sister-in-law Tatiana Schucht, obtained books and journals for his friend and provided an important intellectual stimulus for the production of the *Prison Notebooks*. He acted as a link between Gramsci and the leading Communists who were still at large, and he made consistent attempts to obtain Gramsci's freedom.[3]

These factors should be recorded in order to indicate Sraffa's political allegiance. In some ways it is this very allegiance which guided Sraffa in his theoretical research. This is not to say that his communist friend exercised specific influence on this research, nor that it was Gramsci's influence which led to Sraffa's gradual movement from interest in the problems of applied economics to interest in those of a theoretical nature in the first half of the twenties. However his friendship with Gramsci does help us to understand that the stimulus for, and sustenance of, years of solitary research undoubtedly sprang from an ideal, a strong political involvement.

Nor does it seem possible to attribute to Keynes any particular influence on Sraffa's research. However he did play a decisive role in securing for Sraffa the best possible conditions for his work.

As already noted, Sraffa had met Keynes for the first time in August 1921. He had been preceded by a letter from Mary Berenson, a friend of both Keynes and Gaetano Salvemini. She introduced him as 'a young friend of the Salveminis, who think very highly of him'. Until this time, and for some time to come, Sraffa had been largely concerned with monetary questions. His graduation thesis, debated in November 1920 with Luigi Einaudi, was entitled 'Monetary Inflation in Italy During and After the War'. Immediately after his graduation Sraffa worked for a brief period, before the advent of fascism, to help set up an office of Labour Statistics for the Milanese Socialist administration.

Some time later, Keynes requested from Sraffa a description of the running of the Italian banking system. The first article, 'The Bank Crisis in Italy', published in the *Economic Journal* for June, 1922 is a strongly worded and accurate indictment of the rescue of the Banca Italiana di Sconto, and concludes with an account of the pliability of the Government when confronted by important financial concerns:

> Even if [the banking] laws were not futile in themselves what could be their use as long as the Government is prepared to be the first to break them so soon as it is blackmailed by a band of gunmen or a group of bold financiers?

This article passed without comment. But when, in December, the second article (on the Italian banking system after the First World War) was published in four languages in the widely distributed Supplement of the *Manchester Guardian* dedicated to the Reconstruction of Europe, it was Mussolini himself who reacted. Pressure was put on Sraffa's father Angelo to obtain a retraction – which he did not get.

With these articles and his graduation thesis completed, Sraffa began his academic career as Professor of Political Economy in the Jurisprudence Faculty of the University of Perugia. He remained there until January 1926, when he obtained a chair at Cagliari University. The journey between Perugia and Milan, where Sraffa had settled with his family, and then the journey to Cagliari, were a handicap for the young professor's research. But the obligation to run a general course in Political Economy directed Sraffa's attention to the academic school dominant in Italy at that time – Marginalism, in Maffeo Pantaleoni's Marshallian version.

Amongst other things, Sraffa was occupied with the translation into Italian of Keynes's *Tract on Monetary Reform*. But his main interests were shifting from the field of applied economics to that of theory and he was working on a critique of the Marshallian theory of value. His argument is set out in a long article 'On the Relationship Between Cost and Quantity Produced' published in 1925 in *Annali di Economia*.

Sraffa's claim is that the Marshallian theory of value is invalidated by a logical contradiction between two of its most fundamental elements – the concept of perfect competition and the use of intersecting demand and supply curves to determine price and quantity produced. In particular, Sraffa criticised the tendency to establish a functional relationship between unit cost and quantity produced – that is, the idea that it is possible to determine precise laws of returns to scale.

As Sraffa reminds us, in classical political economy the 'law' of diminishing returns was associated mainly with the problem of rent (theory of distribution), while the 'law' of increasing returns was associated with the division of labour, that is, with general economic progress (theory of production). Marshall, and other neoclassical economists, attempted to merge these 'laws' into a single 'law' of non-proportional returns, utilizing it in the field of price theory to establish a functional connection between costs and quantity produced. This relationship constituted the basis of the rising supply curve as opposed to the corresponding downward-sloping demand curve derived from the 'law' of diminishing marginal utility. Sraffa admitted that changes in the level of production in one industry can lead to changes in unit cost. However, as he showed, these changes derive from causes that also have an influence on costs in other industries (the existence of scarce factors of production for decreasing returns and economies of scale for increasing returns). Consequently, changes in the costs of the industry in question will mean changes in costs of comparable size in other industries, and cannot be considered in isolation as Marshall does with his partial equilibrium method.

At Keynes's request the problem is taken up again in an article aimed at the Anglo-Saxon public and published in the *Economic Journal* in 1926. This article, shorter and somewhat less detailed than the Italian one, was sufficient to earn Sraffa a good deal of prestige in the English academic community for the 25 years preceding the publication of *Production of Commodities by Means of Commodities* (1960) and his critical edition of Ricardo's works. This article also embodied traces of the theory of imperfect competition, although the development of this theory by students like Joan Robinson was a far cry from the road along which Sraffa was to pursue his research.

In the summer of 1927, Sraffa moved to England, having been offered a lectureship at Cambridge University. This offer came from Keynes, who had taken it upon himself to find work for Sraffa in England, and saw to all the organisational problems involved.

CAMBRIDGE

At Cambridge, Sraffa was received into King's College, then dominated by Keynes. Only in 1939, after Dennis Robertson's transfer to London, did Sraffa take up a post at Trinity, of which he has remained a fellow. Keynes also managed to delay Sraffa's lectures for a year, until Autumn 1928, to give him time to get used to his surroundings. In 1930, as Secretary of the Royal Economic Society, he arranged for Sraffa to be allocated responsibility for the critical edition of Ricardo's works. The following year he had him made librarian to the Marshall Library (a post which Sraffa only relinquished in the 1970s) and Director of Research at King's College. Consequently Sraffa no longer had to give lectures and, therefore, had more time to devote to research. Together Sraffa and Keynes – both avid bibliophiles – collaborated to have reprinted a rare pamphlet – 'An Abstract of a Treatise on Human Nature' – at the same time offering decisive proof of its attribution to David Hume.

For three years, from Autumn 1928, Sraffa gave a course of lectures at Cambridge on the history of the theory of value (in addition to less important one on the running of the German and Italian banking systems). His classes were followed by students like Joan Robinson and Richard Kahn. It was probably during the preparation of these lectures and as a result of the only partial comprehension of the fundamental message of the 1926 article by the English public that Sraffa realised the enormity of the task already undertaken in his criticism of the Marshallian theory of value and which led to the more than 30 years of research concluded in 1960 with the publication of *Production of Commodities by Means of Commodities*.

In effect, Sraffa had set himself the daunting task of completely overturning views universally held by economists of the time. His conception of this objective was far more radical than that which Keynes attributed to his own research. In fact the aim was the rehabilitation of the classical economists' analysis of political economy (taken up and developed by Marx) with the critical edition of Ricardo. An additional aim was to resolve a crucial analytical problem left unanswered by these writers - the determination of relative prices and their relationship with the distribution of income between wages and profits. Sraffa does this in *Production of Commodities by Means of Commodities* (1960), simultaneously developing a decisive criticism of the foundations of the marginalist theory of value (in all its forms, not simply the Marshallian version). It was an attempt, then, to eliminate a false scheme of knowledge, which had been given a favourable hearing during its long development because of its apologetic conclusions - the rationale it appeared to give to the capitalist system - and also to reconstruct on a sound basis an analysis far more useful in understanding the real world (a necessary premise for direct action to change it).

As mentioned above, all other activities were subordinated to Sraffa's research. As soon as possible, he ceased lecturing, and gave up his post as director of research at King's. But concentration on research did not lead to isolation. Sraffa was a key figure in the group of economists commenting upon, criticising and encouraging Keynes on his long trek towards the *General Theory*. Joan Robinson, Richard Kahn and James Meade were members of this group. Even more important (for those interested in such matters) is the influence Sraffa exerted on the Austrian philosopher Ludwig Wittgenstein, and on his transition from the logical atomism of *Tractatus Logico-Philosophicus* to the mature ideas expressed in *Philosophical Investigations* (1972) - ideas which have an important influence on contemporary philosophy.[4]

Sraffa produced very little in the field of economics during the time of preparation of his major works. In 1930 he published a short critical note (and an even shorter counter-reply) to an *Economic Journal* article in which Robertson tried to defend Marshall's value theory with an argument based on a series of evolutionistic analogies between economics and the natural world. Again in 1930 he published a short piece on a philological question related to Ricardo in the *Quarterly Journal of Economics*.

More important was an article published in 1932 in the *Economic Journal* – a critical review of a book by Hayek in which the liberal economist tried to develop, within the context of the Austrian School, a theory of prices and levels of production for a modern economic system in which financial activities had a role to play. Sraffa's article is important both as a critique of an alternative ('Austrian') theoretical framework to that which Keynes was in the process of developing in the same period, and as an original contribution to the development of Keynesian thought. He develops the concept of own rates of interest, the importance of which Keynes was to stress in the crucial Chapter 17 of the *General Theory*, the chapter on 'the essential properties of interest and money'.

THE YEARS OF PREPARATION

During the years 1927 and 1960, however, the greatest attention was dedicated to research on the structure of classical political economy and price theory. In 1928, as Sraffa himself later informed us, 'a draft of the opening propositions of this paper (i.e. *Production of Commodities*)' was available. The draft was discussed with Keynes, who was correct in foreseeing the difficulties Sraffa would encounter in directing his readers' attention to the absence of any hypothesis about returns to scale in his analysis of price. In the following years the research proceeded quietly with none of the analytical discussion which, for example, preceded Keynes's *General Theory*. Only a few Cambridge mathematicians (Ramsey, Watson, Besicovitch) were consulted on the mathematical aspects of the problems encountered. The results arrived at in the course of the research were subjected to meticulous verification and refinement before Sraffa considered it appropriate to make them public:

> Whilst the central propositions had taken shape in the late 1920s, particular points . . . were worked out in the thirties and early forties. In the period since 1955, while these pages were being put together out of a mass of old notes, little was added apart from filling gaps which had become apparent in the process.[5]

Sraffa's caution was justified by the size of the task he had set himself and therefore by the necessity of refraining from making initial errors. Otherwise, minor mistakes or failure to present a complete analysis could compromise the reaffirmation of the classical school and the defeat of the marginalists.

The same care was lavished upon the critical edition of Ricardo's works. With Keynes's help, Sraffa set up a meticulous 'manuscript hunt' which led to the discovery in 1930 of a chest containing letters addressed to Ricardo from his correspondents. Many searches yielded nothing, but an enormous amount of secondary information was amassed, allowing Sraffa to form a very full and detailed picture of the cultural and human conditions of Ricardo's time. Then, in July 1943, after 13 years of work and with six volumes already drafted, letters of great significance from Ricardo to James Mill were retrieved from an Irish castle. Amongst the letters was a fundamental essay on which Ricardo had worked in the last fortnight of his life. With Maurice Dobb's help in the final stages, the undertaking was concluded between 1951 and 1955 with the publication in ten volumes of the *Works and Correspondence of David Ricardo*, followed in 1973 by an extremely accurate volume of indices. In the meantime, 30 years after that first draft, a thin volume – almost a pamphlet – came out in 1960 his *Production of Commodities by Means of Commodities – Prelude to a Critique of Economic Theory*.

SRAFFA ON RICARDO

As indicated above, the role played by the critical edition of Ricardo in the total research programme is that of facilitating – after a century of misinterpretation and distortion – the rehabilitation of the classical economists' analysis, based on the concept of surplus.

To understand the interpretative U-turn that this involved, we must look at the situation at the time when Sraffa began his work. In fact in the twenties Ricardo's theories seemed to be of little interest to economists. They were not lacking in justification for this attitude. Whether Marshall's interpretation (according to which Ricardo is an imprecise and partial forerunner of modern theory) or that of Jevons (according to whom Ricardo was responsible for a pernicious deviation of economics from the path of true science)[6] is accepted, there is no need to waste time reading his work. This was, for example, the opinion of economists of the calibre of Robertson and Hicks, as we discover from their correspondence with Keynes.[7] At best, a few economists accepted the Ricardian theory of rent (as providing the basis for the principle of diminishing returns) or the Ricardian monetary theory or the comparative-cost theory of international trade. The Ricardian labour theory of value was, in general, neglected by theorists and regarded by historians of economic thought as merely an object of antiquarian interest. The Ricardian conception of the economic process, based on the concept of surplus, was completely submerged.

One indication of this situation is the way in which the Royal Economic Society handled the work on the critical edition of Ricardo. In 1928 this responsibility was entrusted to Professor Gregory of the University of London, an economic historian whose main interest was in monetary problems. Gregory did not commit himself very deeply to the task, and in 1930 was pleased to pass it on to Sraffa.

Nevertheless there was a certain amount of anticipation among Sraffa's friends concerning the outcome of his work. Publication was announced several times (notably by Keynes in his essay on Malthus, written in 1933).[8] We can see that this anticipation was more than justified when the edition finally appeared. It is unanimously agreed to be a model of philological rigour. More than this, the edited texts, the notes and especially Sraffa's introduction to the first volume of the *Principles of Political Economy and Taxation* restored Ricardo (and in his wake the whole of classical political economy to a central place in economic theory, freeing the interpretation of his thought from the travesties of the marginalists.

Drastically simplifying Sraffa's exposition, we can distinguish two successive analytical stages in Ricardo's work. The first culminates in the *Essay on the Influence of a Low Price of Corn* (1815), in which Ricardo uses what would now be called a 'one-commodity model'. A certain quantity of grain is used as a means of production (seed-corn and subsistence wages for workers involved in the productive process); a larger quantity of grain is obtained as output. After reconstituting the initial supply of means of production, a surplus is therefore obtained; it goes to the property-owning classes (i.e. profit to capitalists and rent to landowners). If land with different degrees of fertility is used, competition between capitalists to rent the best land means that rent is paid for the best land equal to the difference between the surplus obtainable from this land and that obtainable from the poorest land currently being cultivated. This is the so-called Ricardian theory of Rent, which Ricardo actually took from Malthus, Torrens and West. As less and less fertile land is taken into cultivation as a consequence of population growth, the surplus from the least fertile land diminishes, as does the rate of profit. At the same time rents increase, while wages remain constant in real terms at the subsistence level.

Accumulation, which is dependent upon profit, slows down. To favour capitalists (and, therefore, economic growth), it was necessary to favour corn imports – in opposition to the land-owners over the distribution of the surplus This is the root of Ricardo's liberalism.

The second stage – that of the *Principles of Political Economy* (successive editions published in 1817, 1819 and 1821) – is the one in which Ricardo abandoned the one-commodity model, having taken Malthus's criticisms, and adopted the labour-embodied theory of value (according to which the value of each commodity is given by the quantity of labour directly or indirectly necessary for its production) to measure income and capital. From this he obtains the rate of profit as a ratio between aggregates of heterogeneous goods. In this sense, the theory of value had a subordinate and functional role relative to the theory of distribution, and allowed the latter to emphasize the conflict of interest between social classes (workers, capitalists and landowners) in the distribution of income. Nevertheless, within the labour theory of value there remained one problem which Ricardo had already tackled in the *Principles* and more directly in his later writings. This is the problem of the invariable standard of value and of the relationship between absolute and exchange values. In his Introduction to the *Principles* (1951) Sraffa offers a contribution which is not just interpretative but also theoretically innovative. This is a contribution which has perhaps not yet provoked all the attention it should have done, not least in relation to the problem of the links between the classical economists and Marx. As Sraffa pointed out, Ricardo attributes two meanings to the invariable standard which need to be clearly separated. The first is that of having invariable value with respect ot its own means of production when distribution of income between wages and profits alters with no change in technology. The second is that of invariable value with respect to technological change over time. Having separated the two problems, Sraffa shows in *Production of Commodities by Means of Commodities* (1960) how it may be possible to resolve the first by constructing a 'standard commodity' – a composite commodity in which the product and the whole of the means of production are made up of the same commodities, in the same proportions. As for the second problem, it is obvious that the measurement in terms of labour content retains some meaning, but it is also clear that the risk of metaphysical or subjective views increases (work as 'toil and trouble', as sacrifice). All the same, it is a problem on which economic theory has made no new progress after Sraffa's contribution.

PRODUCTION OF COMMODITIES BY MEANS OF COMMODITIES

The most important inheritance Ricardo and the classical economists left us is that of the representation of the economic system as a circular flow of production and consumption based on the concept of the surplus, which Sraffa brought to light again in his edition of Ricardo's work and which he perfects analytically in *Production of Commodities* (1960).

This book, as already noted, has a dual purpose: that of providing the basis for criticism of the marginalist theory and that of analytically perfecting the classical economists approach. This explains some apparent 'openings' in the book which have deceived the many interpreters who have thought it possible to reduce Sraffa's analysis to a special case within the marginalist theory. In fact, if we introduce into Sraffa's analysis two hypotheses which he does *not* make use of – those of constant returns to scale and equilibrium between demand and supply for all commodities we arrive at the above interpretation. On the one hand this is necessary if we wish Sraffa's analysis to serve as a logical internal criticism of marginalist theory and have the destructive strength that an external criticism could not claim. On the other hand, as far as the constructive contribution to the theory of price and distribution is concerned, those hypotheses violate Sraffa's own conceptual framework.

This framework is closely connected to that of the classical economists. In Sraffa's analysis, as in that of the classical writers, the equilibrium condition on which the determination of production prices is based (the classical 'natural prices') consists simply in the equality of the rate of profits in each sector. This hypothesis, together with the consideration of the physical costs of production (that is of the quantity of the various means of production necessary to obtain a given quantity of production) is sufficient to determine the relationship between distributive variables, rates of profits and wages, and prices of production. This is, therefore, an approach based on objective data, in complete opposition to the marginalist theory which is based on consumer 'preferences'.

If we wish to summarise the conceptual framework of the Sraffian and classical analyses, it is enough to record the following factors:

(i) The relation between prices and distributive variables is determined at each point in time by current technology.

(ii) This datum is valid only for the moment under consideration, for technology undergoes continuous change. Analytically the situation of a certain economic system is considered as it might appear from a 'photograph' taken at a given moment.

(iii) All economic magnitudes which are not the object of the analysis may be considered as data, and the theoretician can concentrate his or her attention on the virtual (hypothetical) movements of magnitudes and on their mutual relationships which appear as 'isolated *in vacuo*'.

(iv) In the case of *Production of Commodities* (1960), Sraffa has chosen the relationship between production prices and distributive variables (rate of profits and wage rate) as the objects of the analysis. All other variables (technology, levels of output, structure of industry etc.) are taken as data.

(v)  This choice, however, does not imply an *a priori* refusal of the possibility of analysing the problems of technological development, levels of output, strategy of the firms and so forth. This choice simply stems from the necessity of analysing the different problems one by one, and each in isolation.

(vi) The necessary assumptions and methods of analysis are not necessarily identical for all problems; for each of them only what is relevant should be included, leaving aside those elements which, as Ricardo said, simply 'modify' the analysis but do not change it substantially.

SRAFFA'S METHOD AND RESULTS

Sraffa develops his analysis of prices within this conceptual framework. The first step is the demonstration that in a system of subsistence production which 'produces just enough to maintain itself' and where 'commodities are produced by separate industries', there must be a 'unique set of exchange values which, if adopted by the market, restores the original distribution of the products and makes it possible for the process to be repeated; such values spring directly from the methods of production'.[9]

If the economy produces a surplus, that is, an excess of commodities produced over commodities used up in the production process and as workers subsistence, then the distribution of this surplus must 'be determined through the same mechanism and at the same time as are the prices of production'.[10] If the wage rate is allowed to be higher than the subsistence level, relative prices and one of the distributive variables (wage rate or rate of profits) may be simultaneously determined, given the technology and the other distributive variable. The higher the wage rate, the lower the rate of profits.

Sraffa then analyses 'the key to the movement of relative prices consequent upon a change in the wage! As the classical economists and Marx already knew, this key lies 'in the inequality of the proportion in which labour and means of production are employed in the various industries!. If these proportions were to be the same in all industries no price change could ensue, while 'it is impossible for prices to remain unchanged when there is inequality of "proportions"'.[11]

In the course of his analysis, taking up the classical distinction between necessities and luxuries, Sraffa introduces the terms 'basic' and 'non-basic' commodities. The former are commodities directly or indirectly necessary to all the productive processes of the system; the latter are not used as means of production, or are used only in their own production or that of other non-basic commodities. This categorisation is important in the case of technological change. If the technique of production related to a basic commodity changes there are general repercussions on all relative prices and on the relationship between wage and profit rates; while if the change simply concerns the technique of producing a non-basic commodity, the repercussions are restricted to the exchange ratios concerning non-basics and do not extend to the exchange ratios between basics or to the relationship between wage and profit rates.

As mentioned earlier, Sraffa also constructs a particular analytical tool – the standard commodity – which enables him to resolve, after suitable redefinition, the Ricardian problem of the 'invariable standard of value'. The analysis of prices of production is completed by the examination of the case of joint products (into which category the case of fixed capital – where commodity output plus a 'used machine' are jointly produced – can be placed) and the case where there are non-reproducible scarce factors like land. The book concludes with a chapter on choice between alternative methods of production at different profit rates, and some appendices in which Sraffa specifically likens himself to the classical economists.

The constructive aspect of the book therefore consists of the solution of a number of problems which the classical economists and Marx left unresolved. It is concerned with questions which are crucial for the acceptability of the classical economists' theoretical formulation. In addition the solution of these problems does not involve substantial modifications to the classical writers' frame of reference.

The criticism of marginalist (or neoclassical) theories is represented by a series of propositions, which can be used as a basis for a criticism of neoclassical attempts to think of capital as of a uni-dimensional magnitude, independent of distribution. This concept of capital is essential to all versions of the marginalist theory (including disaggregated versions like that of Walras), in order to determine the rate of profits as the 'price' of a specific factor of production, homogeneous in nature, identified with 'capital'. This criticism destroys the attempts, developed in the course of a century by marginalist economists, to resolve the problem of distribution between wages and profits as part of the theory of long-run equilibrium prices, based on data such as technology, availability of resources and consumer tastes.[12]

CONCLUSIONS

At this point we may come to some provisional conclusions. Summarising what has gone before, we can distinguish three directions integrated with each other in the more than fifty years of Sraffa's research: the criticisms of the marginalist theory, with its basis in a subjective conception of value; the rediscovery of the conceptual and analytical picture of the classical framework, based on the conception of the productive process as a circular flow of production, distribution and consumption and on the notion of surplus; and the integration and partial modification of this analysis with new contributions to the theory of prices of production and their effect on the distributional variables.

For all three areas, the results Sraffa arrived at are considered by many economists as conclusive; but, as is normal in any science, agreement is far from unanimous and the force of tradition is still strong. So, from the publication of *Production of Commodities by Means of Commodities* in 1960 the debate has become ever livelier and has extended into many other areas – from the history of economic thought (in particular the interpretation and evaluation of Marxism) to the pure theory of international trade. But, above all, the rediscovery and integration of classical theory accomplished by Sraffa in the particular but vital area of the theory of value has re-proposed the classical framework as the basis for research in all fields of economic science, from the theory of the firm to that of distribution, from the theory of growth to that of technical change – with results of notable interest. A complete evaluation, however, is not possible; we can only say that the Sraffian revolution has not yet reaped all its fruits.

NOTES

1. R. E. Quandt (1961), p. 500.
2. Cf. the bibliography in the appendix to A. Roncaglia (1978a), which also includes a full list of Sraffa's writings. This chapter draws from this book, where my interpretation of Sraffa's analysis is illustrated, as from A. Roncaglia (1978b).
3. Cf. P. Spriano (1977).
4. Cf. L. Wittgenstein (1972), p. viii: 'Even more than to this [Ramsey's] criticism I am indebted to that which a teacher of this university, Mr. P. Sraffa, for many years unceasingly practised on my thoughts. I am indebted to *this* stimulus for the most consequential ideas of this book'. On the relationship between Wittgenstein's thought and Sraffa's implicit methodology, cf. A. Roncaglia (1978a), Chapter VII.
5. P. Sraffa (1960), p. vi.
6. Cf. W. S. Jevons (1879), last lines of the Preface to the Second Edition; A. Marshall (1920), Appendix i.
7. D. Robertson's letter, 3 Feb. 1935, in Keynes (1973) vol. XIII p. 504; J. Hicks's letter, 9 Apr. 1937, vol. XIV p. 81.
8. J. M. Keynes (1973), vol. X, p. 97.
9. P. Sraffa (1960), p. 3.
10. Ibid., p. 6.
11. Ibid., p. 12–13.
12. For a short survey of the debate on capital theory following the publication of Sraffa's book, cf. A. Roncaglia (1978a), Chapter VI.

REFERENCES

Jevons, W. S., 1879 *The Theory of Political Economy* (2nd edition) (Macmillan).
Keynes, J. M., 1973 *The Collected Writings* (Macmillan).
Marshall, A., 1920 *Principles of Economics* (8th edition) (Macmillan).
Quandt, R. E., 1961 'Review of Production of Commodities by Means of Commodities', *Journal of Political Economy*, vol. 61.
Ricardo, D., 1951 *The Works and Correspondence of David Ricardo: Principles of Political Economy and Taxation*, ed. P. Sraffa (Cambridge University Press).
Roncaglia, A., 1978a *Sraffa and the Theory of Prices* (Wiley).
—— 1978b 'La rivoluzione di Sraffa', *Mondoperaio* n. 9.
Spriano, P., 1977 *Gramsci in carcere e il partito* (Editori Riuniti).
Sraffa, P., 1925 'On the Relationship between Cost and Quantity Produced', *Annali di Economia*.

Sraffa, P., 1926 'The Laws of Returns under Competitive Conditions', *Economic Journal* Dec.
—— 1951 Introduction to Volume One of *The Works and Correspondence of David Ricardo* (Cambridge University Press).
—— 1960 *The Production of Commodities by Means of Commodities* (Cambridge University Press).
Wittgenstein, L., 1972, *Philosophical Investigations* (Translated by G. E. M. Anscombe) (Basil Blackwell).

# Index

257